PASTOR'S COMPLETE MODEL LETTER BOOK

Stephen R. Clark
and
Anne C. Williman

A James Peter Book
James Peter Associates, Inc.

PRENTICE HALL
Englewood Cliffs, New Jersey 07632

Prentice-Hall International (UK) Limited, *London*
Prentice-Hall of Australia Pty. Limited, *Sydney*
Prentice-Hall Canada, Inc., *Toronto*
Prentice-Hall Hispanoamericana, S.A., *Mexico*
Prentice-Hall of India Private Limited, *New Delhi*
Prentice-Hall of Japan, Inc., *Tokyo*
Simon & Schuster Asia Pte. Ltd., *Singapore*
Editora Prentice-Hall do Brasil, Ltda., *Rio de Janeiro*

© 1989 *by*

PRENTICE-HALL, Inc.
Englewood Cliffs, NJ

10   9   8   7   6   5   4   3
Printed in the United States of America

Library of Congress Cataloging-in-Publication Data

Clark, Stephen R.
  Pastor's complete model letter book.

  1. Church correspondence–Handbooks, mauals, etc.
2. Clergy–Correspondence–Handbooks, manuals, etc.
3. Form letters.   I. Williman, Anne C.   II. Title.
BV652.9.C58   1989   651.7'52'0242   88-25489
ISBN   0-13-653312-4

ISBN 0-13-653312-4

PRENTICE HALL
BUSINESS & PROFESSIONAL DIVISION
A division of Simon & Schuster
Englewood Cliffs, New Jersey 07632

Contents

Chapter 2 Letters to Other Members 31

Chapter 3 Letters to Nonmembers 85

Chapter 4 Letters to Church Staff 99

Chapter 5 Letters to the Community

Chapter 6 Letters to the Media   165

Chapter 7 Letters to Vendors 175

Chapter 8 Letters for Special Occasions 181

Chapter 11   Letters to Colleagues

Chapter 12 Letters of Policy and Doctrine 243

Acknowledgments

All scripture quotations are from the *New King James Bible* unless otherwise noted.

We appreciate the many who assisted us in the preparation of this book. Special thanks to:

Rev. Jeff Dybdahl, Central College Presbyterian Church, Westerville, OH.

Rev. Martin Holman, Fremont Baptist Temple, Fremont, OH.

Rev. Richard Steele, Jr., Gibson Heights-Second United Presbyterian Church, Youngstown, OH.

Rev. Loren Schwiebert, Living Word Fellowship, Tiffin, OH.

Rev. Donald Blanton, First Assembly of God, Findlay, OH.

Introduction

In this book you will discover a treasure trove of model letters readily adaptable to virtually every situation requiring a letter. These situations occur daily in infinite number and variety for you, the minister. In spite of advanced communications technology—telephones, computer mail, satellite communications—the need to "get it in writing" has not faded. In fact, each year the Post Office sets new records for the number of pieces of mail handled.

Writing these letters is just as costly as it is to mail them. They cost you time and money. Think for a moment. How much time do you expend on an average letter? Ten minutes? Fifteen? Twenty? Thirty? Surely, you think, no letter takes thirty minutes to write! And you're right. Many take longer, especially when you have to start from scratch.

Consider the steps to writing a letter, and then add up the time involved. First, you have to think about what you are going to say. Then you must decide how you will say what you want to say. Next, you either write your own first draft, or dictate it to your secretary. If you dictate, then your secretary must type up the first draft for you. Then, you must go over your draft for accuracy and clarity and make the necessary changes. Next, you or your secretary types up the final draft, which you must proofread once more. Finally, if there are no further corrections needed, the letter is signed, folded, placed in an envelope, addressed, and put into the mail. It's easy to see how an average letter can easily cost you thirty minutes or more to write.

But how does that translate into dollars? An annual salary of $25,000 yields an hourly rate (based on forty hours per week) of around $12. Let's assume your secretary is making $5 per hour. If you each spent fifteen minutes producing one letter, it's costing you $4.25 per letter, not including the cost of postage and stationery! And that's actually a very conservative estimate. It's been estimated that the average business letter costs over $10 to produce. Can you and your church afford to spend that much time and money producing one letter? Do you really want to?

After all, as a minister, your time is already at a premium. Your congregation expects you to be available to minister to their needs twenty-four hours a day. You want to be available because that's what you've been called to do. You have more pressing needs on your church budget than having to spend up to $200 to $500 or more each week just writing letters and memos!

This book is an answer to your prayers for help with your letters. You will discover over 400 examples of letters used by ministers for virtually every occasion and need. In many instances, all you'll need to do is insert the appropriate names and information. Letters, forms, memos, and other writing chores that once took hours now will take only a few minutes. The savings in time to you and in money to your church will be tremendous.

This is a practical book of model letters designed to specifically meet your needs—the needs of a dedicated and active minister. It is a daily reference book you will use to draft all of the letters, memos, and other written communications that are a vital part of your position. It is a book which will free your time and allow you to more effectively do what you've been called to do—minister.

This is not a book that will gather dust on your bookshelf. Rather, it is a volume which will occupy a featured position on your desk, next to your Bible and most-used commentaries and references. It is a book you'll use and appreciate every day of your ministry.

Stephen R. Clark

Writing Letters Right

While this book offers model letters which will meet all of your routine and most common needs, there will be unique situations during your ministry which will require special attention. You may be required to write a letter pertaining to a very sensitive or personal situation, or be asked to contribute an article or editorial to a publication. Whatever the writing opportunity is, it's a challenge you can easily meet.

While the letters in this book serve as excellent examples fitting most situations, there will be times when a "form letter" will seem too impersonal or inadequate for the special need at hand. The ten "commandments" that follow will serve to help you produce effective and powerful letters and other written communication.

While all ministers are speakers, not all are writers. Good speaking skills don't translate easily into good writing skills. So, for many ministers—and others—writing can be an annoying task or a "necessary evil." But it doesn't have to be so, nor should it be. When you sit down to write, keep in mind Colossians 3:17: "And whatever you do in word or deed, do all in the name of the Lord Jesus, giving thanks to God the Father through Him."

Writing a letter, a memo, or anything else should be a special joy for you because it's another opportunity to minister. It is in this spirit that the following guidelines are offered.

1. BE SMART—"If any of you lacks wisdom, let him ask of God, who gives to all liberally and without reproach, and it will be given to him." (James 1:5) Before picking up your pen or touching a typewriter, stop and think about what you want to say in your letter. Think it through carefully. The more sensitive the situation, the more care you need to take. The best help you can get is from God. Don't just think—pray before you write.

2. BE ON TARGET—"Among all this people there were seven hundred select men who were left-handed; every one could sling a stone at a hair's breadth and not miss." (Judges 20:16) Be sure you're writing to the right audience or person. Don't send a letter to teens that was aimed at adults, and vice versa. Keep your reader in mind as you write. Also, don't send a letter to an assistant that needs to go to an administrator, or to a group when it should go to an individual.

3. BE ACCURATE—"But he who does the truth comes to the light, that his deeds may be clearly seen, that they have been done in God." (John 3:21) A minister's effectiveness depends upon credibility. Be absolutely sure you've got all of the facts straight. Every church has a well-greased grapevine, and information is easily distorted, especially if it was wrong to begin with. Check your facts. Make sure

you have the right names, dates, times, and places. When you're sure you're right, check again.

4. BE COHERENT (logical)—"But Peter explained it to them in order from the beginning. . . ." (Acts 11:4) "Let all things be done decently and in order." (1 Corinthians 14:40) Incoherence or poor logic is a common problem in writing, so I've given two Scriptures to emphasize its importance. The easiest method of organization is to tell your "story" chronologically—in the order events occurred or will occur. If you've got several items or points to cover, outline first. If you can't rank them chronologically, rank them in order of importance. Number each item in your letter if necessary. Be sure to make smooth transitions from one thought to another.

5. BE CLEAR—". . . do not use vain repetitions as the heathen do. For they think that they will be heard for their many words." (Matthew 6:7b) Keep it simple. Never use a long word where a short one will do. Just as God ignores heathen prayers loaded with "fancy language," so will your reader! Other than observing the basic rules of grammar, write the way your reader talks.

6. BE KIND—"Finally, all of you be of one mind, having compassion for one another; love as brothers, be tenderhearted, be courteous." (1 Peter 3:8) Never write a letter when you're angry. If you do, don't mail it. Set it aside so you and your letter can cool off. Always be as considerate of your reader as you want them to be toward you. Try to see the situation from their point of view. We all make mistakes. Sometimes anger is a reasonable reaction to a situation. But always be careful how you let your anger be expressed.

7. BE YOURSELF—"Two men went up to the temple to pray, one a Pharisee and the other a tax collector. The Pharisee stood and prayed thus with himself, 'God, I thank You that I am not like other men—extortioners, unjust, adulterers, or even as this tax collector. I fast twice a week; I give tithes of all that I possess.'

"And the tax collector, standing afar off, would not so much as raise his eyes to heaven, but beat his breast, saying, 'God be merciful to me a sinner.'

"I tell you, this man went down to his house justified rather than the other; for everyone who exalts himself will be abased, and he who humbles himself will be exalted." (Luke 18:10-14) The moral of this parable is, don't put on airs, whether you're dealing with God or people. Be yourself. Be honest. Be straightforward. Don't use words or a style that you wouldn't use in a conversation with your best friend.

8. BE BRIEF (concise)—"And I appeal to you, brethern, bear with the word of exhortation, for I have written to you in few words." (Hebrews 13:22) Have a point. Get to the point. Stick to the point. And then sign off. How many two-or four-page letters do you read all the way through? Don't write letters longer than they need to be.

9. BE WILLING TO REVISE—"And the vessel that he made of lay was marred in the hand of the potter; so he made it again into another vessel, as it seemed good to the potter to make." (Jeremiah 18:4) Seldom is any good writing achieved in the first draft. As all good writing, letters deserve special care, not only out of consideration for your reader, but also for yourself. Letters convey in print an image—your image. The more personal or sensitive or special the situation, the more carefully they must be thought out. Always have someone else proofread for typos, misspellings, and other errors. A little mistake can cost you and your church a lot of respect.

10. BE BRAVE—"And David said to his son Solomon, 'Be strong and of good courage, and do it; do not fear or be dismayed, for the Lord—my God—will be with you. He will not leave nor forsake you, until you have finished all the work for the service of the house of the Lord.' " (1 Chronicles 28:20) While many are intimidated by having to write, it need not be a fearful task. With forethought and planning, anyone can write an effective and powerful letter. Using this book as a resource, you should never be at a loss for words or a format for your letters. Have an important letter to write? Be brave—and do it!

All-Purpose Letter Writing Outline

This letter is based on the AIDA formula. The letters in the acronym stand for ATTENTION, INTEREST, DESIRE, and ACTION. The formula is useful applied to any kind of writing.

Keeping this formula in mind and, using the following outline as a quick reference, you will have no trouble writing effective letters for every purpose.

Date (Month, Day, Year)

Name of Recipient, Title
Name of Company/Organization
Street Address or P.O. Box
City, State, Zip Code

Salutation (Dear [Name],)
Opening . . . A brief greeting or introduction if needed. Many letters do not need an opening.
P1. ATTENTION—Gain the reader's immediate attention by stating the purpose of the letter. Why are you writing? Get to the point.
P2. INTEREST—Maintain the reader's interest by stating why you're writing to him or her. How is your reader related to your purpose?
P3. DESIRE—Arouse the reader's desire to respond to your letter. What's "in it" for the reader? What's the reader going to gain by responding to your letter?
P4. ACTION—What exactly do you want the reader to do? How? When? Where? If you're asking for money, how much? Or, what action are you going to take on behalf of the reader? In other words, how are you or the reader supposed to fulfill the purpose of this letter?
Closing . . . In one or two sentences, restate your purpose in writing and the action desired from the reader. Then thank your reader for his or her time and response, and sign off. Many letters don't need a closing.

Sign-Off (Sincerely,)
Your Signature
Your Name
Your Title
(If not included on your letterhead, type your church's name, complete address, and phone number here.)

Your Initials (uppercase)/your secretary's initials (lowercase)

P.S. If needed.

CHAPTER 1

Letters to Members of All Ages

The letters in this chapter are examples of some of the most common a minister will find it necessary to write. Many deal with what may seem mundane announcements, yet are actually vital pieces of information. It is important to keep congregations aware of both big and small events, so they can in turn be involved in the life of the church.

Some letters also deal with the hard issues—disciplining a troublesome member, announcing the resignation of a pastor, and so on. Yet most deal with the good news of Sunday school promotions, wedding plans, new programs, and more.

It is always important, whether the news is good or bad, that the message be communicated clearly, accurately, and truthfully—and in the appropriate tone. These letters achieve each of those goals.

1 / TO ADULTS ABOUT ADVANCEMENTS

It is my privilege to inform you that as of December 1, our district supervisor, Dr. Roy Piersman, will assume the office of executive board member for the denominational office in California. I'm certain you will want to join me in wishing him God's best as he advances to this new position. Dr. Piersman has been a great help to me personally, and I will miss his work on the district level. But as an executive board member, he will have even more opportunities for service to the Lord.

If you want to convey your congratulations to him, his new address will be:

As of now, a replacement for district supervisor has not been named. When one is, I will inform you.

Sincerely,

Pastor

2 / TO ADULTS ABOUT AGENDAS

As you know, the parish is in the process of constructing a new building in which to meet. A meeting has been set for Tuesday, October 18, at 7 P.M. to discuss the various aspects of the project.

On the agenda will be the following:

Blueprints of the proposed building will be displayed and discussed. The architect will be on hand to explain them.

A list of what jobs men in the parish can do will be presented, and a system of when they can work will be set up.

The finances for the project will be reported and ideas for additional fund raising will be developed.

As you can see, this will be an important meeting. Please make every effort to be present.

Sincerely,

Father
St. Mary's Church

3 / TO ADULTS ABOUT ANNOUNCEMENTS

Pentecost was the first great ingathering of the Church. On that day when the disciples of Christ went into the streets of Jerusalem with the power of the Holy Spirit upon them, the witness which they gave brought some 3,000 persons into the infant Church. It was the beginning of the Christian movement, which was to spread into all the known world within the next fifty years, to win an empire within 300 hundred years, to carry the message of salvation to Europe, Asia, and America in the following centuries.

We are heirs of the witness, and this coming Pentecost, Sunday, May 22, we wish to see another ingathering of men and women into the Church. At that time, we will receive members through the young peoples' communicants' class, the adults' communicants' class, and transfer of membership from other congregations.

But we would also like to extend an invitation to come to all; those who are regular in worship, those who love the Church but don't get out to worship as often as they would like, and those who once found the fellowship of the Church to be uplifting but have somehow drifted away.

Will you help make Pentecost 19XX another great ingathering of the Church? That first Pentecost of the Church brought in 3,000 persons. We would like to have 300 in worship here that Sunday to proclaim our part in the Church. Come and be a part of it.

Sincerely,

Pastor

4 / TO ADULTS ABOUT APPOINTMENTS

This is to inform you that Father James Murphy, who has served our parish so faithfully for the past four years, has received a new appointment. As of April 1, he will begin serving in St. Luke's parish in Columbus.

As difficult as it is to see him go, I am confident that he will be more than able to handle the new challenges of his position. I am also certain that he will miss St. Mary's and those of you whom he has come to know and love. If you feel inclined to express your appreciation for his service to him, I encourage you to do so.

As of the present, no successor has been appointed to fill Father Murphy's position. When one is named, I will inform you.

Sincerely,

Father
St. Mary's Church

5 / TO ADULTS ABOUT CONDOLENCES— ON DEATH OF A SPOUSE

A letter of condolence is one of the most difficult things to write, but it must be done. Usually it may be brief, offering empathy, not pat answers, and the availability of the clergy to assist the survivors during the progression of the grieving process.

The entire St. Mary's parish joins me in extending heartfelt sympathy to you at the tragic passing of your husband. There is no bond so deep as that of a man and his wife, and to break that bond through death is to inflict unspeakable pain on the remaining spouse.

Though we cannot fully understand the trauma you are experiencing, be assured that you are in our prayers. Our Heavenly Father will be with you to strengthen and support you as you go through these stressful days of adjustment.

The grieving process, especially for the loss of a mate, is a lengthy one, and if at any time you feel the need to talk, please call me. I am available at any hour.

May God bless and sustain you.

Sincerely,

Father
St. Mary's Church

6 / TO ADULTS ABOUT CONGRATULATIONS— ON JOB PROMOTION

It was great news to hear about your promotion from assistant professor of English to associate professor. This advancement is certainly well-deserved, and I am confident that you are fully qualified to handle it.

As you know, your profession is yet another aspect of your life in which you can demonstrate your faith. May God grant you many opportunities to do so!

Again, congratulations from myself and the parish. Madonna College is blessed to have you as part of the faculty.

Sincerely,

Father
St. Mary's Church

7 / TO ADULTS ABOUT DISCIPLINARY ACTION

A letter concerning problems caused by a member which are severe enough to require disciplinary action must be handled delicately. Notice the restating of the warning that the actions must stop, the expression of concern for the individual, and the offer to further discuss the situation at any point.

I regret that in spite of the talk we had last week, you have continued to do the very things you were advised to stop. As I informed you at that point, if you continued to attack my person and my authority as pastor, you could expect consequences.

Therefore, you are hereby relieved of all positions you hold in the church. Obviously, it isn't fair to the congregation or to me for you to continue serving at this time.

I truly hope that you will reconsider your stand and again be able to resume service and fellowship here. Even though we have had our different viewpoints, you have been a valuable part of the church and I don't want to lose you.

However, as long as you hold your current beliefs about me and my ministry, it is impossible for you to remain a leader here. I pray that you would seek God for a peaceable solution to this problem, and that you will soon be fully restored at First Church. As always, I am more than willing to sit down and talk with you at any time.

May God bless you.

Sincerely,

Pastor

8 / TO ADULTS ABOUT ELECTIONS

Greetings in the Name of Christ!

As a result of the general elections held on October 22, the following members have been selected to serve on the council at First Church:

Richard Arnold, 989-6767
Ernest Johnson, 989-4003
Carl Myers, 989-4466
Helen Potter, 989-0012
Sidney Young, 559-3367

Feel free to contact any of these individuals at their home phones listed above. In agreeing to be on the council for the next two years, they are reaffirming their desire to serve Christ and their fellow members.

For your convenience, other council members are:

Joyce Adams, 989-7866
Peter Brockway, 989-0223
Martin Hsu, 989-4241
Manuel Ortiz, 989-6655
Jeff Ziegler, 989-0077

We extend our congratulations to the new council members, and we are confident that they will work together with the rest of council in accomplishing what Christ has called First Church to do.

Yours because of Him,

Pastor

9 / TO ADULTS ABOUT ENCOURAGEMENT— WHILE WAITING TO ADOPT A CHILD

It has been several months since I sent my recommendation about you to Catholic Social Services, and I am certain that by now you have completed their process of applying for the adoption of a child. All that is left for you to do is to wait until they have a baby available for you.

Naturally, this is the most difficult part. Perhaps it seems to you that you will never receive the son or daughter for which you have waited so long. But I want to assure you that you continue to be in the prayers of myself as well as many others in the parish. You will get just the right child that our Heavenly Father has for you, at exactly the right moment. This time of waiting can be useful in preparing yourselves for the challenge of parenthood.

If at any time you feel the need to talk, please call me. And if there is some way I can help with the process at the agency, I am more than willing to contact them on your behalf.

May God bless you and uphold you during this time.

> Looking forward with you to the time of rejoicing to come,

> Father,
> St. Mary's Church

10 / TO ADULTS ABOUT EVALUATIONS— OF CHURCH AT YEAR'S END

Looking back over the year we have just finished, I am praising God for all He has done in First Church. Are you aware that:

— Thirty-six adults united with our fellowship, through confession of faith or transfer of membership?

— Seventeen young people joined the church at the completion of communicants' class?

— Twenty-three children and adults underwent the sacrament of baptism?

— Twenty couples were married?

In addition, our average Sunday morning attendance went from last year's figure of 198 to 245. In Sunday school, attendance increased from an average of 89 to 140 people. The weekly offerings went from last year's figure of $730 to $905 this year.

Programs for youth, women, and senior citizens flourished, and we can rejoice that we were able to donate over 500 pounds of food to those who needed it.

All in all, 19XX was a good year for First Church. However, we should not be satisfied with our past achievements. It is time to continue to move forward. In the coming year, I would like to see more people attending the home Bible study groups, a greater commitment to personal prayer among members, and many more persons led into a relationship with Christ.

Yes, there is much to be done, but we can go on to meet the task with the Lord as our strength. Let's trust Him to make this new year the best yet!

Looking forward,

Pastor

11 / TO ADULTS ABOUT INFORMATION

As Christmas approaches, St. Mary's will again hold a live Nativity in the church parking lot. Our youth will be playing the roles of the Blessed Virgin, the shepherds, etc., but we are in need of live sheep and/or a donkey for the display. If you have access to these animals and could loan them to us, please contact my office.

The hours for the live Nativity will be 6 to 8 P.M. on the nights of December 12, 13, 19, and 20. We hope you will be able to attend and bring your children.

May your Advent season be full of the joys of this special time of year.

Sincerely,

Father
St. Mary's Church

12 / TO ADULTS ABOUT INSTRUCTIONS

Gratitude is an attribute that God wants us to cultivate. It's very easy for us to forget to thank Him for the blessings of good health, family and friends, a home, and the freedom to worship our Heavenly Father.

In addition to verbally expressing our thanks to God, we can demonstrate it by helping others less fortunate than ourselves. One way of doing this is by contributing to Canned Foods Days, which will be held on Saturday and Sunday, November 20 and 21. Baskets for the food will be placed by the doors of St. Mary's on those days.

Especially needed are canned goods such as tuna, fruits, and peanut butter. The items collected will be divided between the Rockview Referral agency, the Samaritan House, and needy individuals in the parish.

Please consider the plight of these people and contribute to Canned Goods Days. I, and they, thank you.

Sincerely,

Father
St. Mary's Church

13 / TO ADULTS ABOUT MEETINGS—TO VOTE ON PURCHASE OF NEW BUILDING

As you probably know, our family at First Church has been seeking a new building in which we might carry out our ministry. We are now ready for your vote on whether or not to purchase the old Panel-Ply building.

A meeting has been scheduled for Sunday, October 12, after the morning service. At that time, we shall present a resolution that requires your action. This is your official notice of that membership meeting. All members over eighteen years of age may vote.

If you cannot attend but would like to cast your vote, please contact me.

In addition, I would ask that you continue in prayer about the building, that we would have the wisdom to know if this is God's will for our congregation.

In His service,

Pastor

14 / TO ADULTS ABOUT NEWSLETTERS— TO UPDATE MAILING LIST

The church newsletter is an important link for our members and friends at First Church, and we are more than willing to send it to anyone who wishes to receive it.

However, some who have wanted to get it in the past may no longer be interested, for any number of reasons. Therefore, we are updating our mailing list. Enclosed you will find a card with space for your name and current address. If you desire to continue receiving the newsletter, please mail or return the card to the church by February 1. Anyone whose card is not back by then will be automatically taken off the mailing list.

It is not our intention to drop the names of any of our members or friends who are interested in the newsletter. But it is not good stewardship to keep paying postage for mailings that people don't want.

We appreciate your cooperation in this matter. Whether or not you wish to remain on the mailing list, we wish God's best for you today and every day.

Sincerely,

Pastor

15 / TO ADULTS ABOUT PROBLEMS— CONCERNING PARKING

Recently, a problem concerning parking has developed of which you should be aware. As you know, Dr. Johnson has been kind enough to permit St. Mary's parishioners to use his parking lot across from the church. His only stipulation was that it be used by a maximum of ten cars, none of which were to be located on the grass surrounding his office.

However, for a number of Sundays, there have been approximately fifteen cars in his parking lot during the 11 A.M. Mass, as well as sometimes for other services. Dr. Johnson has brought the matter to my attention, since the grass is starting to show signs of wear.

I am certain that this reminder to you will result in no further problems with too many cars in Dr. Johnson's lot. Your cooperation is greatly appreciated.

Sincerely,

Father
St. Mary's Church

16 / TO ADULTS ABOUT PROCEDURES— TO BORROW CHURCH PROPERTY

It has come to my attention that many in the congregation are unfamiliar with the procedure for borrowing church property. As a result, a number of items have been taken without informing the proper people. When this happens, and a particular item is needed, there is no way to find out where it is.

To help eliminate this problem, let me state the approved church policy:

If any person or organization wishes to borrow any equipment, permission must be obtained from the president of the Board of Trustees. He is James Montag, (address and phone). He is to have a current list of everything loaned out. Once it is returned, he is to check it off the list.

Preference will be given to members, and all equipment must be used for purposes in keeping with the official beliefs and policies of the church.

Anything that is lost or damaged will be the responsibility of the person who requested to borrow it.

Thank you for your cooperation in this matter. I am certain that there will be no further problems.

Sincerely,

Pastor

17 / TO ADULTS ABOUT QUESTIONNAIRES— TO ASK FOR HELP IN FILLING ONE OUT

For a number of years, First Church has met at 9:30 A.M. for worship, with Sunday school following at 10:30. Recently, the idea of holding the worship service at the later time has been discussed by the Administrative Board. However, before deciding, we would like your opinion.

Please complete the enclosed questionnaire and bring or mail it to the church by March 31. At the April 27 meeting of the Board, the results will be presented and a final decision made. In order for this decision to accurately reflect the wishes of the congregation, we need to know what you want.

Thank you for your help in this matter. Working together, we can certainly come to a place of agreement on the hours of the Sunday services.

Sincerely,

Pastor

18 / TO ADULTS ABOUT RESIGNATIONS— RESIGNATION OF PASTOR

It's important to inform the church membership of a decision to move to a new position before it has gone through the church via word of mouth. The letter doesn't need to go into detail about why such a choice has been made. Note how the following letter reveals both the pastor's eagerness to assume the new job and regret at leaving.

It is with mixed feelings that I write this letter. As of 1/1/XX, I will no longer be pastor of First Church. I have accepted a position as senior pastor at Faith Memorial Church in Weston, and I will be assuming my new duties there on January 15.

Naturally, I look forward to the work in Weston with great anticipation. There will be many opportunities for ministry as well as for personal growth there. Yet, leaving the congregation at First Church is extremely difficult for me. No group of people could have been more supportive to me and my wife. I question if I will ever feel as close to a church family as I do here.

But there is no doubt in my mind and heart that it is time for me to move on to this new challenge. I wish each of you the very best as you seek God and obey His leading in your life. As you have always done for me, encourage and help your new pastor. And be certain that you are in my prayers.

Sincerely,

Pastor

19 / TO ADULTS ABOUT SCHEDULES— ABOUT NEW SUNDAY EVENING SERVICES

The book of Revelation tells us that as the ages go by, the distinction between the righteous and the unrighteous will increase until the last great battle between them. We don't know when this battle will take place, but we can make a decision about which side we'll be on when it does happen. Will you and your family make the decision to stand as Christ's people throughout the following months?

One way you can act on your commitment to be the righteous is to plan to attend the new series of Sunday evening services now being scheduled.

The first Sunday of each month will be devoted to a service of worship through song. Individuals from our church will be sharing their vocal talent with us, and as a congregation we will sing a number of hymns. You will even have a chance to request your favorites.

The second Sunday will be Church Family evening. After a potluck supper, a film appealing to the entire family will be shown.

A special service will be held on the third Sunday of each month. This will include guest speakers and musical groups.

The fourth Sunday will be in the hands of different lay groups within the church, such as the youth and the women's association.

When there is a fifth Sunday in the month, nothing will be scheduled, in order that you may spend the time with your family.

I'm excited about this new series and I hope that you will be too. Decide now that you will be a part of Sunday evenings at First Church. I'm certain that it will only strengthen your commitment to Christ.

Sincerely,

Pastor

20 / TO ADULTS ABOUT SPECIAL EVENTS— ABOUT UPCOMING SERVICE WITH VISITING MUSICAL GROUP

Greetings in the Name of Our Lord!

"O sing unto the Lord a new song: sing unto the Lord all the earth" Psalm 96:1 (KJV).

First Church is going to be praising the Lord in song on Sunday evening, March 29, when we host the New Life Singers from Erie, PA. The service begins at 7 P.M.

A group of fifteen musicians and vocalists, ages eighteen to thirty, the New Life Singers have traveled across most of the eastern United States, presenting their message that Jesus truly brings a changed and different life to those who let Him into their hearts. Their style varies from Southern Gospel to contemporary Christian, and the enthusiasm and vitality of the group has ministered to congregations everywhere for the past five years.

Plan on joining us for this exciting and inspiring evening of song, and bring a friend. You can expect to receive a blessing!

In Christ,

Pastor

21 / TO ADULTS ABOUT THANKS—UPON RECEIVING CONGREGATIONAL CHRISTMAS GIFT

A thank-you note is always gratefully received. If an actual gift is involved, it should specifically be referred to; if it is cash, as in the following example, the amount ought not to be revealed, but to state the intended use is in good taste.

As my wife and I opened the envelope presented to us from the congregation at the Christmas Eve service, we were once again overwhelmed by the generosity of God's people. Thank you, dear friend, for your part in the gift. We realize that for many, it meant a sacrifice; perhaps one less meal in a restaurant or a smaller present for your spouse. Believe me, it is appreciated!

After much thought and discussion, Mary and I have decided to use it to purchase a new arm chair. If you've been in our living room lately, you know how much it is needed. We expect to have it in the next month; after then, please feel free to stop in and see it.

We are so pleased with the gift, but even more so, we cherish what it means—the love, prayers, and support of our congregation. May God bless you abundantly!

With our deepest appreciation,

Pastor

22 / TO CHILDREN ABOUT ADVANCEMENT— MOVING INTO THE NEXT AGE GROUP CLASS FOR SUNDAY SCHOOL

Fall is here again! School's started, leaves are beginning to change in color, and the weather's getting cooler.

Things are happening at First Church, too. You will be moving up to a new Sunday school class. Promotion Sunday will be on September 21, and on that day you will become a part of the fifth and sixth grade class. The class meets in room 104, and Mrs. Havens is the teacher. The Sunday school hour is from 9 to 10 A.M.

We're sure that you'll have fun and learn a lot in your new class. Hope you'll be able to make it every week!

See you in room 104,

Pastor

23 / TO CHILDREN ABOUT ANNOUNCEMENTS

If you see people and trucks from the Channel 12 TV station around St. Mary's next Sunday, don't be surprised. The station has received permission to do a program on "Growing Up

Catholic,'' and they will be asking some questions of several children from our parish. If they stop you as you are leaving Mass, you should politely answer their questions.

When we know the day and time the show will be broadcast, we will tell you.

Blessings,

Father
St. Mary's Church

24 / TO CHILDREN ABOUT CERTIFICATES

Attention all girls and boys who attended Vacation Bible School! Certificates saying that you were a part of the fun and learning at this year's VBS are ready for you now. They can be picked up in the church office at any time, along with a number of art projects completed on the last day of VBS.

We would appreciate it if you could get them as soon as possible. Thanks!

Sincerely,

Pastor

25 / TO CHILDREN ABOUT CONDOLENCES— ON THE DEATH OF A MOTHER

The loss of a parent is extremely traumatic. The following letter acknowledges the validity of the questions such a child may have, and expresses the willingness to talk it out, without guaranteeing answers.

It doesn't seem fair, does it? Just when you needed her, your mother is gone. Maybe you feel angry at her or even at God, for letting her die. Or you could be wondering if she'd be alive now if you had done or thought something differently. You might be confused and asking yourself, "Why? Why did this happen?"

All of those thoughts would be very normal for you to have. In fact, the grown-ups who loved your mom are probably feeling the same things. No one would be mad at you for thinking them. And if you are, it would be good for you to talk to someone about your feelings.

If you want to share them with me, I would be glad to listen. Just call me and we can get together. I don't promise to have a lot of answers (even adults don't always know everything, especially when it comes to a death), but we can talk it out. I join the rest of the parish in telling you how sorry I am at your great loss. My prayer for you is that our loving Heavenly Father will comfort you and your family.

Sincerely,

Father
St. Mary's Church

26 / TO CHILDREN ABOUT CONGRATULATIONS

Now that you have reached the third grade, we at First Church feel you have come to an important point in your life. You have a firm grip on reading, and so you are ready for your very own Bible. Reading God's Word is very important, because you find out what God is like and what He wants you to do.

To help you learn the Bible, we want to give you one especially written for boys and girls. On Sunday, September 18, we will ask you to come up to the front of the church during the 10:30 A.M. worship service. Then you will get your Bible.

We hope that you will read it every day and do what it says. Congratulations on taking this big step!

See you on the 18th,

Pastor

27 / TO CHILDREN ABOUT DISCIPLINARY ACTION

I am sorry to tell you that for the next month, you will not be permitted to attend your Sunday school class. In spite of repeated warnings from your teacher, Mrs. Ross, that your in-class behavior must change, you have continued to create problems by talking to and poking your classmates. I have also personally spoken with you, but you have apparently chosen to keep it up. So we have no choice but to remove you from the class for a time. For you to remain would simply not be fair to the others in the class who want to learn.

During class time in March, you will be required to stay in the church office. We hope that by the end of the month, you will be willing to act as you should in your class. At that time, you may return to your room. But remember, I will not hesitate to take you out of class again if your behavior is not what it should be.

I have talked to your parents about this, and they are in agreement with me. Believe me, neither they nor I like doing this. But at this point, we can see no other way to go.

I do feel that you don't really want to be like this, and I am praying that God will help you to change. If you want to talk, please call me.

Sincerely,

Pastor

28 / TO CHILDREN ABOUT ENCOURAGEMENT— WHEN A PARENT REMARRIES

Many children face a stepparent entering their families, but there still is a time of adjustment for everyone involved. The following letter is written on a positive note, assuring the child that the problems which arise will work out. Yet it recognizes that the stepmother will never take the place of the deceased, and that the child may have to deal with negative emotions.

By now, you are probably busy helping with the wedding plans. You haven't said what you think about your dad getting married again, but I wanted you to know that if you have some mixed feelings, it's OK.

I'm sure you've been told that your soon-to-be stepmother is not trying to take your mother's place. No one can ever do that. You will always love and miss your mom.

But you can grow to love your stepmother too. It may not be easy at first. After all, since your mom's death, you and your dad have been on your own. And you've done pretty well.

Now this lady you hardly know will be moving into your house and doing things your mom used to do. You could feel sort of angry at her. Or you might be mad at your dad for marrying someone else. If you feel this way, don't be upset. Lots of kids have gone through the same thing when their parents remarried.

But remember, God has brought Marie into your dad's life. He wants to make you a family—not just like the one you had, but a new family. If you let Him, He can help change any bad feelings you have. It will take time. There will be problems, just as with anyone beginning relationships. Yet they can be worked out, if the three of you want them to be.

If you ever want to talk to someone about all of this, call me. I am praying for you during this difficult time of adjustment.

Sincerely,

Father
St. Mary's Church

29 / TO CHILDREN ABOUT EVALUATIONS— OF VACATION BIBLE SCHOOL

How did you like Gospel Bill? What was the most fun in Vacation Bible School last week? What didn't you like? We want to know!

So that we can plan for next year, we need to find out just how you felt about it. Please take a minute right now and answer the questions on the back of this letter. Then bring or mail it back to the church by Sunday, July 7. You can give it to your Sunday school teacher or put it in the offering basket.

Thanks for your help!

Sincerely,

Pastor

30 / TO CHILDREN ABOUT INFORMATION— CONCERNING ESTABLISHMENT OF NEW CHILDREN'S CHOIR

Do you like to sing? If you do, we have just the place for you! Starting in January, the Cherub Choir will be forming for girls and boys in grades two through six. We will be practicing once a week for about forty-five minutes, and we will sing during morning worship five or six times a year. The director will be Mrs. Diane Williams.

When we find out more details, we will let you know. But you can start practicing singing right now!

Hoping you'll want to be a part,

Pastor

31 / TO CHILDREN ABOUT INSTRUCTIONS

Several months ago, you were given a little plastic bread loaf to take home from Sunday school. Your teacher told you that you could put money in it and that after a while, you would bring it back to church. Then the money would all be put together and given to One Great Hour of Sharing. It would help hungry children to get food.

I hope that you have remembered to put some quarters, dimes, nickels, and pennies in your loaf, because now it is time to bring them back to church. All loaves need to be here by Sunday, October 22. That day, we will be breaking them open and seeing how much money we have to help the poor children.

Please make sure that your Sunday school teacher has your loaf by then. If you do not have a loaf, you can still bring in some money to be used for this project. You can also ask your parents if they would like to give anything.

Thank you for your help, and remember that hungry boys and girls are counting on you.

Sincerely,

Pastor

32 / TO CHILDREN ABOUT MEETINGS

It was great to have you join us for Kids' Club last night. We hope that you had fun and learned more about Jesus too.

Remember, Kids' Club meets every Thursday at 7 P.M. in First Church's Fellowship Hall.

Boys and girls in grades one through six are welcome to come for a time of stories, crafts, games, and a snack.

Ask your parents right now if you can come back next week. You'll be glad you did!

See you then,

Pastor

33 / TO CHILDREN ABOUT NEWSLETTERS— ESTABLISHMENT OF CHILDREN'S PAGE

Attention boys and girls! Starting in January, First Church will be putting out a newsletter just for you. It will be on the back page of the regular church newsletter, and it will have fun things for you to do and read. There will be a story, puzzle, or dot-to-dot, and some ideas for things you can do to help others at home or at church.

The newsletter will also list things that you would want to know about, like Kids' Club special activities or children's services.

How can you get this great newsletter? Simple! If your parents get the regular newsletter, you will already get the children's newsletter. If your parents don't get it, just tell your Sunday school teacher or Kids' Club leader that you want it.

Don't forget, your very own newsletter will be in the mail soon. Be on the lookout for it!

Working for Jesus,

Pastor

34 / TO CHILDREN ABOUT PROBLEMS

The following letter is intended to be sent to all children in the Sunday school who are beyond nursery age. The problem—too much noise as youngsters pass the adult classrooms—and the desired change in behavior are clearly defined. And although the consequences of further misbehavior are specified, the certainty of no more problems is conveyed.

Are there problems at First Church? Yes, but we think they can be solved. You see, during the Sunday school hour, some boys and girls go down the hall past the rooms where the grown-ups are meeting. Instead of walking quietly, they talk in loud voices and make too much noise with their feet. They laugh and clap their hands. Even when their teacher tells them to stop, they keep doing it.

All the noise makes it hard for the grown-ups to hear their lesson. It has to end. As your pastor, I'm asking you to listen to your teacher and be VERY quiet when you're in the hall during Sunday school. It's not fair to make others who want to learn miss their lesson.

I've spoken to all the Sunday school teachers about this, and any boy or girl who keeps doing it will have to come talk to me. Jesus would not want you to disobey. I'm expecting to see a big change this Sunday, and I'm certain that you won't disappoint me.

Sincerely,

Pastor

35 / TO CHILDREN ABOUT QUESTIONNAIRES— TO COMPLETE ONE ON FAVORITE ACTIVITIES

What do you like to do? Swimming? Roller skating? Eating pizza? Whatever it is, we want to find out.

Once again, the Sunday school department is planning the annual get-together for all the boys and girls who have been learning about Jesus each week. We decided that we would do what *you* like this year. With this letter is a questionnaire listing some things kids have fun doing. Please answer the questions about what you think we should do. Also fill in (or have your parents do it) the best day and time for you to attend. Then mail or bring the paper back to church by Sunday, April 22.

When we have all the papers, we will decide what most boys and girls would like to do. Then we'll let you know the plans.

Don't forget—we need your help to make this the best Sunday school outing ever!

Sincerely,

Pastor

36 / TO CHILDREN ABOUT RESIGNATIONS

This is to let you know that after next week, I will no longer be leading the Tuesday evening children's meeting.

During the past two years that I've been in charge of it, I have really enjoyed getting to know you boys and girls. As I've played with you, sang with you, done crafts with you, and taught you about Jesus and the Bible, I've learned a lot. I hope you have too.

Because the adult home Bible study group has grown so much, it will now be dividing into two. I will be leading the new group, so I can no longer go to the children's meeting. Mrs. Joyce Ransom has offered to take my place. I'm sure she'll do a great job and that you will all help her.

I'll miss having the time with you each Tuesday, but I know you will be in good hands.

God bless you,

Pastor

37 / TO CHILDREN ABOUT SCHEDULES— FOR VACATION BIBLE SCHOOL

Have you met Gospel Bill? If you haven't, you're in for a treat! That cowboy is coming to First Church by way of videos for this year's Vacation Bible School. He has lots to teach us about Jesus and living for Him. But Gospel Bill is also just plain fun.

We hope you plan to join the good times, beginning Monday, June 10, at 9 A.M. VBS will last all week and be out at 11:30 A.M. each day, except Friday, June 14. On that day, a picnic lunch will be held after classes for all the girls and boys involved. Tell your parents to pick you up at 1 P.M. Friday.

The closing program for VBS will be held during morning worship on Sunday, June 16. You should be at the church by 9:30 A.M. so you can practice your part before the service begins at 10.

Invite your friends to join you at Vacation Bible School. Gospel Bill is ready to meet you!

See you then,

Pastor

38 / TO CHILDREN ABOUT SPECIAL EVENTS— UPCOMING PUPPET SHOW

Many places of worship hold occasional special services for boys and girls. A letter such as the following generates excitement in the children, which they will hopefully pass on to their parents, the ones who are usually in charge of transportation.

Hi Boys and Girls,

Peaches, Freddy, and Bubblegum are coming your way soon! Tell your mom and dad to mark the calendar right now, because the special children's service on Sunday evening, March 21, is one you won't want to miss.

Pam Donoghue and her puppets will be ready to meet you at First Church, starting at 7 P.M. Called "The Puppet Lady" by children where she lives, Mrs. Donoghue has been bringing her friends Peaches and the others to churches for ten years. You'll laugh at the funny things they do and say as they learn about Jesus.

Don't miss this special evening service just for you!

See you then,

Pastor

39 / TO CHILDREN ABOUT THANKS— FOR ASSISTANCE AT FESTIVAL

You may not realize it, but you were an important part of the St. Mary's festival last weekend.

If you manned a booth with your parents, if you watched your younger brothers and sisters so that Mom and Dad could work, if you set up chairs or threw away trash, you helped make the festival the great success it was. And if you could do none of that but still attended, you also did a lot, because you were needed to enjoy the games, food, and fun.

Thanks for whatever you did! By working together as the parish did last weekend, we help each other. I'm proud of what St. Mary's can do.

Sincerely,

Father
St. Mary's Church

40 / TO TEENS ABOUT ADVANCEMENT—INTO NEXT AGE LEVEL CLASS FOR SUNDAY SCHOOL

Good News! Now that you are beginning your sophomore year, you are invited to become a part of First Church's senior high Sunday school class.

The class meets in room 109 starting at 9:30 A.M. Bob and Cathy Davis are the teachers. I'm sure that you'll find them easy to talk to, fun to be around, and deeply committed to the Lord. They want to help you learn more about your faith, as well as to mature in your walk with Christ.

If you have been attending the junior high class, move on up to room 109. If you haven't been coming, how about starting next Sunday? You'll be glad you did!

Hope to see you there,

Pastor

41 / TO TEENS ABOUT AGENDAS— FOR YOUTH GROUP

Where will you be the evening of Sunday, October 4? I hope you're planning on attending the youth meeting. We have plenty of important things to discuss.

On the agenda are:

— Making final plans for Youth Sunday, October 18. We still need two teens to read Scripture and one more usher.

— Deciding which money making project to do in October, selling candy apples or have a slave day.

— Writing a group letter to the child we sponsor in Mexico.

— Brainstorming about how we as a youth group can help fight pornography in our city.

Because of all of this, we really need each member of the youth group to be present. Can we count on you?

Sincerely,

Pastor

42 / TO TEENS ABOUT ANNOUNCEMENTS— CANCELLATION OF YOUTH GROUP

Because of the illness of Bob Myers, CYO will not be meeting this week. We trust that Mr. Myers will soon be well enough to fulfill his responsibilities as youth leader.

Keep in mind that the canoe trip planned for May 20 will take place at that time, even if Bob is unable to go. It's not too late to sign up for it.

Sincerely,

Father
St. Mary's Church

43 / TO TEENS ABOUT APPOINTMENTS— TO SET UP PERSONAL CONFERENCES

Congratulations on successfully completing membership class at First Church! As you will remember, however, before you can actually join the church, you need to meet with me personally to talk about your own relationship with Jesus.

I have set Monday, March 2 at 4 P.M. for your appointment. Please come to my study at that time. Plan on spending about twenty minutes with me.

If for some reason you won't be available then, call the church office to reschedule.

If you don't want to be considered for church membership now, you may cancel your appointment. But I would be more than willing to meet with you anyway just to talk about any questions or concerns you may have.

Looking forward to having some one-on-one time with you,

Pastor

44 / TO TEENS ABOUT CONDOLENCES—ON THE ATHLETIC TEAM'S LOSS IN TOURNAMENT PLAY

While this type of loss isn't like losing a loved one, it would be a great tragedy to a teen member of the team. Writing a letter like this expresses the church's caring for the individual, especially important during adolescence when religion often becomes personal, not just something of one's parents. Also conveying pride in the athlete's ability to participate in sports, the letter builds self-image and confidence at a time when the teen may be lacking in them.

To say that last night's game was a great disappointment is such an understatement that it's almost better to say nothing. But we at First Church wanted you to know that although Riverbend High is now out of the district tournament, we are proud of you.

Throughout the basketball season, you have worked hard with the team, doing your best to help make it a winning season. And you've succeeded. With a fourteen win, two loss record, no one can say otherwise.

We realize it must be a severe blow not to get to attend the regional tournament. But you can be sure that everyone in Riverbend thinks you (and the entire team) did a great job. Remember, God can use a defeat in your life too.

Looking forward to seeing you out on the court next season,

Pastor

45 / TO TEENS ABOUT CONGRATULATIONS— ON ATHLETIC HONOR

On behalf of everyone at First Church, we would like to congratulate you on your being named to the district all-star basketball team. This honor is certainly well-deserved; we know how hard you have worked over the years to do your best on the court. Yet you still found time to be faithful to the church in attendance, serving as an officer in youth group and singing in the youth choir.

We just wanted you to know that we're proud of you, and we're eager to see how the Lord is going to continue to use you in His service over the years. May you always keep Him first in your life.

Again, our congratulations.

Sincerely in Christ,

Pastor

46 / TO TEENS ABOUT DISCIPLINARY ACTION— TO CONFIRM VERBAL DISCUSSION OF

As I stated in our talk yesterday, I wanted you to have a written record of what was said.

Vandalizing the mens' room at the church shows a serious lack of respect for the parish, myself, and God. You will be required to pay for the damages, and you will work twenty hours under the janitor to make up for what you have done.

After speaking with you about this, I believe that you are sorry and will not do such a thing again. However, I must remind you that if you do, more severe consequences will take place.

I have talked to your parents, and they agree with what I have decided to do.

Of course you will still have to deal with this in confession, which I expect you to do soon. May God help you to do what is right.

Sincerely,

Father
St. Mary's Church

47 / TO TEENS ABOUT ELECTIONS—RESULTS OF

Just in case you missed it, youth fellowship elections were held at the May 21 meeting. Next year's officers will be:

President, Jim Watson;
Vice-president, Kathy Burton;
Secretary, Joyce Matthews;
Treasurer, Sean Detterman.

Congratulations to these young people! We are looking forward to a great new year as all of us work together with the officers. Please keep in mind that they can't do anything without the support and participation of each member of the youth fellowship. Plan now to be an active part of it in the fall!

Sincerely,

Pastor

48 / TO TEENS ABOUT ENCOURAGEMENT— TO VICTIM OF TERMINAL DISEASE

Dealing with cancer patients (and others with fatal illnesses) is another difficult but necessary aspect of the ministry. The following letter would not be appropriate to send to everyone, but in this case, where the teen is well known by the pastor, candidness is acceptable.

I'm angry! Seeing the cancer drain your energy, invade more and more of your body, and tear you away from the things and people you love makes me furious. And I'm sure that your own anger must surpass mine.

All I can say is that I am praying for you continually, that the Lord would give you the strength you need, both physically and spiritually. You are in the middle of a great battle, and at times (or maybe even most of the time), you must feel very alone in your struggle.

But believe me, you haven't been forgotten. Many of the people at First Church have been and are faithfully praying for you too. We are asking God for a miracle.

In the meantime, you must keep on fighting. That doesn't mean you can't ever feel down or that you should pretend that everything is fine. But don't give up. God's love for you is just as strong as it ever has been, and He understands better than anyone else what you're going through.

I know I've told you before, but I want you to know that I still am available any time you need to talk. I promise to listen, not give pat answers, and to let you be whatever you need to be.

Sincerely,

Pastor

49 / TO TEENS ABOUT EVALUATION—PERSONAL

As the new years starts, it seems like an appropriate time to do a little self-evaluation. How would you answer the following questions?

1. Am I attending Sunday school faithfully?
2. Is Sunday morning worship a priority for me?
3. Have I been active in youth fellowship?
4. Do I devote time each day to personal prayer and Bible study?
5. Do I look for chances to share my faith with the people in my life?
6. Am I growing in my relationship with the Lord?
7. Am I involved in some kind of service to others on a regular basis?

Don't worry—you don't have to tell anyone how you answered these questions. But if you're like most of us, you realize that you could stand some shaping-up in the areas mentioned. Why not decide right now to do something to strengthen one of them today? It could be that you need to make more of an effort to attend youth group. Or maybe your biggest weakness is not taking time to pray and read the Bible. By setting goals and working one step at a time, you can change. And when would it be better to do so than the present?

While all of the areas mentioned are important, I admit that I would especially like to see more of you at the youth meetings and in Sunday school. So if you haven't been for a while, why not try it again? You'll be glad and so will I!

Sincerely,

Pastor

50 / TO TEENS ABOUT INFORMATION— CONFIRMING RESERVATION AND GIVING DETAILS FOR YOUTH RETREAT

We are delighted to acknowledge your reservation for the fall youth retreat to be held October 23–24 at Camp Mary Orton. The youth committee has been working hard to plan a fun as well as spiritually challenging weekend.

In order to ensure that everyone has a great and meaningful time, we want to remind you of the rules First Church has set up for youth activities.

1. No alcohol, smoking, or drugs.
2. Lights out by 11:30 P.M. and quiet by 12:30. Please be considerate of those around you trying to sleep.
3. No radios, tape decks, or boom boxes.
4. No running off from the group. You're expected to be at all scheduled activities.
5. Everyone helps clean up.

With your cooperation, we're confident that this retreat will be the best ever! Come expecting to be blessed!

In His Service,

Pastor

51 / TO TEENS ABOUT INSTRUCTIONS— CONCERNING YOUTH RETREAT

It's hard to believe, but the fall youth retreat is only a week away! The youth committee is excited about the program planned, and we hope you are too.

Please be at First Church's rear parking lot at 4 P.M. sharp on Friday, as it is important that we leave on time. In addition to your sleeping bag, Bible, and toiletries, you are asked to bring snack food to share on Friday night. Soft drinks will be provided.

We will be back at First Church at approximately 8 P.M. on Saturday evening. Make sure you will have transportation home.

See you on the 23rd at 4 P.M.!

Expecting a great weekend,

Pastor

52 / TO TEENS ABOUT MEETINGS— SPECIAL OFFICERS' MEETING

Just a reminder that the youth group officers will be meeting before youth group on Tuesday, May 2. Please make every effort to be in the library at 6 P.M. We will be discussing the upcoming summer camp-out, and we need the input of each of you in order to make several important decisions.

Counting on seeing you there,

Pastor

53 / TO TEENS ABOUT NEWSLETTERS— CHANGE IN YOUTH PAGE

Calling all teens! As of September, the Teen Happenings page of First Church's monthly newsletter will have a new look. In addition to the usual activities calendar, we are expanding it to include original writings and art work by youth. If you have drawings, poems, short stories, or other work you would like to share, submit it to the church office. We will try to use two or three items a month. If possible, they should somehow reflect your faith.

Please seriously consider what you can contribute. Your work can not only show what talented youth we have in our church, but it can minister to needs.

Anything to be considered for the September newsletter should be submitted by August 15. Thanks for your cooperation—without it, this new venture cannot succeed!

Sincerely,

Pastor

54 / TO TEENS ABOUT PROBLEMS— THROWING SNOWBALLS

Once again, the high point of winter—snow—has arrived. I know many of you have been looking forward to it for some time, and I also know that snow seems to be just waiting to be formed into snowballs and thrown.

But a few teens in our parish got a little carried away with the snowball war after the 11 A.M. Mass last Sunday, and the end result was that an elderly lady was hit with a snowball. I realize that this was an accident, but the lady did not appreciate having snow all over her clothes. In addition, she could have fallen and been injured.

Because of this, I must insist that no snowballs be thrown within a quarter mile radius of the church. I would also like to see the person who threw the snowball which hit Mrs. Groves apologize to her.

Thank you for your cooperation in this matter.

Sincerely,

Father
St. Mary's Church

55 / TO TEENS ABOUT PROCEDURES— FOR ELECTION OF OFFICERS

At the next meeting of the youth fellowship, we will be holding elections for new officers. Here is the procedure which we will use:

For each position, the youth council will present two names of those who are considered capable and willing to serve.

In addition, nominations from the floor will be accepted. Anyone may nominate a person, including himself/herself, but the nomination must be seconded from someone else present. A maximum of two names per office will be accepted from the floor.

After nominations have been closed by a motion and a second from the floor, members may vote for one name for each position.

When the voting is completed, the written ballots will be tabulated and the winners announced at the end of the meeting.

Be thinking now who you would like to lead the youth group next year! We already have some great ideas for programs and projects for then, and if you are dedicated to God and willing to serve Him in this way, we need you to accept the challenge of being an officer. Even if you don't want to run, please make sure to come and vote. Let your wishes be made known!

See you then!

Pastor

56 / TO TEENS ABOUT QUESTIONNAIRES

What do you want CYO to be? Would you like roller skating? A hayride? Horseback riding? What subjects would you like to learn about? Getting along with parents? Dating? Handling peer pressure?

As we plan activities for next school year, we are trying to set up a schedule that you will be excited about. But in order to do so, we need your cooperation. Please fill out the enclosed questionnaire, indicating what interests you, and bring or mail it to the church by Sunday, May 28.

Thanks for your help. We expect to have such a great CYO planned that every teen in the parish will participate!

Sincerely,

Father
St. Mary's Church

57 / TO TEENS ABOUT RESIGNATIONS— OF YOUTH OFFICER DUE TO ILLNESS

As you may already know, Kerry Wilson has been having a struggle with his health for some time. In spite of the cancer, he has been doing an outstanding job as president of the youth group.

But now, as his condition is worsening, Kerry has informed me that he can no longer handle the responsibilities of his office. Rather than hold back the group in any way, he has decided to resign. He has assured me that as his health permits, he will continue to attend meetings. But he feels someone else needs to take over the leadership position that he has held.

Although I'm sorry to see Kerry take this step, I understand and agree with his decision. This is a very difficult place for him to be in; I know how dedicated he is to the youth group.

At the next meeting, we will be taking nominations for a new president. In the meantime, I hope that you will make an effort to encourage Kerry in some way. Let him know that although he can no longer serve as an officer, he is still an important part of our youth group.

Sincerely,

Pastor

58 / TO TEENS ABOUT SCHEDULES— FOR YOUTH RETREAT

In only one more week, the youth retreat will be here! I hope you're as excited as I am. Here is the schedule for Friday and Saturday's activities:

Friday: 4:00 P.M.—Meet in church parking lot.

5:00 P.M.—Arrive at camp. Time to unload gear and find out where things are.

6:00 P.M.—Dinner. Girls in cabins one and two set up; boys in cabins five and six clean up.

7:00 P.M.—First Session. Bring your Bible, pen.

8:00 P.M.—Break for Recreation.

8:45 P.M.—Share Groups.

9:00 P.M.—Second Session.

9:45 P.M.—Wrap-up.

10:00 P.M.—Snack and free time.

12:00 midnight—Lights out.

Saturday: 8:00 A.M.—Breakfast. Set-up, boys in cabins seven and eight; clean-up, girls in cabins three and four.

8:45 A.M.—Personal morning devotions. Find a place by yourself.

9:00 A.M.—Third session.

10:00 A.M.—Sharing groups.

10:30 A.M.—Fourth session.

11:15 A.M.—Free time.

12:15 P.M.—Lunch. Set-up, boys in cabins five and six; clean-up, girls in cabins one and two.

1:15 P.M.—Fifth session.

2:15 P.M.—Share groups.

2:45 P.M.—Wrap-up.

3:00 P.M.—Free Time.

4:30 P.M.—Pack up.

5:00 P.M.—Leave camp. Stop at restaurant on way home.

6:45 P.M.—Arrive at church. Make sure someone is there to pick you up.

As you can see, we have a lot planned. Come expecting to have a great time and to be challenged in your faith!

See you soon,

Pastor

59 / TO TEENS ABOUT SPECIAL EVENTS— YOUTH SEMINAR

What are your plans for Saturday, March 24? I hope you're free, because CYO has a great opportunity on that day.

We have been invited to attend an intraparish Drug Information Day to be held in Dayton, Ohio. Over thirty parishes have been asked to participate, and the day begins at 10 A.M. with a general session about the problem of illegal drugs among teens.

After a luncheon, the group will be broken down into smaller workshops dealing with problems such as how to help a friend who uses drugs. This will be followed by a time for socializing.

The day ends at 4 P.M., and we plan on being back to St. Mary's by 7 P.M.

Because of the importance of the topic, the parish will pay for any teen who wishes to attend the seminar. Your only cost will be money for a meal on the drive home.

I would encourage you to plan on going if at all possible. The drug problem is a serious one, and I'm certain we will gain from the information presented.

As soon as possible, I will let you know how to go about signing up for the trip. In the meantime, mark your calendars!

Hoping you can go,

Father
St. Mary's Church

60 / TO TEENS ABOUT THANKS— FOR HELP WITH FESTIVAL

You deserve a note of appreciation, so here is one! Your work at the St. Mary's Festival last weekend was outstanding; the children's rides and games were a great success. I can imagine it must have taken a good bit of time to organize all of them, as well as to make sure each was running smoothly during the festival.

I look forward to being able to count on your help for next year's festival.

Thanks again for all you did!

Gratefully,

Father
St. Mary's Church

CHAPTER 2

Letters to Other Members

While the letters in Chapter 1 were aimed more at the general membership, the letters in this chapter are directed more toward specific individuals and groups, and specific situations.

Here are letters of encouragement to the woman who has suffered a miscarriage, and words of congratulations to a member who has just received a job promotion. They express the pastor's wish to minister to the whole person, not just to a person's "spiritual" needs.

These letters help the minister relate to members where they live, touching their hurts and their joys, and expressing the minister's true, human, yet godly, genuine concern for church members. It's in letters such as these where spiritual principles are brought down to earth and made real and practical.

1 / TO COUNSELEES ABOUT AGENDAS—FOR MEETING OF ABOUT-TO-BE-MARRIED COUPLES

To all couples planning to be married at First Church this summer:

You are invited to a special meeting to be held on Saturday, May 29 for the purpose of discussing wedding procedure. The church wedding coordinator, Marge Smithers, and I will be on hand. Come to the church lounge at 3 P.M. to find out all about the following:

- Options for the ceremony, including a sample ceremony and ideas of how to make it uniquely yours;
- Suggested wedding music and when it can be used during the service;
- Various decorations for the church you may want to consider, such as aisle runners, candles, pew bows, and flowers;
- Preserving your wedding day through tape and video recordings;
- Holding your rehearsal dinner and reception in the church Fellowship Hall, with or without catering by members of the church.

There will also be time for questions, and the meeting will be over in about two hours. I hope that you will be able to attend; it should prove to be very helpful in planning your special day.

In His Service,

Pastor

2 / TO COUNSELEES ABOUT APPOINTMENTS— TO CANCEL SESSION

As you know, we were scheduled to meet together for premarital counseling on Tuesday, May 3. However, due to the serious illness of my mother, I must fly to Lincoln today and will be unable to keep our appointment. Please inform Roger about this for me.

Since I do not know what will happen with my mother's condition, I cannot reschedule you and Roger at this time. But as soon as I am back in town, I will contact you and we can set up something agreeable to all of us. I expect that to be some time within the week.

I apologize for any inconvenience to you, but I trust you will understand.

Sincerely,

Pastor

3 / TO COUNSELEES ABOUT CONDOLENCES—ON A MISCARRIAGE

A pregnancy loss is usually traumatic, and a letter like this acknowledges that along with the other problems of the individual who has been undergoing therapy, it may well be overwhelming. The letter assures the counselee of both the pastor's compassion and availability.

I was so sorry to hear of your recent miscarriage. Losing a baby is never easy, but with the other problems you have been dealing with, it is even worse to have something else with which to cope. Though I realize that nothing I can say will bring back your child, I want you to know that you are in my prayers. God alone has to be your strength as you walk this difficult path before you; He will not fail you.

In addition, I am available to resume our sessions together at any time you are ready. If you wish to wait a week or so, that is fine; however, I would encourage you to come talk about your feelings as soon as you can.

May the Lord grant you His peace and His comfort during these days. He alone can heal the pain you feel.

Sincerely,

Pastor

4 / TO COUNSELEES ABOUT CONGRATULATIONS—ON JOB PROMOTION

Congratulations on your recent job promotion! I'm confident that you will do excellent work in your new responsibilities, and that your superiors were showing good judgment in offering you the new position in Rochester.

Since you will be relocating out of state, it's obvious that we will no longer be able to continue our counseling sessions. While I can refer you to several qualified counselors in your new city, I personally feel that you have made sufficient progress in dealing with your divorce. Naturally, the wounds of a broken marriage may take years to heal, but you seem to have reached the point where you can make the rest of the journey to wholeness on your own. Therefore, I am recommending that you discontinue counseling at this time.

Of course, if you think you do need more professional help, I will stand by your decision; you yourself know what is best for you. Let me know what you want to do.

Again, let me say how pleased I am to hear about the promotion. I am certain that God has given you a new start. May He bless you in every way.

In His service,

Pastor

5 / TO COUNSELEES ABOUT DISCIPLINARY ACTION— CONCERNING BEHAVIOR OF COUNSELEE

It has come to my attention that you have again ignored my requests for confidentiality regarding your counseling sessions with me and the other two women.

When I arranged for the three of you to be in a group session, I felt it would prove helpful to all of you, since you are all in the same circumstances. But the value of the time together has been greatly decreased, if not totally eliminated, by your insistence on revealing details of the things discussed to others outside the group.

As you know, I have asked you several times not to do this. I have explained to you the unfairness of such behavior to the other members of the sessions. Yet you have persisted in this behavior. Therefore, I have no option but to inform you that you will not be permitted to attend any further group sessions.

Believe me, I regret having to take this step, but I believe that you leave me no choice. However, if after a month you feel you could keep the private details shared inside the group, I will reconsider letting you participate. In the meantime, I hope that you will seek God to determine why you are doing this, and that He will help you change.

As always, I am available to discuss this or other matters at any time.

Sincerely,

Pastor

6 / TO COUNSELEES ABOUT ENCOURAGEMENT— WHEN DOWN

After our appointment today, you seemed discouraged. I can understand how it may seem like your problems are overwhelming and that nothing is changing. Perhaps you are feeling like it isn't even worth trying to fight anymore.

But let me assure you that progress is being made. Though the circumstances still look bad, God is in control, and He will continue to help you survive even this distressing situation in which you find yourself. I know it doesn't seem possible to you, but as time passes you will begin to feel better.

So please don't give up! Together, you and the Lord will make it. And I will continue to be here if you need my help too. You are in my prayers.

Sincerely,

Pastor

7 / TO COUNSELEES ABOUT EVALUATIONS—
OF COUNSELING SESSIONS

It's risky to invite criticism, even in the name of evaluation, but it's also valuable in a counseling situation. Here the pastor asks that specific aspects of their sessions be examined. In this letter, the pastor is honest enough to admit that things may not be perfect, and that if they are bad enough to warrant it, there are alternatives.

Now that we have been meeting with each other for four months, I feel it would be good to step back and look at what has been happening in our sessions. Before our next appointment, I would like you to evaluate what you think are the strengths and weaknesses of our time together.

Are you satisfied with the progress you are making in dealing with your problem? Do you feel you have developed a sense of trust in your relationship with me? Are you coming away from our appointments thinking clearly about what steps you should take during the week?

Please think about these questions in order that we may discuss them at your next session. At that time, we should be able to determine if we ought to continue. If not, I can recommend several other good counselors whom you may wish to try.

I look forward to hearing your opinions about these matters.

Sincerely,

Father
St. Mary's Church

8 / TO COUNSELEES ABOUT INFORMATION—
CHANGE OF LOCATION OF SESSIONS

I wish to inform you that from now on, counseling sessions with me will take place in the church library instead of in my office. With the noise and confusion of the telephone, people coming and going, and Marge typing, it has proved to be impossible to have the quiet and confidence needed in a counseling session. Therefore, until the remodeling is completed and I am again in a private office, I will meet with you in the library. While this may be somewhat inconvenient, I am certain it will be better than where we have been.

Thank you. See you at your next appointment in the library.

Because of Him,

Pastor

9 / TO COUNSELEES ABOUT INSTRUCTIONS— WHAT TO BRING TO SESSIONS

Let me take this opportunity to remind you that for this week's counseling session, you will need to bring your Bible and your list of communication goals for the month. As usual, I have you scheduled for Thursday at 10 A.M.

I am looking forward to seeing you at that time. If you have any questions before then, feel free to call me.

Sincerely,

Pastor

10 / TO COUNSELEES ABOUT PROBLEMS— LACK OF CONTACT

At this point, it has been over a month since I have heard from you. Therefore, I am assuming that you no longer wish to receive counseling from me.

If you feel that your problem is solved, then I rejoice with you in the great work that God has accomplished in your life. In that case, further counseling may not be necessary.

However, if the problems you had been experiencing are still causing a significant amount of stress in your life, it does not seem like an appropriate time to stop seeking professional help.

Of course, it is completely up to you to choose what course of action you want to pursue. But I need to know what you decide. Is there some other problem of which I am unaware? Could another counselor do more at this point to minister to your needs? Please contact me and help me understand what is going on. I deeply care about what happens to you and I am praying that God will aid you in determining exactly what you should do now.

I hope to hear from you very soon.

Sincerely,

Pastor

11 / TO COUNSELEES ABOUT PROCEDURES— TO BE MARRIED IN THE CHURCH

I am delighted to hear that you and David have decided to marry in First Church. The following is the standard procedure here:

Select a wedding date and time and clear it with the church wedding coordinator. Also, determine if you want to use Fellowship Hall for the rehearsal dinner and/or reception and if you want the women's group to cater either affair for you.

Contact me to set up appointments for premarital counseling. I prefer to spend three one-hour sessions with the couple as well as one with each spouse-to-be alone. Sessions should begin about two months before the ceremony and be completed several weeks in advance of the wedding.

The sessions concern these topics:

First week—general plans for the wedding, both the bride and groom-to-be.

Second week—the financial end of marriage, both the bride and groom-to-be.

Third week—the sexual side of marriage and the Biblical responsibilities of the wife, the bride only.

Fourth week—the sexual side of marriage and the Biblical responsibilities of the husband, groom only.

Fifth week—communication, both bride and groom-to-be.

Sixth week (if needed)—problems and/or questions, both or either.

Assignments for each week will be made, such as reading or working out a tentative budget.

In setting up this schedule, I am attempting to do all within my power to aid you in starting off your marriage in the best possible way. Please feel free to contact me with any questions or concerns. I look forward to meeting together with you and David.

Sincerely,

Pastor

12 / TO COUNSELEES ABOUT RESIGNATIONS— RELOCATION OF COUNSELOR

It is with great regret that I must inform you that I will no longer be able to continue our counseling sessions. As of November 1, I have resigned as pastor at First Church to assume a new position in Atlanta. Because of the distance involved, I believe it would be in your best interests to find a counselor in this area.

I realize that it is difficult to begin opening yourself up to someone, and that doing so again with a new counselor is equally difficult. I am sorry to put you in this position, but I feel that God would have me take this job. Just as He has blessed our time together, I have confidence that the Lord will aid you in finding another counselor who will be able to minister to you.

I do think it is important for you to continue seeking help. You have been making great progress, and you will keep on improving if you persist in treatment. I can suggest Rev. William Myers at Faith Memorial Church or Dr. Bruce Boxer, a psychologist, both of whom I highly recommended. I will be glad to contact either one for you.

Let me know what you want to do. It has been good working with you, and I continue to pray that God will minister to every area of your life.

Sincerely,

Pastor

13 / TO COUNSELEES ABOUT THANKS—FOR GIFT

Thank you so much the fruit basket you left at the rectory for me last night. It will be greatly enjoyed and you can be certain that it won't last long!

In your note, you indicated that you felt I have helped you. I am glad you feel that way, but the progress you have made is really a result of God and you working together. I have played only a small part. Nevertheless, your gratitude is appreciated. I look forward to seeing you continue to move toward complete wholeness.

Again, thank you for your thoughtful gift.

Sincerely,

Father
St. Mary's Church

14 / TO COUPLES ABOUT AGENDAS—
FOR NEXT MEETING OF GROUP

Where will you be at 7 P.M. on Tuesday, February 1? I hope you're already planning to be at the Couples Club meeting at the church that night.

As you may recall, this is an important meeting. Plans need to be made for the Lenten service the Club will be leading; we should set a date for the spaghetti dinner fund raiser; and ideas are still needed for the retreat. In addition, some new business has arisen which must be taken care of at once. I won't tell you what it is, but I will guarantee that it is exciting and it affects you personally. You'll have to come on the 1st to find out what I mean.

So mark your calendar now and plan on being a part of the February agenda. You won't regret it!

In Him,

Pastor

15 / TO COUPLES ABOUT ANNOUNCEMENTS—
CONCERNING SWEETHEART DINNER

Instead of just telling about the upcoming dinner, the following letter piques the couples' interest by an appeal to leaving their usual lifestyle for something special. Then it gives enough details to intrigue even more without spelling out the entire evening.

Calling all sweethearts! Have you been longing for a special night out with your best girl or guy? A time away from the kids and the ordinary cares of day-to-day living?

Then we have just the thing for you! The Couples Club is planning a Sweetheart Dinner for all the married couples in the church. To be held on Saturday, February 14, at 7 P.M. It will include romantic music, candlelight, and a gourmet menu selected just for you. After the dinner, a surprise program will be presented which will top off the evening. The cost for all this? A mere $4 per person.

However, limited seating is available, so you must call in your reservation to the church office as soon as possible.

Don't miss this unique opportunity—plan on joining us for the Sweetheart Dinner on Valentine's Day.

In His Name,

Pastor

16 / TO COUPLES ABOUT CONDOLENCES— ON LOSS OF BUSINESS

Most people think of sending condolences only on a death. But there are many other times of stress when such a note would be appreciated. Doing so shows concern for all aspects of a member's life.

I was saddened to hear the news yesterday that you will definitely have to shut down and sell your business. After all the time, effort, and money which you put into it, you must feel a great sense of loss. Perhaps you are also uncertain as to what direction you should go in order to support your family.

I wish I could somehow turn your financial situation around so that none of this would be happening. Of course you know that I can't. I can only say that if you are experiencing these feelings, you are reacting in the way that anyone else would, and that even in this God is with you. Though He may seem very far away, He can provide the comfort and strength that you need during this stressful time.

You will be constantly in my prayers, and if I can do anything to help you, either in the way of a new job or just in listening, don't hesitate to contact me.

Sincerely,

Father
St. Mary's Church

17 / TO COUPLES ABOUT CONGRATULATIONS— ON OPENING OF NEW BUSINESS

Congratulations on the grand opening of your new business! I'm sure that during the long months of preparation, it seemed as if this day would never come. But your hard work has paid off, and now you really are standing in your store, ready to meet the public.

Surely God will bless you both and your business as you dedicate it to Him and use it for His glory. Again, my very best wishes for success. I'll be in soon to check out Walters' Paints and Wallcoverings for myself!

Sincerely,

Pastor

18 / TO COUPLES ABOUT ELECTIONS— MISTAKE IN RESULTS OF

My face is red! I can't explain how it happened, but somehow, during the elections last week at Couples Club, the ballots were miscounted. We announced that Walt and Cathy Jones were elected president, when actually Ken and Tina Morganstein had the highest number of votes. Apparently, some of the ballots were put aside by mistake and this caused the problem.

Believe me, I feel terrible about the mix-up, and I apologize to Walt and Cathy, as well as to Ken and Tina. (No other officers were affected by the added votes found). It won't happen again!

Your embarrassed pastor,

19 / TO COUPLES ABOUT ENCOURAGEMENT— UPON AGREEING TO LEAD SEMINAR

I was delighted to hear that you have decided to help lead a seminar for Catholic engaged couples. As I told you before, you two have many qualities which could assist young couples planning for marriage, and I am confident that you will find the experience to be beneficial. Not only will you have the opportunity of aiding others, but you will probably find that being a part of the seminar will be enriching for you too.

At first, it may seem to be frightening to stand up before a group and lead discussions about something so personal as your marriage. But I believe that you will find it becomes easier the more you do it.

Maybe you feel unqualified. You shouldn't. No one is expecting that your own relationship be perfect; there is no such marriage. Your willingness to take part in the seminar, and your basically well-adjusted union are all the qualifications you need.

Again, I want to thank you for stepping out in this new direction for you. God will bless you for it. If you have any questions, feel free to contact me.

Sincerely,

Father
St. Mary's Church

20 / TO COUPLES ABOUT INFORMATION— NEW ADDRESS OF OFFICERS

As of November 1, the address of Bob and Cathy Myers will be 201 North Main Street. Their telephone number will remain the same as it has been, 445-2231. If you need to contact them about any aspect of Couples Club, they are available at their new home. Serving as president of the group means they are eager and willing to hear from you. Why not stop over to see their house? At the same time, you can share your feelings about the group. Need directions? Call them or call the church office.

Sincerely,

Pastor

21 / TO COUPLES ABOUT INSTRUCTIONS—ABOUT WHAT TO BRING TO POTLUCK DINNER

The Couples Club Potluck supper has been scheduled for Saturday, September 12, at 6:30 P.M. It will be held in Fellowship Hall, and beverages, rolls, and ham and chicken will be provided. Please bring your own table service and $1.00 per person toward the meat.

In addition, each couple should bring the following:

If your last name starts with A – H, bring a salad, I – O, bring a vegetable, and P – Z, bring a dessert.

We are looking forward to a great time together as we begin a new year of Couples Club activities. Even if you haven't been an active part of the group in the past, why not start coming now? You'll be glad you did!

In His love,

Pastor

22 / TO COUPLES ABOUT MEETINGS— MEETING TIME MOVED

This is your official notice that because of Lent, the March meeting of the Couples Club will be moved from its regularly scheduled night. Instead of gathering the second Wednesday of the month, we will be meeting the second Tuesday, March 12, so as not to interfere with the Lenten service at the church on the 13th.

As originally planned, the meeting will begin at 7 P.M. at the home of Kathy and Ron Schultz, 112 Main Street. The program will remain unchanged.

See you there!

Because of Him,

Pastor

23 / TO COUPLES ABOUT NEWSLETTER— ASKING FOR CONTRIBUTIONS FOR

Perhaps you've noticed that the church newsletter has recently assumed a new look. In an effort to make it more readable, we have added some artwork, more information about groups within the church, and some short devotional pieces. All this is possible because of the extra page that has been added.

As a result of this, we are now able to offer to you, the members of the Couples Club, the opportunity to use the space of one-half page every month. How you use that space is up to you. You may choose to include more detailed write-ups about your meetings. Or maybe you'll want to use original pieces, such as poetry or short articles by members of your group. You may have other ideas of how best to use the space. Or you could decide you would prefer not to have the extra space. It's up to you.

Please think about this, and be prepared to discuss it at the next Couples Club meeting.

Sincerely,

Pastor

24 / TO COUPLES ABOUT QUESTIONNAIRES— ON COMPLETION OF

After members have been urged to fill out and return an opinion questionnaire, a follow-up letter such as the following should be sent. In addition to sharing the totaled results of the questionnaire, it thanks members who participated and promises that changes will be made, based on what has been expressed.

———————————

Thank you for completing and returning to the church the questionnaire about future plans for the Couples Club. Here are the compiled results:

1. the purpose of the group—
    32% of respondents felt it is mainly for learning.
    12% said it's for service to others.
    10% thought it's for fellowship.
    36% wrote that all three purposes are equal.

2. activities that should be done more—
    50% said social things like the summer picnic, bowling party.
    23% wanted more guest speakers.
    10% wanted more personal sharing and prayer time.
    17% wanted an ongoing service project such as sponsoring an overseas orphan.

3. activities that should be done less—
    62% wrote less business meetings.
    10% said fewer fund raisers.
    28% wanted less Bible study.

4. meetings last—
    15% said too long.
    10% said too short.
    75% said just right.

As you can see, no one will be able to be completely happy all the time, but we are going to do all we can to satisfy as many members as possible. Again, we appreciate your help with the questionnaire. Plan on being an active part of Couples Club this year and see how great it can be!

Sincerely,

Pastor

25 / TO COUPLES ABOUT RESIGNATIONS—REQUEST TO FILL IN AFTER RESIGNATION OF OFFICERS

As you probably know, Bob and Joyce Wilson will be moving to Pittsburgh at the end of this month. While we are pleased at Bob's job promotion, it will certainly be a big loss for First Church to see the Wilsons go.

The Wilsons' relocation will also mean that the Couples Club is without a president. Tim and Betty Moore have told me that they don't feel they can assume the office at this point, although they are willing to continue in the position of vice-president.

I was wondering if you two might consider accepting the appointment of president. You have been an active part of the group for some time, and you have a good rapport with the other members. I feel you would make excellent leaders. Would you prayerfully think about it?

Because the Wilsons are leaving so soon, I do need to have an answer from you within a week. Please contact me when you decide. If you have any questions about the responsibilities of the president, call Bob, Joyce, or myself.

May God bless you in every way.

Serving Jesus,

Pastor

26 / TO COUPLES ABOUT SCHEDULES

Thank you for signing up for bearing the offertory gifts. As you know, bringing up to the altar our Lord's Blood and Body as well as the financial gifts to Him is a solemn responsibility and a privilege in which everyone in the parish should be encouraged to share.

The schedule for the next three months is as follows:

Jan. 4—Ron and Jane Ponce

Jan. 11—Howard and Bonita Abbott

Jan. 18—Terry and Glenna Rosford

Jan. 25—Vince and Sarah Wells

Feb. 1—Dick and Betsy Snyder

Feb. 8—Jim and Becky Wood

Feb. 15—Dennis and Sheryl Mast

Feb. 22—Morris and Tonya Wickert

Mar. 1—David and Donna Bowersox

Mar. 8—Frank and Fran Joyce

Mar. 15—Dennis and Cathy Summers

Mar. 22—Austin and Marty Stein

Mar. 29—Lance and Yvonne Kaufman

Please mark your calendar; you are responsible for being there the week you are scheduled. If you cannot serve for any reason, switch with someone else on the list.

Again, my appreciation for your willingness to help.

Sincerely,

Father
St. Mary's Church

27 / TO COUPLES ABOUT SPECIAL EVENTS— MARRIAGE SEMINAR

Marriage is the most challenging and yet also the most rewarding relationship in your life. Isn't it worth doing all in your power to help yours grow?

You need to plan to attend the Dr. George Maxwell seminar coming to Cincinnati. To be held Saturday, May 2, in Riverfront Stadium, it will feature the renowned marriage and family expert Dr. Maxwell in one of his rare personal appearances. You may never again have the chance of hearing him live; I heartily encourage you to do all you can in order to attend.

Because of this rare opportunity, I have arranged to charter a bus to Cincinnati for the day. Tickets for the seminar are $10 for the day, and the charge for the bus will be only $3 per person, with the church picking up the remaining cost for the bus.

If you are interested in going, please contact the church office as soon as possible, as we have only a limited number of tickets to sell. Additional details of the seminar will also be available there.

Again, let me urge you to prayerfully consider going. It will be well worth your time and money.

In Him,

Pastor

28 / TO COUPLES ABOUT THANKS— FOR HELPING OTHERS

On behalf of the congregation, I would like to thank you for opening your home to the refugee family from Thailand which the church is sponsoring. During their first weeks here, it is crucial that they be in a warm caring environment which will aid them in their adjustment to their new lives. You are providing that kind of help.

I realize that it isn't easy to have people you don't know move in. You too will have to get used to different ways of doing things, different words, and an entire different lifestyle. But it will be well worth all you have to give, as the _____ family sees the love you share in Christ's name. It may be the very thing that brings them to a saving knowledge of Him.

Soon, the month or so that you have them in your home will be over and they will be in their own home. But the family will never forget all you did for them. Neither will God; you will have your reward from Him.

May the Lord strengthen you and give you both wisdom and patience in abundance during this time. Again, my thanks for your sacrificial giving.

Sincerely,

Pastor

29 / TO PARENTS ABOUT ADVANCEMENTS—CHILD MOVING INTO NEXT AGE LEVEL SUNDAY SCHOOL CLASS

Next Sunday, September 9, is Promotion Sunday and your child _____ will be moving to a different Sunday school room. His/her new class meets in room _____, and the teacher is _____. If you are not sure where this class is, check the church map in the lobby or ask in the church office.

If your child has been an active part of Sunday school, I hope that he/she will continue to do so in the new class. His/her teacher is anxious to have him/her join the fun and the learning this fall.

Perhaps your child has not attended Sunday school regularly. If so, I would like to take this opportunity to encourage you to begin coming each week. Every child needs a spiritual education in addition to the one he/she receives at school.

I hope to see your child in his/her new classroom this Sunday.

In His service,

Pastor

30 / TO PARENTS ABOUT AGENDAS— OF INFORMATIVE MEETING

As the time of First Communion approaches, you may have questions about how it is done at St. Mary's, especially if this is your oldest child. Therefore, a meeting for parents of the children taking their First Communion next month is being planned for Tuesday, April 15. It will be held at 7 P.M. in St. Mary's Hall.

Topics to be discussed include:

— What your child should wear and where to get it;

— The significance of the Sacrament and how it is explained to your child, in case you wish to talk about it with him/her;

— Appropriate behavior during the service, including when the taking of photographs is permissible;

— Suggestions for making the time especially meaningful for your child;

A chance to ask questions.

I hope that you will make every effort to attend this meeting.

Sincerely,

Father
St. Mary's Church

31 / TO PARENTS ABOUT ANNOUNCEMENTS— REPAVING OF PARKING LOT

During the week of May 4, the parking lot behind St. Mary's will be repaved. The contractor expects to do the work early in the week, so that by Saturday it will be ready to use.

However, if unforeseen circumstances arise, such as rain, it is possible that the new pavement may not be completely dry. Should this occur, the parking lot will be blocked off.

In that event, please make sure to keep your children away from the blacktop. I'm certain you do not want their clothing stained any more than we want tar on the inside of the church.

Thank you for your cooperation.

Sincerely,

Father
St. Mary's Church

32 / TO PARENTS ABOUT APPOINTMENTS— TO DISCUSS PROBLEM CHILD

As you know, your son Robert was caught vandalizing the men's room at St. Mary's yesterday. This is an extremely serious situation which indicates a lack of respect for the parish, myself, and God. I feel it most necessary to discuss the matter with you (without Robert) at your earliest convenience. Therefore, I have tentatively set aside time tomorrow night, April 2, at 7 P.M., to meet with you. If this is not possible, please contact me to set up another appointment. However, I must stress again that this is an urgent problem that needs to be dealt with as quickly as we can.

I'm sure you share my concern and I look forward to discussing it with you. Thank you for your cooperation.

Sincerely,

Father
St. Mary's Church

33 / TO PARENTS ABOUT CERTIFICATES— MISPLACEMENT OF

I was delighted to be able to minister the sacrament of Infant Baptism to your daughter Megan Katherine last Sunday. As you know, in the confusion of the day, her baptismal certificate was mislaid, and I was unable to present it to you following the sacrament. I enclose it with this letter; please accept my deepest apologies for any embarrassment or inconvenience it caused you.

I must admit this is the first time in all my years as a pastor that I have made such a mistake. In the future, I vow to be more organized!

May God bless you and Megan in a special way.

In the Name of Our Lord,

Pastor

34 / TO PARENTS ABOUT CONDOLENCES— DEATH OF INFANT

On Saturday, October 27, we were deeply saddened by the sudden death of your son, (name). Especially when a young child is taken away, we sense our human helplessness to answer the age-long question of why this happened. We cry out to God, frustrated in our lack of comprehension. But even though in this life we may never have a full explanation, we do have the assurance that He is with us. He understands our pain, and He brings comfort and hope in the midst of it. In the assurance of Jesus Christ's death and resurrection, we are confident that we will meet (name) again.

Dear friends, this may be the greatest tragedy of your lives. Please know that we at First Church are standing with you. You are in our prayers, and we are ready to listen to you when you feel like talking. Realizing the grief process is a lengthy one, we fully understand that for a while you may not be able to carry out the church responsibilities you have taken on. But remember that there is always a place for you here.

In Christian love,

Pastor

35 / TO PARENTS ABOUT CONGRATULATIONS— ON AWARD RECEIVED BY CHILD

It is with pleasure that I congratulate you on your son Andy's qualifying as a National Merit Scholar. This is a great honor, and you have every reason to be immensely proud of him. The parish and I are proud of Andy too—he is a fine boy, not only scholastically, but in all areas of his life. His devotion to St. Mary's has always been evident, whether he is serving as altar boy, attending a CYO meeting, or helping with the annual festival. I am certain that he will go on to accomplish much as he attends college and chooses a career.

Only rarely does the parish get blessed with a National Merit Scholar, and we are delighted that Andy is one of them. May God bless him and you, as your years of raising him pay off.

Sincerely,

Father
St. Mary's Church

36 / TO PARENTS ABOUT DISCIPLINARY ACTION— AGAINST CHILD

When disciplinary action is necessary, it should be confirmed in writing even after it has been agreed upon verbally. In this example, the parents are thanked for their cooperation, and are assured that the matter is considered closed.

Thank you for coming in yesterday to discuss with me Robert's vandalism of the men's room. As we decided at that time, he will be responsible for giving me the sum of $10 a week from his paper route money, until the total amount of the repairs has been paid.

In addition, he will be required to spend twenty hours helping the janitor. This will be done over the next month, beginning on this Saturday morning at 9 A.M. He and the janitor will work out the times for the rest of his work.

I believe that Robert has repented and that we will have no further problems with him. I consider the situation closed.

Thank you for your cooperation in this unpleasant matter.

Sincerely,

Father
St. Mary's Church

37 / TO PARENTS ABOUT ELECTIONS— CONGRATULATIONS ON ELECTION OF CHILD AS YOUTH GROUP OFFICER

As you know, your daughter Marcia was elected vice-president of the Youth Fellowship at the last meeting. May I take this opportunity to congratulate both you and her?

Serving as an officer in the YF is a great responsibility as well as a privilege. That her peers chose her for this position indicates their confidence in her to carry out the duties of the vice-president, who is the program chairman. I share that confidence, and I look forward to being able to work closely with Marcia and the other officers in the upcoming year.

Thank you for your encouragement and support, both of which Marcia will need throughout her term of office.

Sincerely,

Pastor

38 / TO PARENTS ABOUT ENCOURAGEMENT— ON RUNAWAY CHILD

I wish I could somehow say something so profound that it would immediately give you all the comfort and answers you need—something that could reassure you that David will come back home, that he will turn around his destructive behavior, and that he will stop causing you so much pain.

But I think you realize that I cannot do that. All I can tell you is that I feel a little of the hurt you are in the midst of, and I'm praying for you. God alone must be your strength; He can minister to you in such a way that, although circumstances may not change, you will be able to handle the stress.

Remember too that the parish is not forgetting you. In the three weeks since David ran away, a number of people have asked about him and have told me they are especially praying for you and for him. I believe that our Heavenly Father is watching over your son, even though you don't know where he is or what he's doing. We must continue to believe that God will use this difficult situation in a positive way for both him and your family.

Keep in mind that I am always available to talk, should you feel the need, and that I'm more than willing to help in the search for David by contacting people, etc. May God bless you and minister to you in a mighty way.

Sincerely,

Father
St. Mary's Church

39 / TO PARENTS ABOUT EVALUATIONS— OF SUNDAY SCHOOL PROGRAM

From time to time, I feel it is appropriate to evaluate how the church programs are progressing. Discovering weak points, as well as finding out where we are doing well, strengthens the overall work of the church.

With that in mind, I would like to ask for your help in evaluating the Sunday school classes which your children attend. Please fill out the enclosed form and return it to the church by Sunday, May 2. Keep in mind that your child's teacher and I are not looking for compliments but an honest critique of what you think of the class your child attends.

Possibly the most important part of the form is the space for suggestions. I would appreciate it if you would especially take the time to think about what improvements you would like to see. It is not possible to do every thing that every parent suggests, but if for example, you strongly feel more Scripture memorization or less music would help, write it down.

Thank you for your cooperation.

Sincerely,

Pastor

40 / TO PARENTS ABOUT INFORMATION—ON POSSIBLY CONTROVERSIAL YOUTH PROGRAM

In dealing with a sensitive subject like the one here, being open about exactly what is going on helps cultivate acceptance of the study. Notice how the letter writer is sympathetic to parents who do not provide sex education to their children, while attempting to get their support for the program.

Perhaps you noticed in the church bulletin last week that the youth group will begin a three week study on "Ethics and Sex" this Sunday.

Although your child receives information on the physical aspects of sex in school health and biology classes, the ethical and spiritual side of it is neglected. Personally, I feel that these matters should be discussed at home, and I realize that some parents do so. But for others, doing so is a source of difficulty, either because of lack of knowledge or the awkwardness of the topic.

Therefore, we are beginning the program as a help to you, the parent, as well as to your teen. It is to supplement the teaching you give, not relieve you of your responsibility in this area.

Today's youth hear much about responsible sex, that is, preventing or ending pregnancy and avoiding sexually transmitted disease. But God has a different view about such things than what most teens believe. In our course, we'll see just what the Bible says about sex and why He designed it only to be in the context of marriage. We hope you will make every effort to encourage your son/daughter to attend.

Sincerely,

Pastor

41 / TO PARENTS ABOUT INSTRUCTIONS

As you know, your child will be receiving First Communion at the 11 A.M. Mass on Sunday, May 13. Please have your son/daughter at the school at 10:30 A.M., so that he/she may line up and be ready to come into church with the group. The children will be sitting together in the front pews.

Rehearsal for the service will be on Saturday, May 12 at 2 P.M. Have your child at the church on time so that we can begin the practice promptly. It should last about a half an hour. As I'm sure you realize, it's extremely important that your son/daughter attend the practice in order for him/her to know where to stand, etc. during the Mass.

First Communion is a major step in the life of your child, and I encourage you to acknowledge it as such by taking photographs, inviting your relatives, and if possible, holding a reception afterwards.

May God bless you and your child as he/she begins to participate in the Blessed Sacrament.

Sincerely,

Father
St. Mary's Church

42 / TO PARENTS ABOUT MEETINGS

Your child's religious education is one of your major concerns. Here at First Church, we want to supplement what he or she receives at home and assist you in any way we can. Therefore, we would like to invite you to attend a meeting with the Sunday school teachers on Tuesday, September 29, at 7 P.M.

We will be sharing the general goals of First Church's Christian Education program. You will also have a chance to meet your child's teacher and hear what specific objectives he or she has set for the year. The meeting will be dismissed promptly at 8 P.M., at which time refreshments will be served in Fellowship Hall.

It is important that we jointly look at which direction we are going in our Sunday school, and we need you to be a part. Together, we can do everything possible to guide your child in the process of spiritual maturation.

Sincerely in Christ,

Pastor

43 / TO PARENTS ABOUT NEWSLETTERS—RECOMMENDATION OF

How often have you wondered how you're doing as a parent? Did you handle your toddler's fears right? Should you let your twelve-year-old daughter date? What should you do about the fourth grade bully who beats up on your son every week?

So many of the questions we deal with every day are difficult to answer, especially within a Christian context. Things that would be acceptable for many people aren't for us believers. That's why many parents' magazines aren't very helpful for us.

Recently I have come across a small monthly newsletter for Christian parents which has been extremely helpful for me personally in raising my children. Called simply "Christian Parenting," it had articles in the last issue on the questions asked at the beginning of this letter. Concerning children ages birth to eighteen, the articles are practical and easy-to-read, as well as being written from a definitely Christian viewpoint.

Because I think so much of "Christian Parenting," I have asked the Board to pay one-half of the subscription fee for any parent in our church who wishes to receive it. They have agreed to do this, which would mean your cost would be $5 per year.

If you are interested in this helpful parenting tool, please fill out the enclosed subscription blank and return to the church with your money by Sunday, February 21.

Should you wish to see a copy of it before deciding, I will have some available in the church office. But I am convinced that if you subscribe, you will be delighted as I am with this newsletter.

Sincerely,

Pastor

44 / TO PARENTS ABOUT PROBLEMS—CONCERNING BEHAVIOR TO AVOID

If you attended the 11 A.M. Mass last Sunday, you are aware that we had a problem with some of the children in the parish. At that time, a small child accidentally knocked over a lighted candle. Fortunately, an adult quickly realized what had happened and righted the candle before any real damage occurred.

While I am thankful that the incident ended promptly, it does make it clear that occasionally youngsters are not being watched carefully enough during the services. I have no problem with parents standing at the back of the sanctuary and letting their toddler walk around there during the service, as long as the child is relatively quiet and well-supervised. But I cannot permit it if the adults don't properly watch the youngster. We must not risk having something more serious than last Sunday's incident. Please do everything within your power to cooperate in keeping our church a safe place for everyone.

Thank you.

Sincerely,

Father
St. Mary's Church

45 / TO PARENTS ABOUT PROCEDURES— FOR NURSERY

As the result of some recent problems we have had with babies left in the nursery, we have established a new procedure to use when leaving your child there.

1. You must sign a registration card, filling out all applicable information. If your child is in the nursery regularly, you must still fill out a new card the first week of every month that you are present. Each additional Sunday of the month, you must initial the card so that the nursery helpers know that nothing has changed.
2. Please attach a name tag to your child and his/her diaper bag before leaving the nursery, and pick up a location number to take with you into the sanctuary.
3. When you enter the sanctuary, hand your location number to the usher nearest where you will sit. Then he or she can quickly find you if you are urgently needed by your child.

I realize that these measures do take time, but if they are followed they will eliminate some of the difficulties we have experienced. Our main concern is for the safety and happiness of your baby.

Your cooperation is greatly appreciated.

Sincerely,

Pastor

46 / TO PARENTS ABOUT QUESTIONNAIRES— ASKING FOR HELP FILLING ONE OUT

Parenting has to be one of the toughest jobs in the world. Not only is there no real training for the task, but the rewards often seem far-removed, if not totally nonexistent. And everyone has his or her own opinions about what's right or wrong.

That's why First Church has begun a Sunday school class geared just for the needs of parents with children ages birth to high school. It will meet in room 109, with experienced parents Ben and Mary Moore as teachers.

But in order for this new class to really help you, we need to know exactly what you would like to cover. Should we go through a book on parenting by a popular author such as James Dobson, or would you prefer a totally Bible-centered class? Do you want a lecture on some phase of parenting which is troubling you, or would a discussion group be more helpful?

Fill out the enclosed questionnaire in order to make your views known, and return it to the church by Sunday, September 2. We are excited about the possibility of ministering to your unique needs as parents, and we want your input as we plan.

Thank you for your cooperation.

Sincerely,

Pastor

47 / TO PARENTS ABOUT RESIGNATIONS— REQUESTING ASSISTANCE IN FILLING SPOTS AFTER RESIGNATIONS

Several of our Sunday school teachers have informed me that they are resigning as of the end of the school year. While I hate to see these faithful people leave, they have served well and deserve a rest.

Therefore, First Church is in need of some new teachers, and I wondered if you might consider volunteering. Openings for teachers are in the classes for four and five year olds, fifth and sixth grade, and junior high. If your child is in one of these classes, you may feel more comfortable teaching another age.

Teaching Sunday school is a big responsibility. It involves time, energy, and effort. But it is also a rewarding experience, as you touch lives for the Lord Jesus.

If you would like to accept this challenge, please contact me at once. You may teach only for the summer, or if you prefer you may take a class for a longer length of time.

Please pray and ask the Lord if He wants to use you as a teacher at this time. If many people help with teaching our faith to our young, no one will have to do it for too long.

Sincerely,

Pastor

48 / TO PARENTS ABOUT SCHEDULES— NEW NURSERY SCHEDULE

Thank you for offering to serve in the nursery again this quarter. The schedule for fall is as follows:

September 6—Joe and Terri Moore
September 13—Rick and Randi Johnson
September 20—Sam and Joyce Miller
September 27—Bob and Kathy Burton
October 4—Keith and Tammy Sours
October 11—Dean and LaDonna Distel
October 18—John and Sally Myers
October 25—George and Betsy Adams
November 1—Tom and Joan Smith
November 8—Ron and Betty Young
November 15—Kay Benson and Mary Bare
November 22—Chuck and Charlene Dynes
November 29—Debbi Wilson and Mandy Fox

If you cannot work the week that you are scheduled, please switch with another name on the list. It's your responsibility to make sure someone is present to supervise the children.

You may bring a small snack, such as crackers, for the children if you want, but it's not necessary.

Again, thanks for your help. Without the willingness of the parents to help, we would not be able to operate the nursery. You are appreciated!

Sincerely,

Pastor

49 / TO PARENTS ABOUT SPECIAL EVENTS— CHURCH PARENTS' WORKSHOP

If you had all the time and money in the world, wouldn't you invest a large portion to learn how to be the best parent you could be? After all, your children are a focal point in your lives, and you have a great responsibility to bring them up to be productive, mature workers for Christ.

Well, you don't need that much time or money to take a step toward improving your parenting skills. Plan now to attend First Church's Family Workshop Day on Saturday, April 17, from 9 A.M. until 3 P.M. The cost for the day is $10. which includes lunch.

Leading the workshop will be author and teacher Dr. William Westminster. For twenty years he has been traveling across the country presenting practical ideas for parents. Sessions included are the preschooler, elementary years, adolescence, the single parent, and sharing your faith with your children.

More information about the workshop will be shared within the next month, but for now, mark your calendar for April 17. You won't be disappointed.

Sincerely in Christ,

Pastor

50 / TO PARENTS ABOUT THANKS— FOR REDECORATING NURSERY

I would like to extend my personal thanks to you for your recent help with the redecorating of the church nursery. The bright murals on the walls, the repainted furniture, and the repaired and cleaned toys all contribute to making it a cheerful, warm place. And where else would we want our babies and toddlers to be? Even at this early point in their lives, they need to view coming to church and Sunday school as a pleasant thing to do. You have helped accomplish this goal, and with the aid of the parents and others who take nursery duty, we will succeed in reaching out in love to the little ones of the church. Long after your child is out of the nursery, your work will continue making a difference.

Again, my appreciation for a job well done.

Gratefully,

Pastor

51 / TO SINGLES ABOUT ADVANCEMENTS— AS OFFICER OF SINGLES GROUP

Now that the year is ending, I'd like to express my appreciation to you for a job well done. You have served faithfully in the position of vice-president of the Positive Christian Singles, and your hard work has played a vital role in making this a great year for the group.

As you know, the policy of PCS is that the vice-president moves up to the office of president the following year. All the officers are advanced in this way, so that each spring only a new secretary need be elected. Since you are aware of this, I trust that you are willing to serve as president for the coming year. If not, please contact me at once so that other arrangements can be made.

Should I not hear from you within the next week, I will assume that you can and will be the PCS president for 19XX. Congratulations on your advancement! I am confident that you will be able to do just as well next year in your new position as you did this past year as vice-president.

Sincerely,

Pastor

52 / TO SINGLES ABOUT AGENDAS— CHANGE IN PLANNED AGENDA

Did you realize that several families within our own church are living in poverty? I have learned that they are housed in buildings with quite inadequate heat, and with the recent cold weather, it is imperative to get them relocated into warmer facilities as soon as possible. This could actually be a matter of life or death for them.

The church council has told these two families to be prepared to move within the week. At that time, we would like to have housing for them to rent. At the very least, we will move them into others' homes temporarily until something more permanent can be found.

I have asked all the groups of the church to make this need a priority, both in prayer and in giving. Therefore, the officers of PCS have decided to change somewhat the agenda for the next meeting.

As much business as possible will be postponed to a future time, in order that we may discuss ways in which PCS can help in this situation. Bring any ideas for fund-raisers which could be carried out within the next two weeks and/or ideas about where inexpensive but decent housing is available.

In order for us to accomplish as much as possible, it's important for you to attend. Please plan on being there!

Thanks, in the name of our Lord, Who desires that we reach out to the needy in His name.

Sincerely,

Pastor

53 / TO SINGLES ABOUT ANNOUNCEMENTS— OF ORGAN DEDICATION

The wait is over! After all the long months of looking forward to the day when the new organ will be here, we can at last rejoice in knowing that it is ready to be delivered. The company has informed me that the organ will be installed the week of May 2.

To allow plenty of time, we have set May 16 as the Sunday in which we will dedicate the organ to the glory of God. We will have a special service, with the organ accompanying the choir. Afterwards, there will be a brief demonstration by the organist for anyone who cares to stay, followed by refreshments in the Fellowship Hall.

Since you are a part of the Positive Christian Singles who donated a sizable gift towards the purchase of the new organ, I'm sure you'll want to be a part of that special day.

See you then,

Pastor

54 / TO SINGLES ABOUT APPOINTMENTS— TO POSITION

I'm delighted to hear about your recent appointment as Singles Coordinator for the district. It is certainly a great honor to be selected for this position, and I'm confident that you have both the ability and the enthusiasm for the job. You are already greatly appreciated for your faithfulness in serving as one of the leaders of the Singles program here at First Church; now all the churches in our area will be able to benefit from your work.

Again, congratulations from the entire church as well as from myself personally. May God give you the wisdom and strength that you need to provide outstanding leadership in this new and challenging responsibility.

In His service,

Pastor

55 / TO SINGLES ABOUT CERTIFICATES—
ON CORRECTION OF

Even with the best of intentions, mistakes happen. In the following letter, the pastor apologizes but goes on to focus on the achievement for which the certificate was presented. _____

It has come to my attention that the certificate you recently received for completion of the Basic Bible Study series, Part Two, was incorrectly filled out. I apologize for the misspelling of your name; I know from firsthand experience how irritating that can be.

But let me assure you that although your certificate wasn't made out right, it in no way lessens the achievement you have accomplished. Completing the course demands a great deal of time, effort, and commitment, and I am personally proud of you for doing it.

Your new certificate, with your name spelled correctly, is enclosed. Again, please accept my regrets that this happened, as well as my congratulations on your hard work.

Sincerely,

Pastor

56 / TO SINGLES ABOUT CONDOLENCES—
DEATH OF PARENT

It was a source of great sorrow to me to hear of the death of your mother yesterday. At a time like this, words mean very little, but I did want to let you know that I am praying especially for you during this difficult situation.

Losing a parent is always a big blow, but I know that it is even more painful for you because of the close relationship you had with her. Yet, you can take comfort knowing that you gave her loving, devoted care for the last years of her life, even though it meant great sacrifices on your part. By living with her, you gave up a good deal, particularly in the past six months when she was so ill.

Now in the midst of the grief you feel, you can be assured that you did everything possible for her. May God reward you abundantly for that, even as He walks with you through the pain of being separated from her.

If you need to talk, I am available.

Sincerely,

Father
St. Mary's Church

57 / TO SINGLES ABOUT CONGRATULATIONS— FOR RECEIVING AWARD

Congratulations on your selection as Single of the Year by the District Council!

In informing me of this honor, the District Superintendent expressed how pleased he has been to work with you over the past year. Your insights and hard work have lightened his load, and he felt that no one else was as qualified as you are for the annual award.

I am certain that he will contact you soon to inform you of when and where the award will be presented.

In the meantime, let me say again how happy I am to hear about this honor. May the Lord continue to help you to excel in your position.

Because of Him,

Pastor

58 / TO SINGLES ABOUT DISCIPLINARY ACTION— INDIVIDUAL'S IMMORAL BEHAVIOR

I dislike having to send you this letter, but it seems as if I have no choice. It concerns your relationship with Melvin Evans.

As you know, I agree with the denomination's position on adultery. I have discussed this with you at some length, and while you say you believe that what you are doing is wrong, you have still made no obvious steps to break off the relationship.

Therefore, it appears that another step must be taken. On Tuesday evening at 7 P.M. I and several of the elders will be calling on you. As before, I will attempt to convince you of the necessity of breaking off your relationship with Melvin. If you want, we would be more than willing to help you decide upon some practical things you can do to end it.

I must warn you that this is the final contact the church will be making with you. If you continue to openly practice this sin, we have no choice but to ask you to leave the fellowship of First Church.

Believe me, this is an extremely difficult position in which I find myself. I have no desire to hurt you or to have you cast out. But we who believe the Bible to be the Word of God can do no less than what the Scriptures teach.

Keep in mind that God loves you very much, as do we. There is always room for you at our church, once this relationship is dissolved. The Lord and we are eager to do anything we can to help you.

I am not saying that we have already achieved perfection; I'm certain you could find many things that don't measure up in myself as well as anyone else in the church. Yet we are aware of our shortcomings and are working to change them by the power of God.

I personally am praying that you will be able to see the disastrous situation you are in, and will have the strength to pull away from it. I look forward to out time together Tuesday night. If you want to talk before then, please call.

Love in Christ,

Pastor

59 / TO SINGLES ABOUT ELECTIONS—UPCOMING

YOU are needed at the next gathering of the Positive Christian Singles! Yes, you! Plan now to be at the Thursday, May 13 meeting in the church lounge. We will be electing officers for the coming year.

Please prayerfully consider if you might serve in some capacity. All too often, the same people continue leading a group year after year, which sometimes results in stagnation. The officers for this past year have done an excellent job in guiding PCS, but they deserve to have a chance to sit back and let others take over. Perhaps you are among those whom God would like to use this year.

Even if you feel you are not to be involved in the group's leadership, we still want you to make every effort to attend the meeting. Come and cast your vote! Without it, your wishes won't be known.

Oh, yes, following elections and a brief business meeting, PCS will be having a pizza party. Don't miss it!

See you then,

Pastor

60 / TO SINGLES ABOUT ENCOURAGEMENT—UPON DECIDING TO FURTHER ONE'S EDUCATION

I understand that you have recently decided to return to school to pursue your master's degree in middle eastern history, with the eventual goal of teaching on the college level. While you are taking on a project which will entail a great amount of work over the next year, I applaud your choice. With God's help, your talents and determination will get you to your destination, I am sure, in spite of any obstacles which may arise in your path.

As you begin this new direction in your life, I wish you the blessings of the Father, Son, and Holy Ghost. May He continue to use you as He sees fit.

Sincerely,

Father
St. Mary's Church

61 / TO SINGLES ABOUT EVALUATIONS—REQUEST FOR EVALUATION OF ASSISTANT PASTOR

For the past year, Jeff Blackendale has served as assistant pastor in charge of the singles' ministry. He has done an outstanding job in expanding the program and also in ministering to the individual needs of people.

However, everyone has weaknesses that may be unknown to him/her. Only when a person becomes aware of them can he or she work to do something about them.

Therefore, I am enclosing an evaluation form which I would like you to fill out concerning Jeff's work. This is not meant to be a vicious attack on him, nor is it to pick at small details of his life style or personality. Yet, I feel it is of value to have you who work with him the closest do these forms, so that he may find out what, if any, overall weaknesses are affecting his job performance. I am also looking for his strengths, in order that he may realize what he's doing right.

Please seal your completed form in an envelope addressed to my attention, and return it to the church by May 1. You need not sign your name to it unless you want to do so. The forms will be totally confidential; only I will read them.

Thank you for your time.

Yours in Christ,

Sr. Pastor

62 / TO SINGLES ABOUT INFORMATION— CONCERNING GROUP

When visitors and new members show an interest in specific groups in the church, having an informative letter on file to give them is perhaps the best way to get the facts out. This example includes the purpose of the group, who may join, meeting times and places, and where to get more details.

Thank you for your request for information about Positive Christian Singles. An outreach of First Church, it was begun in 1979 to minister to the special needs of the singles in the church and community. All unmarried people over the age of twenty-two, including divorced and widowed, are welcome.

The groups meets about twice a month with a two-fold purpose. One is to simply have fellowship with others, which is why we schedule activities such as attending concerts, touring museums, and having ski trips.

More importantly, we strive to learn more about God and His purposes in our lives. We believe it is only through a personal relationship with His Son Jesus Christ that we will find fulfillment in a life style that many of us would not have chosen. To this end, we have teachings by myself and others, who may or may not be a part of the group. We have discussion and sharing groups, and we include praying for each other's needs as a portion of each meeting.

Currently, PCS meets in the church lounge on the first and third Tuesdays of the month. The meetings usually run from 7 until 9:30 P.M., and include refreshments.

If you have any questions about the group, please feel free to contact Ted Burns, the current president, at 888-9494, or myself. We can provide you with a current schedule of PCS activities for the next few months.

May I extend a personal invitation to you to attend our next meeting?

Sincerely,

Pastor

63 / TO SINGLES ABOUT INSTRUCTIONS

As you know, the Positive Christian Singles group is holding a Pancake Supper on Saturday, Nov. 1, from 5:00 to 7:00 P.M. This project is to raise money which will go to the needy child in Chile whom we sponsor.

We are asking each member of the group to sign up to bring a food item as well as to volunteer to work at the supper. If you have not seen the list of food needed, call Mary Williams as soon as possible. At this point, we have a number of people coming at 4:00 to set up and serve, but we have only a few who plan to come at 6:00 and clean up. Can you help? Contact Ron Majors.

While we have sent out publicity about the supper, we can always use more. How about putting up a notice at your place of employment? You could invite your friends to meet you there.

With all of us working together, the Pancake Supper can't help but be a great success!

See you then,

Pastor

64 / TO SINGLES ABOUT MEETINGS— CHANGE OF LOCATION

This is to let you know that the PCS meeting for April 17 has been moved to the home of Ann Marshall, 401 Jefferson St. The church lounge where we usually meet is unavailable on that evening.

If you need directions to Ann's apartment, call her at 939-2231 (home) or 939-4460 (work). Or you may contact the church office.

The meeting will still start at 7 P.M., and the program will remain the same. The May meetings will again be at the church.

In His service,

Pastor

65 / TO SINGLES ABOUT NEWSLETTERS— CORRECTION OF

As you might have noticed, last week's church newsletter stated that the Positive Christian Singles would not be meeting this week.

This is NOT correct. As scheduled, the PCS will have a regular meeting on this Tuesday, September 17. The program will be on self-image.

However, the meeting planned for the following week, September 24, has been cancelled, due to the unavailability of the speaker who was to address us about the Suicide Hot Line. It is to be rescheduled for some time in the future.

The October 1 regular meeting will be held as usual.

Please mark your calendar with the change. I'm sorry for any inconvenience this error may have caused you; I promise to be more careful in the future!

In Christ,

Pastor

66 / TO SINGLES ABOUT PROBLEMS— NEGLECT OF DUTY

Recently I have noticed that problems have developed in several areas that might involve you. A number of singles have generously volunteered to serve as ushers, nursery workers, and Sunday school teachers. The help is greatly appreciated, and I'm delighted that so many are willing to serve the church in these ways.

However, it seems that lately some of the workers have not shown up when they were scheduled to assist. I can understand that when you're single, you have more flexibility than most of the rest of us. I believe you should take advantage of that by going off when you please as much as possible. In later years, you probably will not be able to do so.

However, you must realize that when you just do not come, your absence creates problems. Someone must be found at the last moment to fill in for you. For Sunday school teachers, this means no time to prepare a lesson. This is hardly fair to the person asked to take your place. Nor is it good for the children and/or people you are helping. Service which has not been prepared for tends not to be the best.

I am not asking you to stop going away when you want to do so, but I am saying you must make sure you have a replacement.

Please, if you cannot serve where you are supposed to at any particular time, contact the appropriate person in charge at least two days in advance, a week if possible. To do anything less is to treat the church with great disrespect.

I am certain that much of this problem has been the result of simple ignorance. Now that it is clear what is expected, I'm sure we'll have no further difficulties.

Sincerely,

Pastor

67 / TO SINGLES ABOUT PROCEDURES— TO APPLY FOR POSITION

Thank you for volunteering to serve as a counselor at the District Singles Conference in March. The procedure is:

1. Meet these qualifications: a personal relationship with Christ, active member of the church, age twenty-five and over, secure and comfortable in your status as a single.
2. Fill out the enclosed application and return it to me for my recommendation.
3. Submit the completed application to the district office.
4. If you are accepted, you will be notified no later than February 1. A training session will be held sometime that month.

I appreciate your interest in the program and I hope that you will be able to participate. Please contact me if you have any questions.

Sincerely,

Pastor

68 / TO SINGLES ABOUT QUESTIONNAIRES

In order to more fully meet your needs as a part of Positive Christian Singles, we have come up with the enclosed questionnaire. There is no need to sign your name, but we would appreciate it if you would answer the questions about who you are, what your greatest struggles are, and what your major interests are. By compiling the responses, we hope to find out exactly what the average PCS member is all about.

Please return the questionnaires to the church by February 15. Thank you for your cooperation.

Because of Jesus,

Pastor

69 / TO SINGLES ABOUT RESIGNATIONS— OF SINGLES PASTOR

As many of you know, I have been dating Maria Gomez for some time. Recently, we have felt the Lord speaking to us about getting married, and we have set the date of January 31 for our wedding.

Since Maria lives and works in Tampa, we have prayed about which one of us should relocate. At this point, we have decided that I will be the one to change jobs. Therefore, as of January 21, I will no longer be Singles Pastor at First Church. I have begun the process of looking for a position in the Tampa area.

While I am excited about my new life, I truly regret having to leave all the great people at First Church. In the years that I have overseen the Singles program, I have gained much in terms of experience, understanding, and genuine friendships. I will miss each one of you.

Please be assured that although I am marrying, I will not lose my concern for the needs of singles. In fact, I hope to find another church who needs an assistant pastor to work with the singles ministry. Having waited this long to get married myself, I'll always remember the difficult years before God brought that special someone into my life.

I am certain that First Church will continue to have a vibrant outreach to the singles in the church and community. May God bless you.

Sincerely,

Pastor

70 / TO SINGLES ABOUT SCHEDULES—CHANGE IN

Due to problems beyond our control, there has been a change in the plans for the Singles Retreat next weekend. Instead of leaving at 4:30 P.M, as announced in the original schedule, the bus will now leave at 5:30 P.M. Please be sure to be in the church parking lot at that time. Because of the later departure time, we will need to leave at precisely 5:30; if you aren't there, you will have to drive yourself to the retreat.

The rest of the revised schedule is:

5:30 P.M.—depart

7:00 P.M.—arrive at hotel

7:30 P.M.—dinner

(The rest of the schedule remains the same.)

I hope the change won't inconvenience you, but it is necessary. It won't affect the exciting and spiritually enriching weekend we'll have. See you then.

In His service,

Pastor

71 / TO SINGLES ABOUT SPECIAL EVENTS

Special opportunities come along only occasionally, and when they do, it's time to take advantage of them! That's why I'm sure you'll want to attend the all-diocese singles conference planned for Saturday, October 16.

To be held at St. Matthew's Church in Lima, it will be led by Father Peter Grant of St. Bartholomew's parish. The central theme will be "The Special Needs of the Single—the Church Reaches Out."

Further details as far as cost, reservation deadline, and seminar topics will be available in several weeks. In the meantime, mark your calendar for October 16. You'll be glad you did!

Sincerely,

Father
St. Mary's Church

72 / TO SINGLES ABOUT THANKS— FOR HELPING OTHERS

It has recently come to my attention that you have opened your home to a woman who had no place to sleep. Knowing you, I'm certain that you had no intention of doing it to gain public recognition. Nevertheless, I felt I wanted to express my personal thanks to you.

It requires sacrifice and selflessness to permit someone else to stay in one's house. It means the disruption of many aspects of your life, especially when the incoming person is not well-known by you. But God Himself will reward you for your kindness; you are clearly demonstrating your faith.

I'm proud to have you as part of the parish. May our Heavenly Father continue to bless and use you.

Sincerely,

Father
St. Mary's Church

73 / TO SPECIAL GROUPS ABOUT ADVANCEMENTS

I was delighted to hear of your advancement to Eagle Scout. This is a great honor, and it required much in the way of time and effort. But now your hard work has paid off—you have finally reached your goal.

We have always supported the Boy Scout troops sponsored by St. Mary's, and encouraged boys in the parish to become active in it. Nevertheless, it isn't often that someone achieves the highest rank that the scouts offer. You are an inspiration to the younger boys, and we are proud to have you as a part of Troop 445.

Again, congratulations on your advancement!

Sincerely,

Father
St. Mary's Church

74 / TO SPECIAL GROUPS ABOUT ANNOUNCEMENTS—OF SIMILAR PROGRAM

From your participation in the "Fit for the King" program, it's obvious that you place a high priority on keeping your body in shape. Because of this, you might be interested in attending a special seminar about health and nutrition to be held at First Church on October 28.

Nancy Jamison, a registered dietician and a member here, will be speaking to the women of the church and community on the topic of "Eating Right—What is it and Does it Make a Difference?" She will be covering topics such as salt and cholestrol consumption, fiber in the diet, the basic food groups, and health foods.

There is no charge for the evening, which will begin at 7 P.M. in Fellowship Hall. It will conclude with samples of healthy snacks prepared by Nancy.

Plan on coming and learning more about another area of your total health!

Sincerely,

Pastor

75 / TO SPECIAL GROUPS ABOUT CERTIFICATES— DISCOVERY OF MISSING ONES

After the last meeting of the Boy Scouts, the janitor found a number of certificates that had fallen behind one of the tables. Since they had been made out to boys just joining the troop with the rank of Tenderfoot, we knew they belonged to you. They are enclosed with this letter in order that you might present them to the scouts who were meant to receive them.

We are glad to have the scouts as a part of First Church!

Sincerely,

Pastor

76 / TO SPECIAL GROUPS ABOUT EVALUATIONS— RESULTS OF

Recently, we surveyed the congregation here to get feedback on the programs and activities currently offered. We thought you might be interested in the results of the questions concerning your group.

Over 58 percent of respondents were aware that Weight Watchers met in the church, and 34 percent knew your meetings were on Tuesday evenings. Eighty-seven percent felt Weight

Watchers was a worthwhile group to use church facilities, and 8 percent had attended one or more meetings. Another 15 percent thought they would like to come or should come.

However, only 12 percent had any idea of what went on during your meetings. Perhaps at some point, some of your members would be interested in presenting a program to the Women's Group about Weight Watchers.

Since First Church believes in the fitness of the total person, body, soul, and spirit, we would like to see more people in the congregation who need help with a weight problem attend your meetings. Maybe by working together with you, we can achieve that goal.

Keep up your good work! May God bless you.

Sincerely,

Pastor

77 / TO SPECIAL GROUPS ABOUT NEWSLETTERS— OPPORTUNITY TO BE ON THE MAILING LIST TO RECEIVE

Welcome, Ladies at the "Fit for the King" Program!

We are delighted to have you come to the exercise program today, and we hope you will become a regular part of it.

Although "Fit for the King" meets in First Church, it is open to any woman in the community, regardless of whether or not she attends this or any other church.

However, information about the program is printed each month in the church newsletter. In addition to notifications about cancellations of sessions or changes in times, general news about fitness and health are listed in the "Fit for the King" column.

Because of this, you may be interested in receiving the newsletter on a regular basis. If so, just fill out your name and address on the bottom of this letter and return it to the church. You will be added to the church mailing list.

Keep in mind that this won't obligate you to do anything; the pastor won't call on you and you won't be pressured to attend worship. It is merely to keep you informed about the program.

Thank you, and enjoy your workout!

Sincerely,

Pastor

78 / TO SPECIAL GROUPS ABOUT PROBLEMS— MISUSE OF BUILDING

It has been great having the "Fit for the King" exercise group meeting in the church gym. I firmly believe that God wants us to take care of our bodies, and regular exercise is an important part of that responsibility, one that far too many Christians ignore.

However, certain problems have recently occurred of which you should be aware. The day after the meeting, the janitor has found lights left on, the side door to the church unlocked, and an abundance of trash and items such as towels left in the gym.

Obviously, these practices are not in the best interests of the church. I'm certain that they were unintentional mistakes, and it is understandable that such things might happen occasionally. But they are beginning to occur every week.

This cannot continue. I must ask each of you to do everything within your power to make sure they don't. Perhaps one person could be appointed to be responsible for checking the lights, the door, etc. Whatever you want to work out is fine, but please do something to eliminate the problems.

Thank you for your cooperation. I'm confident that since you are now aware of the situation, the problems will no longer continue.

Sincerely,

Pastor

79 / TO SPECIAL GROUPS ABOUT PROCEDURES— FOR BUILDING USE

As you know, we have had no set procedure for closing up the church after special groups meet here in the evenings. We have always been pleased to let organizations such as Boy Scouts, Parents Toughlove, and Weight Watchers use the facilities at no charge.

While we are still happy to have the building in use when our regular services are not taking place, we have recently found it necessary to implement a sign-out policy. It is as follows:

Groups are asked to exit through the west door only. By the door will be posted a sign-out sheet. A person responsible for the group is to be the last one out the door. He/she is to sign the name of the group, the date and time, and his/her name on the sheet. In so doing, he/she is indicating that:

1. lights are turned off,
2. heat is turned down (if necessary),
3. the room(s) used have been put back in the shape they were in when the group arrived (trash thrown out, chairs in place, etc.),
4. everyone is out of the church, and
5. the door is locked.

In putting into practice this procedure, we hope to make your use of the building to be as problem-free as possible. Thank you for your cooperation.

Sincerely,

Pastor

80 / TO SPECIAL GROUPS ABOUT QUESTIONNAIRES— URGING THE RETURN OF COMPLETED ONES

It has been approximately one month since the questionnaires about the "Fit for the King" program were distributed, and so far I have only received three completed forms back. I realize that your life is busy and that it's easy to forget one more thing to do. But please make an effort to find your questionnaire, fill it out, and get it back to the church. Only by getting your opinion on things such as possible future programs and specific exercises you like or dislike can we work out problems and make the sessions ones from which you can benefit the most.

Thank you for your help. It is necessary! (If you need another copy of the questionnaire, stop by the church office.)

Sincerely,

Pastor

81 / TO SPECIAL GROUPS ABOUT SCHEDULES— CHANGE IN

During the approaching Lenten season, the "Fit for the King" program will be operating under a slightly changed schedule. Thursday morning sessions will continue at 10 A.M. for Lent, except for during Holy Week (April 4-11). In order for the church to be prepared for Easter, no session will be held that week.

Wednesday evening sessions will be meeting on Tuesdays, so that women may attend the Lenten services Wednesdays at 7 P.M., if they so desire.

The location for both sessions remains the same, and all sessions will go back to their regular schedules the week after Easter, April 12-19.

Thank you for your cooperation.

Sincerely,

Pastor

82 / TO SPECIAL GROUPS ABOUT SPECIAL EVENTS— CANCELLATION OF

We regret to inform you that the All-Day Health Seminar scheduled for Saturday, October 3, has been cancelled. Even with a number of churches going together to put it on, there was not enough interest shown in attending to warrant renting the Civic Center as planned. Perhaps in the future we will try again to do a seminar on a smaller scale.

We are sorry for any inconvenience this may have caused, and we commend you for your "Fit for the King" program and your concern for your physical health.

Sincerely,

Pastor

83 / TO SPECIAL GROUPS ABOUT THANKS— FOR DONATION

To each person in the "Fit for the King" program:

I would like to extend a big thank you to you for your generous contribution to the new organ fund here at First Church. You certainly did not have to make any sort of gift to us for the use of our building for your exercise sessions; it is free to worthy groups such as yourselves. But your thoughtfulness is greatly appreciated. As you may know, we are in dire need of a new organ and have almost two-thirds of the money needed for it. Your donation will make a difference in enabling us to reach our goal sooner.

We are pleased that you meet in First Church, and we encourage you to let your programs develop as the Lord leads. If we may be of any service to you, please contact my office.

Again, my heartfelt thanks on behalf of the entire congregation.

In His Name,

Pastor

84 / TO VOLUNTEERS ABOUT ADVANCES— TO HIGHER POSITION

On behalf of the entire congregation, I would like to personally thank you for your faithful service as an usher over the past few years. People have told me several times how much your warm welcome means to them, and I am always encouraged by your smile as well as your devotion to your position.

You are already aware that Ben Ortiz is relocating to Boston and will no longer be able to serve as head usher. I would like to ask you if you would consider advancing to take his place. I know of no other man whom I would rather have do it.

Pray about it and contact me with your decision. I am hoping you will be able to accept. In any event, be assured that you are appreciated.

Sincerely,

Pastor

85 / TO VOLUNTEERS ABOUT AGENDAS—CHANGE IN

As you may have heard, part of the rectory roof was blown off during the recent windstorm. Due to the urgent nature of this problem, the agenda of the parish council meeting for tomorrow night will be altered.

Instead of beginning planning for the St. Mary's Festival, we will discuss options for the rectory roof, along with whatever else must be taken care of this month. Next month we will start working on the festival.

Since a decision about the roof must be made at this meeting, please make every effort to attend. Thank you.

Sincerely,

Father
St. Mary's Church

86 / TO VOLUNTEERS ABOUT ANNOUNCEMENTS— ON NEW PROCEDURES

When it's important how something is done, it helps to have the specifics spelled out. In the following letter, each step in cleaning the church is clearly listed in a format which could be checked off as it's completed.

First Church is in the process of updating the cleaning list. The following has been developed to help volunteers know what needs to be done to keep the building neat. (A copy will be posted on the cleaning closet door.)

SANCTUARY:

Straighten hymnals and Bibles, turning them right side up and placing two hymnals and a Bible in each rack. Throw away old bulletins and trash.
Vacuum all carpets and dust tile floors.
Dust organ, piano, pulpit, pews, pictures, altar table, and window sills.

FRONT FOYER, REAR FOYER, AND CORRIDOR:

Dust floors, shelves, door trim, and furniture.
Mop floors with clear water.
Vacuum mats and place lost items in box in rear of sanctuary.

RESTROOMS:

Clean toilets, sinks, countertops, and mirrors.
Empty trash and mop floors if needed.
Check toilet paper and paper towel supply.

SUNDAY SCHOOL ROOMS:

Vacuum and dust.
Empty trash.

KITCHEN:

Sweep and mop floor.
Straighten up as needed.

FELLOWSHIP HALL:

Vacuum carpet and straighten up chairs and tables.
Wipe off tables and chalkboards.
Dust window trim, cupboards, piano, and furniture.
Wipe out drinking fountain.

Thank you for your cooperation. The condition of our building reveals much about how we really feel toward our Lord.

In His service,

Pastor

87 / TO VOLUNTEERS ABOUT APPOINTMENTS— TO NEW POSITION

Greetings in the Name of our Lord! I'm pleased to inform you that you have been appointed to fill the unexpired term of the late John Masterson on the Board of Trustees.

Your faithful service to the church over the past five years that you have been a member gives me every confidence that you will continue to do well as a trustee, and I am looking forward to working with you in that capacity.

When I talked with you last month about the possibility of this appointment, you indicated that you would accept it. However, if anything has changed since then which would make your service in this area impossible, please contact me at once.

Your term will expire in December of 19XX. At that time, you will be free to seek reappointment if you desire.

Thank you for your dedication to First Church. See you at the next Trustees meeting, Monday, October 10, at 7 P.M.

Sincerely,

Pastor

88 / TO VOLUNTEERS ABOUT CERTIFICATES— DELAY IN RECEIVING

Thank you again for your hard work in teaching Vacation Bible School last week. The program reached over 150 children, with at least 32 of them making first-time commitments of their lives to Christ. In addition, about 37 others rededicated themselves to the Lord.

As you know, we had ordered certificates for the children for being a part of the 19XX VBS. The certificates arrived yesterday, but upon examining them, we noticed that the company had sent us only half the number we requested. We have contacted the supplier, who has agreed to rush more to us as soon as possible. However, we anticipate about a two-week wait until they arrive.

Therefore, you won't be able to get the certificates to your students as quickly as we had hoped. If you see any of your students, you may want to reassure them that the certificates are on the way.

As soon as they do come in, we will get some to you, which you may fill out and distribute to the members of your class. In the meantime, thank you for your patience.

Because of Him,

Pastor

89 / TO VOLUNTEERS ABOUT CONDOLENCES— UPON INJURIES RECEIVED IN CAR ACCIDENT

I was greatly disturbed to hear about your recent car accident and subsequent hospitalization. Going through such a trauma is never easy; even though your physical injuries may not seem to be long-term, the emotional scars often are. If at any time you want a listening ear, please don't hesitate to contact me.

Let me also assure you that if you do not feel up to teaching CCD classes next week, I will understand. Let me know if you would prefer to wait until a later date to start, and I will find a substitute for as long as you think it necessary. Recovering from a serious accident such as yours may take awhile, and I don't want you to feel pushed into something new until you are physically and emotionally ready.

In the meantime, I am praying for your rapid and complete recovery. May God bless you.

Sincerely,

Father
St. Mary's Church

90 / TO VOLUNTEERS ABOUT CONGRATULATIONS— FOR PRIZEWINNING FLOAT

On behalf of the entire parish, I would like to congratulate you for your efforts on the St. Mary's float for the community Christmas parade. Winning second prize was no small achievement; your hard work certainly paid off.

I realize that constructing a float may not seem like a very spiritual activity, but everything that is done for His glory is of value. And I feel that participating in the parade showed that we as a parish are interested in our community. As always, the church stands ready to help those who need it.

Again, thanks for all you did and congratulations on coming in first runner-up in the float division.

In His name,

Father
St. Mary's Church

91 / TO VOLUNTEERS ABOUT DISCIPLINARY ACTION—CONCERNING PERSONAL BEHAVIOR

As you know, you have been asked a number of times now to restrain from talking to others in the choir during Mass. However, you continue to ignore both the choir director's and my instructions on this matter. Your continual whispering in the choir loft has proved to be distracting and annoying, and at this point I have no choice but to inform you that you will not be permitted to sing with the choir during the month of March.

Believe me, I do not like taking this step, but you leave me no other options. I hope that you will use this time off from the choir to examine yourself to find out why you must continually draw attention to yourself, even during church. Then I suggest that you seek the Heavenly Father's help in changing.

You do make a valuable contribution to the choir, and it is the desire of both myself and the choir director that you return to your place there. But that will not be possible until you are able to change this intolerable behavior pattern you have demonstrated.

May God minister to you in this area. If you feel I can be of assistance to you in any way, please contact me.

Sincerely,

Father
St. Mary's Church

92 / TO VOLUNTEERS ABOUT ELECTIONS— WILLINGNESS TO RUN

Thank you for your willingness to run for the office of president of the Couples Club for the coming year. Along with others who expressed an interest, your name will be placed on the ballot and voted on at the May 16 meeting. If you desire to, you may make a brief (three minute) speech about what you would do if you were elected, but this is not a requirement in order to run. However, you do need to be present at the meeting if you want to be considered for the position.

Again, thank you for your willingness to serve in this capacity. We are greatly in need of dedicated persons like yourself to make the Couples Club the ministry all it can and should be. Be assured that even if you should not be selected as an officer, you will still be an important and necessary part of the group.

Sincerely,

Pastor

93 / TO VOLUNTEERS ABOUT ENCOURAGEMENT— UPON LOW TURNOUT

One look at your face yesterday told me how you were feeling about your Vacation Bible School class. I admit, having only two students show up for you to teach is disappointing, to say the least. But I would like to assure you that even so, you are doing a job that desperately needs to be done. What you say to those two children may affect them for the rest of their lives. And because of your small class size, you will have a greater opportunity than if there were a great number of boys and girls. You will be able to communicate on a very personal level with your students, in which you can really determine where they are in their walks with God. Knowing their individual weaknesses, you can minister directly in those areas.

Let me urge you to join with me in asking the Lord to send more students into your class. But if they don't come, thank Him for His perfect plan and use the time you have with your class to the fullest.

May God bless you.

In Christian love,

Pastor

94 / TO VOLUNTEERS ABOUT EVALUATIONS— REQUEST TO DO ONE

Thank you for your willingness to chair the annual Lawn Fete held last week. I know you spent a great many hours coordinating everything, and your hard work certainly paid off. We had an excellent turnout, plenty of food but not too much left over, and even perfect weather! When the bills are paid, I'm certain we'll see a good-sized profit to benefit the Sunday school department.

As well as everything went, you must be aware of some areas which did not run as smoothly as they could have for whatever reason. As a help to the person who volunteers to chair next year's Lawn Fete, I'm asking you to take a few minutes now while you remember and fill out the enclosed evaluation sheet. By listing what worked and what didn't, we can hopefully take care of any difficulties before they happen again.

Again, my personal gratitude for all you did.

Sincerely,

Pastor

95 / TO VOLUNTEERS ABOUT INFORMATION

Thank you for your willingness to help again with the annual St. Mary's festival. This year it will be held on Saturday and Sunday, June 14 and 15. As usual, we will raffle off a new car, have a German band and polka dancing, and run an assortment of booths for food and games.

Jim and Brenda Watkins have offered to chair the festival this year, and I'm sure they will be contacting you soon about what you would like to do.

With everyone cooperating, I know we will once again have a successful festival. Let me thank you in advance for all you can do in helping to achieve that goal.

Sincerely,

Father
St. Mary's Church

96 / TO VOLUNTEERS ABOUT INSTRUCTIONS

To Those Who Have Volunteered to Clean the Church:

Thank you so much for your willingness to donate your time on Saturday, October 1, as we give First Church its annual cleaning. We plan to begin work at 9:30 A.M., with the first shift ending at noon. The second shift will start at 1 P.M. and clean until 3:30 P.M. (or until everything is done!).

Please sign the sheet on the church office door, indicating when you can work. If you can bring dust rags, ladders, vacuum sweepers, or glass cleaner, it would help. Make sure you come with an ample supply of elbow grease!

Being on the cleaning crew may not seem like a very important service to the Lord, but it's pleasing to Him when we do even the smallest thing in His Name.

Again, our appreciation for your assistance.

Gratefully,

Pastor

97 / TO VOLUNTEERS ABOUT MEETINGS

Thank you for your offer to teach CCD classes at St. Mary's. We are always in need of qualified adults who are willing to devote their time to this important work.

In order to be properly prepared to teach the children, volunteers need to attend a meeting on Tuesday, September 2, at 7 P.M. in St. Mary's Hall. It will last approximately two hours.

If you are unable to come, please let me know as soon as possible. We look forward to having you as a CCD teacher this fall!

Sincerely,

Father
St. Mary's Church

98 / TO VOLUNTEERS ABOUT NEWSLETTERS— DEADLINE FOR

Thank you for offering to be in charge of packing the Thanksgiving food baskets for the needy. I am always touched by the tearful appreciation expressed by the recipients of the baskets; they have so little and yet they are genuinely grateful for the gifts they receive.

Let me remind you that the deadline for news to be printed in the church newsletter is Thursday, October 29. If you want people to sign up to pack and/or deliver the baskets or to remember to bring canned goods to donate, make certain the information is to the church secretary by that time.

I'm confident that you have things well in hand for the project; thank you again for your help.

In His Service,

Pastor

99 / TO VOLUNTEERS ABOUT PROBLEMS— WITH NEGLECT OF DUTY

How do you deal with the situation of a volunteer not doing a good enough job? In an insignificant matter, it could and probably should be ignored. But in this example, the consequences—young children being unsupervised—are too serious to be allowed to continue. Notice how the letter writer surrounds the problem with praise for the volunteer's efforts.

Thank you for your willingness to work in the church nursery. It is a much needed ministry, and it means a great deal to me that you are available to serve in that area.

However, last week when you were in charge, several young children were found wandering in the hall during the service. Naturally, the parents were concerned, not only for the safety of their youngsters, but also for the unintentional damage to the building which they might do.

I'm certain you understand the problem, and that the next time you are in the nursery you will take steps to make sure it does not happen again. Of course we understand that toddlers can move very quickly at times, and that it is sometimes impossible to keep up with them, despite our best efforts. But please do try to keep the children in the nursery in the future.

Again, I appreciate your dedication to the children and your faithfulness in the nursery.

Sincerely,

Pastor

100 / TO VOLUNTEERS ABOUT PROCEDURES— FOR DOING SOLOS

As you know, the adult choir will not be performing again until September. However, we are in need of volunteers to do solos and/or small group numbers during morning worship for the summer months.

If you are interested, the procedure is as follows:

1. Sign up on the list on the choir room door by May 27. Include your name, phone number, what part you sing, and what dates or months you would be available.

2. Within two weeks, the choir director will contact you to set up an appointment to try out. Be prepared to sing one verse of a hymn of your choice.

3. Following your tryout, you will be notified as to whether you will be doing a solo, duet, or larger group number. You will also be given a date(s) when you will be scheduled to minister.

4. Practice times will be set up two weeks preceding the day you sing.

Thank you for your cooperation. We look forward to having you share in the summer music ministry.

Because of Jesus,

Pastor

101 / TO VOLUNTEERS ABOUT QUESTIONNAIRES

As the choir disbands for the summer, I wanted to personally thank you for your dedication to it. It requires a great deal of time and effort to faithfully attend practices and to be at each service to minister in song; rest assured that you are appreciated. I am convinced that the choir adds a great deal to the worship, and that the Lord is pleased by your hard work.

Even at this point, we are making plans for the fall, and we would like your input. Please complete the enclosed questionnaire about your views on what music the choir should sing next. Were the pieces you did this spring too easy or too difficult? Would you prefer some more contemporary Christian music, or are the classical pieces more to your liking?

Return the questionnaire to the church by June 1, along with any comments you have about choir. Remember, we value your opinion and look forward to your participation in the fall.

In His service,

Pastor

102 / TO VOLUNTEERS ABOUT RESIGNATIONS

As you may know, George Monroe has resigned from the Parish Council as of May 1. He is relocating to Chicago, and we will greatly miss him and his family's active participation at St. Mary's.

Naturally, we will need someone to take over George's unexpired term on the council. As a member of the council, you may have suggestions of who might be interested. Please come to the April meeting prepared to nominate someone. We will be voting on George's replacement in May.

Thank you for your assistance.

Sincerely,

Father
St. Mary's Church

103 / TO VOLUNTEERS ABOUT SCHEDULES

I'm delighted that you will be able to participate in the day of ministry, October 4, with our sister church in the inner city, Westport Church. The schedule for the day is as follows:

8:00 A.M.—meet in First Church parking lot to board bus for Westport.

8:45 A.M.—arrive at Westport. Men meet outside for instructions about paving the parking lot; women meet inside to clean interior of church.

10:30 A.M.—coffee break and time of fellowship. Get acquainted with someone from Westport.

11:00 A.M.—resume work.

12:30 P.M.—break for lunch. Westport is providing it.

1:30 P.M.—inner city children arrive for weekly tutoring session. Meet in Fellowship Hall to be assigned to a child.

3:30 P.M.—break for recreation and refreshments with children.

5:00 P.M.—children depart; load bus for return to First Church.

5:45 P.M.—arrive at church. Those who wish may go together to restaurant for dinner.

As you can see, we have a full day planned for us. We are expecting it to be a great one. Not only will we have a chance to fellowship with the people from Westport, but we can show our faith in a practical, positive way to the children and the congregation there.

If you have any questions, feel free to call me. Otherwise, I'll see you October 4.

Sincerely,

Pastor

104 / TO VOLUNTEERS ABOUT SPECIAL EVENTS

Because of your interest and participation in the choir, you are invited to attend a special "Music in the Mass" seminar sponsored by the diocese. To be held on Saturday, November 10, at St. Matthew's Church in Lima, the seminar will explore how music can enhance worship. Leaders of the seminar will be Father Joseph Warner of St. Thomas' Church and Virginia Gomez from St. Peter's Church.

As soon as it is available, I will send you the list of workshops for the day, which will conclude with the celebration of the Mass. In the meantime, I hope that you will plan to attend.

Sincerely,

Father
St. Mary's Church

105 / TO VOLUNTEERS ABOUT THANKS— FOR HELPING WITH CLEAN-UP DAY

On behalf of the entire church, I would like to thank you for participating in last Saturday's church clean-up/fix-up day. The good turnout, the enthusiasm of the helpers, and the number of hours spent working all added up to a great time of accomplishment and fellowship. As good as the church looks now, we are more than ready for the Easter season.

While washing woodwork or painting bathroom walls may not seem especially spiritual, keep in mind that God expects us to be good stewards of the building. And by taking care of it properly, we are fulfilling that trust. We are also revealing our respect and love for the church.

Again, my appreciation for a job well done. May God bless you!

Serving Christ together,

Pastor

CHAPTER 3

Letters to Nonmembers

Every minister is concerned about evangelistic outreach and the social needs of the community. The letters in this chapter address the issues related to these areas, and are aimed at nonmembers.

Here are letters for those who are interested in becoming members, letters for following up contacts made through special events, letters greeting new residents to the community, and letters that help introduce the programs and special personality of the church to the individual.

This is an especially important area of ministry, requiring sensitivity and attention. A newcomer to a church often feels a bit awkward, and needs to be made welcome and given clear directions to classrooms, and other information on the church. Some newcomers may have had very little contact with any church, and need noncondescending care and help in becoming acclimated to church life. Others may have been members elsewhere, and because of a divorce or any number of other sensitive situations have found it necessary to find a new church home. These members need a great deal of love, acceptance, and patience.

The letters in this chapter will help the caring minister to effectively communicate in these kinds of situations.

1 / TO MEMBERSHIP APPLICANTS ABOUT ACCEPTANCE AS A MEMBER

Greetings in the Name of Jesus Christ!

First Church takes great joy in informing you that your application for membership has been accepted. We are confident that having you and your family as a part of our fellowship will be a blessing both for you and for us. In welcoming you into the church, we are confirming that you share the vision of First Church to reach out to the world while ministering to the needs of the Body of Christ here.

You will be informed when a date has been set to officially receive new members into the church. In the meantime, we're glad you are with us. If there is any way that we can be of service to you, don't hesitate to call the office.

In Him,

Pastor

2 / TO MEMBERSHIP APPLICANTS ABOUT DOCTRINE—REQUEST FOR INFORMATION ABOUT

What does First Church teach about baptism? How does First Church feel about communion? Is tithing expected?

Though you have applied for membership at the church, you may still be unclear about exactly what we believe. To assist you, we are enclosing a brochure stating our denomination's position on these and a number of other doctrines.

Please look it over carefully, so that you understand the church's position. We will be discussing many of these issues in membership class, but if you have any questions, feel free to contact my office.

Sincerely in Him,

Pastor

3 / TO MEMBERSHIP APPLICANTS ABOUT INFORMATION

Just in case you didn't hear—plan on using the side (west) door or the door off the parking lot when you come to church next Sunday, November 16. The main entrance is unusable due to the broken door locks.

We are assuming that the front door will again be functional by the following week, but if it is not, we will let you know.

Please accept our apologies for any inconvenience this causes.

Sincerely,

Pastor

4 / TO MEMBERSHIP APPLICANTS ABOUT MEMBERSHIP INFORMATION

First Church is delighted to inform you that you will be officially received as members during the 10:30 A.M. worship service on Sunday, November 3. Please contact the office if for any reason you will not be able to be present.

Though we have been privileged to have you in our fellowship for several months now, we are looking forward to your taking this public step of joining our fellowship. Together, we can make a difference in reaching our community for Jesus, as we grow to be more like Him.

See you on the 3rd,

Pastor

5 / TO MEMBERSHIP APPLICANTS ABOUT MINISTRIES AND PROGRAMS—REQUEST FOR INFORMATION ABOUT

Enclosed you will find a brochure describing the various ministries and programs available at First Church. Since you have been attending our fellowship for several months now, you are probably aware of many of them. But for your convenience, we wanted you to have the complete list.

We trust that you will avail yourself of any which catch your interest. If you have questions, please call the contact person listed for the particular program, or call the church office.

Sincerely in Christ,

Pastor

6 / TO MEMBERSHIP APPLICANTS ABOUT REFUSING MEMBERSHIP

While most churches or synagogues do not often refuse membership to an individual, this does occasionally need to be done. In those cases, the tone of the refusal ought to be one of sincere regret and may include an invitation to apply again if circumstances should change.

I deeply regret having to inform you that, at this point, First Church is unable to accept your request for membership. Our denominational requirements for members are as follows: (pastor supply specifics).

According to the information you supplied to us, you do not meet the following criteria: (pastor supply specifics).

We have no desire to refuse the fellowship of the church to anyone, and you are certainly welcome to continue attending First Church as frequently as you wish. This is by no means a personal rejection of you; as a part of the denomination, we have no choice but to follow their requirements for membership. Keep in mind that at any time we would be happy to reconsider your application, should changes in the aforementioned areas occur.

May God bless you.

Sincerely,

Pastor

7 / TO MEMBERSHIP APPLICANTS ABOUT SPECIAL EVENTS

Because you are a part of the newly formed membership class, I would like to extend to you a personal invitation to attend First Church's annual meeting, to be held on Sunday, March 1.

It will take place at North High School, 445 Washington Street, in the cafeteria, beginning at 5 P.M. with a carry-in dinner. Beverages and rolls will be provided; please bring your own table service and two dishes to share.

Following the meal (approximately 6:30 P.M.), we will move to the auditorium for a presentation concerning the various programs of the church, including the TV ministry, cell groups, progress on the new building, the youth outreach, etc.

After these reports, we will adjourn for a time of fellowship, including use of the gym for any who wish. The evening will conclude about 9 P.M. (There will be no evening worship service that Sunday.)

We hope that you will be able to attend. It will prove to be informative as well as enjoyable.

Yours Because of Him,

Pastor

8 / TO MEMBERSHIP APPLICANTS ABOUT THANKS—ON COMPLETED APPLICATION

We were pleased to recently receive your completed membership application. It is currently under consideration by our board, which will notify you of a decision within the next two weeks.

Thank you for your interest in First Church; we are glad that you want to become an official part of our congregation. I trust this indicates that here you have found opportunities to be ministered to as well as to serve others. If there is any way in which I can be of service to you, don't hesitate to contact my office.

Sincerely,

Pastor

9 / TO NEWCOMERS ABOUT EVANGELISTIC FOLLOW-UP—FOLLOWING NEW COMMITMENT

I was delighted to receive your name from the Follow-up Committee for the recent New Life concert. Your decision to commit your life to Christ is the most important step that can be taken. Not only does it have eternal consequences (you'll have a place with Jesus in Heaven), but you will discover it also means profound changes for the good in your life now.

As I'm certain you were told the night of the concert, it's important to begin reading the Bible and praying to God each day. You also need to share your newfound faith with others, as He gives you opportunities.

Getting involved in a Bible teaching church is also vital. You have already begun that process in choosing to attend First Church. Might I suggest that you now plan on becoming a part of our Sunday school classes? There is one for every member of your family, beginning at 9:30 A.M.

We also have a number of midweek home Bible study groups which meet across the city. This would be an excellent source of teaching and fellowship, on a more personal basis than morning worship. For the name and address of the home Bible study group nearest you, call the church office.

Once again, let me congratulate you on your acceptance of Christ as Savior. You will never regret it! And if I might be of service to you in any way, don't hesitate to contact me.

In His service,

Pastor

10 / TO NEWCOMERS ABOUT INFORMATION

It has been a joy and a privilege to have you as part of our congregation on several occasions. With the Lenten season now upon us, First Church has scheduled a number of special services. For your convenience, they are as follows:

Palm Sunday, March 22, morning worship at 9:30 and 11 A.M. Special music by the children's choir. Message on "Entering Our Jerusalems."

Maundy Thursday, March 26, communion service at 7 P.M. Special music by Barbara and John Gates. Message: "The Passover Lamb".

Good Friday, March 27, prayer service, 12 noon, in chapel.

Easter Sunday, March 29, worship services at 9:30 and 11 A.M. Special Easter Cantata by senior choir. Message: "The Triumph in the Garden."

We hope that you will plan to make First Church an important part of your Easter this year. If you have any questions or concerns about the church, please feel free to call my office.

In the Master's service,

Pastor

11 / TO NEWCOMERS ABOUT INTRODUCTION AND GREETING

A letter to newcomers about a place of worship should be kept brief, preferably one page or less. Note how this example still manages to convey the basic information of who, where, and when. It covers parking and nursery, two big concerns of many people, as well as mentioning the most important beliefs.

Greetings! We are pleased to have you recently become a part of our community. In the event that you are considering churches in the area, let us introduce ourselves.

Located at 55 Main Street, one block west of the public library, First Church is a nondenominational fellowship which was founded in 1932. It has over 300 members with an average attendance of 210 for morning worship and 120 for Sunday school.

Services consist of morning worship, 9:30 and 11 A.M.; Sunday school, 9:30 A.M.; evening praise service, 7 P.M.; and midweek home Bible study groups, various days and locations.

For your convenience, a nursery for children under the age of five is located just east of the sanctuary. It is staffed with qualified workers during all services.

A large parking lot is directly north of the church, and on-street parking is located on the west and south sides of the church.

We believe in the Trinity, the Bible as the revealed Word of God, and the necessity of the new birth for forgiveness of sins and a life of growth in commitment to Him. We welcome people of all ages, races, and backgrounds as we seek to minister in the name of Christ.

We would welcome the chance to serve you in any way. Please feel free to call my office if you have need. We would consider it a pleasure to see you in one of our services.

May God bless you in every way.

Sincerely,

Pastor

12 / TO NEWCOMERS ABOUT MEMBERSHIP INFORMATION

Now that you have joined us for worship on several occasions, I would like to take this opportunity to let you know that a new member class will be forming in two weeks at First Church. It will meet during the Sunday school hour for four weeks. Those completing the class who wish to then join the church will be publicly received on May 16.

Perhaps you feel you are not yet ready to make a commitment to become part of a local congregation. Then I would especially encourage you to attend the class. You will have the opportunity to learn exactly what our denomination teaches. If upon completion of the class you believe that First Church is not the place for you, fine. You are free to go elsewhere. But at least you can make a knowledgeable decision.

If, at this time, you are not interested in going to the class, that is also fine. But I wanted you to be aware of the option.

Thank you, and I look forward to seeing you again.

In Him,

Pastor

13 / TO NEWCOMERS ABOUT MINISTRIES AND PROGRAMS

We have been blessed to have you join us for morning worship for the past two weeks. Hopefully, the time you spent at First Church proved to be spiritually uplifting.

Perhaps you would also be interested in one of our home Bible study groups. The purpose of them is to learn more about applying the teachings of the Word of God to our day-to-day lives, as well as to develop personal relationships of caring and commitment within the Body of Christ.

The home Bible study group which is located closest to your home is at the house of Joe and Maria Weber, 5142 E. Madison Street. It meets on Thursday evenings from 7 until 9 P.M. You would be more than welcome to attend at any time.

If another night might be more convenient for you, please call the church office for the locations of home Bible study groups which meet on other evenings.

Should you have questions about the program or about anything else at First Church, don't hesitate to call me or Joe and Maria at 464-0097.

May God bless you in every way.

Because of Him,

Pastor

14 / TO NEWCOMERS ABOUT SPECIAL EVENTS

Looking for something to do on a Friday night? As a recent new resident of (town), you may be finding it difficult to locate decent entertainment. May I suggest to you the upcoming concert of the contemporary Christian musical group, New Life?

From Wingfield, CA, New Life will be appearing at the high school auditorium, 3339 W. Mountain Dr., on Friday, February 2. The concert will begin at 8 P.M. and tickets are only $2 each. They may be purchased at the door or in the office of First Church.

The group has been touring the country for the past four years, and it consists of four vocalists and six instrumentalists, including percussion and brass. Their musical style has been compared with that of the well-known group Up With People.

I am certain you would find the evening enjoyable. If you have any questions, feel free to call the church office. I hope to see you at the concert.

Sincerely,

Pastor

15 / TO NEWCOMERS ABOUT WELCOME

We were privileged to have you as our guest last Sunday and are grateful you chose to worship with us. We trust that your visit here was spiritually enriching and that you were warmly received.

As a church, we are committed to the person of Jesus Christ, and we base our teaching upon God's revealed word, the Bible. It is our desire that people come to place their trust in Christ to forgive and lead them, and that they grow in their relationship with Him.

We seek to provide regular teaching and preaching of the Bible, meaningful times of worship, opportunities for fellowship, prayer, outreach, and numerous other ministries for people of all ages.

If there is any way we can be of service to you, please contact my office.

Yours because of Him,

Pastor

16 / TO RELATIVES AND FRIENDS OF MEMBERS ABOUT EVANGELISM FOLLOW-UP

From your sister Nancy Thompson, I heard the good news that you recently committed your life to Christ. I share in Nancy's joy as you begin your walk of faith. Indeed, this decision is the most important one you will ever make; it will prove to be life-changing.

Let me encourage you to spend time each day in prayer and reading of the Bible. As you communicate with God, you will grow in Him. It's also vital to regularly attend a Bible-believing church. While we at First Church certainly don't presume to be the only local congregation to help you in your walk with Jesus, we would be more than happy to have you join us on any occasion. Nancy has found the church to meet her needs, and we would welcome the opportunity to minister also to you and your family. If you choose another church, that is fine too; the important thing is to get involved in a fellowship somewhere.

If I may be of any service to you, please call. And best wishes as you pursue the excitement and fulfillment of a life centered around Christ!

Sincerely,

Pastor

17 / TO RELATIVES AND FRIENDS OF MEMBERS ABOUT INFORMATION

Since Betty Morris informs us that you are at home with young children, we thought you might be interested to know that First Church is beginning a program especially for mothers of preschoolers. Called Mother's Time Out, it will consist of planned activities for the youngsters while the moms gather in another part of the church. There will be time for a presentation about an area of concern to parents of young children, discussion, a craft, and informal sharing over refreshments.

The program is to be held every Thursday morning from 9 to 11:30 A.M., and the charge per session is only $1, since the church is underwriting the additional expenses.

We believe there is no higher calling than the raising of our next generation, but we realize that day after day with the clamor of preschoolers can be extremely taxing. Mother's Time Out offers you the chance to get away from your child(ren) for a period of adult conversation with others who understand your needs. We hope that you will give it a try.

Sincerely,

Pastor

18 / TO RELATIVES AND FRIENDS OF MEMBERS ABOUT INTRODUCTION AND GREETING

Welcome to (name of city)!

We recently learned from (name of friend or relative) that you have relocated in the area. Hopefully you are finding our community to be one of warmth.

For many people, adjusting to a new area also means finding a church. We at First Church would like to invite you to visit us. The Sunday schedule includes church school, 9:15 A.M.; worship service, 10:30 A.M.; and Bible study, 7 P.M. In addition, we have a number of programs for every age and interest, such as youth, singles, and women.

First Church is committed to the person of Jesus Christ, and bases its teaching upon God's revealed Word, the Bible. Our vision is to see individuals dedicate their lives to Him and grow in that relationship.

We would consider it a privilege to have you attend one of our services. In the meantime, please feel free to call my office if I can be of help to you in any way.

Sincerely,

Pastor

19 / TO RELATIVES AND FRIENDS OF MEMBERS ABOUT MEMBERSHIP INFORMATION

It has been a joy for us to have you attend worship services with your aunt and uncle for the past few weeks. We trust that you are finding your time at First Church meaningful.

Next month we will be starting a class for potential new members. Perhaps you would be interested in attending. In it, we will specify the denominational requirements or membership as well as the doctrines and beliefs of First Church. Even if you do not know at this time whether or not you wish to formally join the church, you might find it helpful to attend this class. It will make clear to you what your aunt and uncle believe as members here and assist you in deciding if First Church should also be your spiritual home.

If you are at all considering coming to the new member class, please contact me for details about when and where it will meet. We would be pleased to have you become a part of it. May God bless you in every way.

Sincerely,

Pastor

20 / TO RELATIVES AND FRIENDS OF MEMBERS ABOUT MINISTRIES AND PROGRAMS

Over the past several weeks now, we have been pleased to have you joining (friend or relative's name) for Sunday morning worship at First Church. We trust the services have been meaningful to you.

For your convenience, we are enclosing a complete list of our various ministries and programs. Please feel free to attend any of them which interest you, with or without (relative or friend's name.) If you have questions concerning them, call the church office or the chairperson listed under each program.

Again, it's been a joy for us to have you at First Church, and we hope to continue to see you on a regular basis.

Sincerely in Christ,

Pastor

21 / TO RELATIVES AND FRIENDS OF MEMBERS ABOUT SPECIAL EVENTS

We are delighted to have your child attending First Church's Vacation Bible School this week with (name of member). Hopefully the experiences that he/she is having will stay with him/her for a long time.

The children at VBS will be presenting a special program on Sunday, June 15, at the 11 A.M. service. We would very much welcome your attendance, and we hope that your son/daughter will be able to be a part of the program. If so, he/she should be at the back of the church by 10:45, in order to walk in and sit with the other children in his/her class.

Again, we are glad that you chose to accept the invitation of (name of member) for your child. If we can assist you in any way, please contact my office. I hope to meet you at the program.

Sincerely,

Pastor

22 / TO RELATIVES AND FRIENDS OF MEMBERS ABOUT WELCOME

We were privileged to have you attend First Church last Sunday with (name). Hopefully your visit was spiritually uplifting.

We at First Church desire to meet the needs of the congregation, as well as the community, by pointing people to Jesus Christ, the answer to every problem. We preach the Bible as the word of God for today.

We are always happy to have guests at our services, and you are more than welcome to come at any time, with or without (name). If there is any way that we can be of service to you, don't hesitate to call the church office.

Sincerely in Chirst,

Pastor

23 / TO VISITORS ABOUT EVANGELISM FOLLOW-UP

Greetings!

It was our pleasure to have you with us at the recent Christian music concert. Your response at the concert was an important one. You now need to become a part of a caring Christian family.

We at First Church want to extend ourselves to you. If you are not presently attending a Bible-believing church, it would be our joy to have you join us this Sunday.

Our Bible class begins at 9:30 A.M., morning worship is at 10:35 A.M., and our evening worship is at 7:00 P.M.

If you are not from this area, may we recommend that you attend First Church or any other Bible-believing church near you.

In Christ,

Pastor

24 / TO VISITORS ABOUT INFORMATION— ON CHANGE OF SERVICE TIMES

Visitors who have come more than once would need to receive a letter such as this, announcing a change in the time of worship. In addition to keeping the visitor updated with something likely to effect him or her, it shows that the individual has not been forgotten, and encourages another visit.

We have been pleased to have you join us for worship on several occasions now while you are in (name of city) to visit your grandmother. You are more than welcome to come any Sunday you are here.

However, we did want you to know that the times of our services have recently changed. The Sunday school hour is now at 9:15 A.M. instead of at 9:30. From 10:15 until 10:45 A.M. is a time of fellowship over coffee in the lounge. Worship will begin at 10:45 A.M. instead of at 10:30 as it was before. These shifts began last Sunday. We are confident that they will better serve the needs of our congregation.

We look forward to having you with us again at some point in the future, and when you do come, don't forget the different times for our services.

In His service,

Pastor

25 / TO VISITORS ABOUT MEMBERSHIP INFORMATION

During the past several months, you have frequently chosen to worship at First Church on Sunday mornings. Your presence has been a blessing to us, and we trust that our fellowship has ministered to you.

Because of your interest, we would like to invite you to attend a meeting for potential members on Tuesday, October 16, at 7 P.M. To be held in the library, the meeting will explain membership requirements, answer questions, and set up a time for membership classes which is convenient for all who want to attend.

Even if at the present you are uncertain as to whether or not you are willing to take this step toward formal ties to the church, we would very much like to have you at this meeting.

In the meantime, please feel free to contact me at any time if you have questions or concerns.

Sincerely in Christ,

Pastor

26 / TO VISITORS ABOUT MINISTRIES AND PROGRAMS

During the past few weeks, it has been our privilege to have you as a guest during Sunday morning worship at First Church. We are pleased to have had these opportunities to minister to you.

For your convenience, we are enclosing a schedule of all our services as well as programs for various groups such as youth, singles, and women. Please feel free to attend any of the functions listed. If you would like more information about them, call the chairperson listed in the brochure or call the church office.

We would like to be of service to you, and we hope to continue to see you on Sunday mornings.

Because of Him,

Pastor

27 / TO VISITORS ABOUT SPECIAL EVENTS

When hosting special events, a church can check its records to see what visitors attended similar events in the past. Then, a special letter such as the following can be sent to those people who have a better-than-average chance of wanting to come again.

Greetings!

Since you recently attended the Joyful Sounds concert at First Church, we wanted to inform you that the contemporary Christian musical duo of Joyce and Ron Randell are coming here on Sunday, January 23. The service is at 7 P.M., and a freewill offering will be taken.

Having recorded two albums, this husband and wife team have been ministering across the state for the past five years. They have appeared on several Christian TV and radio programs, and their greatest desire is to call the Body of Christ into a deeper walk with the Lord. Come expecting to receive from Him!

We trust that the Joyful Sounds concert was a blessing to you, and we want to extend a personal invitation for you to also hear the Randells.

Hoping to see you there,

Pastor

28 / TO VISITORS ABOUT WELCOME

Please accept this expression of appreciation for your visit to First Church last Sunday. It was kind of you to include our church in your plans for the day, and I sincerely hope you received spiritual inspiration and blessing from our time together in the presence of the Lord.

We understand that you will be unable to attend First Church regularly, since you live outside our city. Nevertheless, we want you to know that the doors of our church are always open to you. If you have occasion to be in (name of city) again, please be assured that a welcome will await you at First Church.

Again, thanks for worshipping with us last Sunday.

Sincerely,

Pastor

Letters to Church Staff

Whether a small rural church, or a large metropolitan cathedral, the pastor relies on a variety of paid and volunteer staff members. And vital to a pastor's effectiveness is open and ongoing communication with staff members. It's important that the pastor's goals and vision for the church be shared with staff members, so that everyone's efforts will be unified and productive.

Here are letters that express the pastor's regret and thanks to a staff member resigning a position, encouragement to a new staff member, and a letter informing the staff of policies and procedures. Since it's crucial that communication between pastor and staff be clear and concise, also included are model employment contracts and letters of discipline. These letters will help the pastor gain the respect of staff, while at the same time communicating appreciation for their service.

1 / TO ASSOCIATE PASTOR ABOUT ACKNOWLEDGMENTS—ACKNOWLEDGE RESIGNATION

Thank you for your letter of 5-21-XX, informing me of your intention to resign your position as youth pastor, effective 8-31-XX. Although it will be difficult to see you leave, I fully understand your desire to go into full-time work with inter-city youth. If that is what God is calling you to do, you must obey.

You have done an excellent job here, and I know I speak for the youth and the rest of the congregation when I say how much you and your wife will be missed. Finding a replacement of your caliber will not be easy.

Yet we rejoice to see this new ministry opening up for you. In all you do for Him, we pray that you will be continually blessed in every way. If I can ever be of any help to you in your new position, please feel free to contact me.

Warmest personal regards,

Pastor

2 / TO ASSOCIATE PASTOR ABOUT BENEFITS— ADDITION OF

I am pleased to inform you that the Church Council has voted to add full dental coverage to the health insurance plans for me and you. This will mean an increase of $XXX per half-year, but the council felt it was a benefit that we should have. I do not yet have a booklet from the insurance company outlining the items covered, but I know it includes an examination and teeth cleaning for each member of the family once every six months at no charge.

Since the church has never before had dental coverage, I am gratified that it is willing to take on this additional expense for our sakes. Hopefully we won't need to use the coverage for fillings, etc., but it's reassuring to have it just in case.

Because of Him,

Pastor

3 / TO ASSOCIATE PASTOR ABOUT CONGRATULATIONS—UPCOMING WEDDING

It was with great delight that I heard the news of your engagement and upcoming wedding. I'm certain that you and Melinda will be greatly blessed as you serve God together, and I wish you joy in this time of preparation as well as when you're married.

You've officiated at enough weddings to know the procedure. You've also counseled enough couples with troubled marriages to know that the step you're taking is no insignificant one. It is a lifelong commitment of two people, irregardless of the trials along the way.

Yet, you know too that the union of a husband and wife who are rooted in Jesus Christ can survive those difficult times and go on to accomplish much.

As a pastor, you have an added responsibility, in that your wife will enhance or tear down your professional life more than she would if you were in almost any other occupation. Yet the support Melinda can give you will help more than it would in most other fields.

I'm sure that you have considered all the possibilities and prayed until you are confident that this is the direction in which God would have you go. Now, you can step forward with assurance.

May the Lord minister to you both in every way. Again, my warmest congratulations.

In His love,

Pastor

4 / TO ASSOCIATE PASTOR ABOUT CONTRACTS AND AGREEMENTS—WHEN HIRED

When there are a number of details which need to be specified, such as in the following contract, an outline is an efficient means of organizing them.

Confirming our conversation of September, 22, on behalf of the Official Board and Congregation of First Church, we wish to extend to you the invitation of joining our staff as associate pastor. As we discussed with you and your wife when you were here, the following statements detail our salary and benefits package for your first twelve months of ministry here.

A. Salary and Benefits
  1. The total package offered is $XXXXXX per year, to be divided as follows:
      a. Hospitalization/Dental: If you choose Plan 1 of the district insurance program and the dental program, this will cost $XXXX per year.
      b. Approximately $XXXX will cover the employer's portion of Social Security taxes. However, once you are credentialed, you may qualify to be exempt from Social Security. The employer's portion will be deducted on a weekly basis.
      c. Since you will be living at the church-owned property at 123 First Lane, $XXX per month will be deducted as rent for this property ($XXXX per year). As you are not

eligible, at this time, to receive the IRS living allowance exemption, you will be required to pay federal tax on this allowance. Once you are licensed, a designated living allowance will be tax exempt. Utilities will be your responsibility.

2. The remainder of the package will be salary. We should look at a designated car allowance for tax purposes once you arrive.

3. All federal, state, and local taxes will be processed through payroll deductions.

B. Relocation and Moving Expenses

1. First Church will pay the cost of the truck rental (U-Haul, Ryder, etc.) and related expenses for moving you and your family to Jacksonville.

2. Utility connection and required deposits will be paid by the church.

C. Professional Expenses

1. All approved ministry-related expenses such as seminars, retreats, and so forth, will be paid by the church.

D. Vacations and Time Off

1. Vacation will be whatever you had last year or two weeks—whichever is greater.

2. You MUST take one day off each week, during the week, and you are encouraged to take a second day off each week whenever possible.

E. Working relationships

1. You will be directly responsible to the senior pastor.

2. A private office will be provided with necessary supplies, equipment, and phone.

3. You have received a general portfolio, and from this will be developed a detailed job description upon your arrival.

4. There will be a weekly meeting with the senior pastor, for the purpose of review and evaluation, goal-setting, and sharing.

5. An annual written report and evaluation of your ministry, along with your goals and objectives for the next year, must be submitted to the church board each December.

F. Family Responsibility

1. Take time to be with your wife and family.

2. We want your wife to be free to pursue her ministry desires as she labors with you.

We are looking forward to your joining us in October and are excited about the days ahead. Our desire is to assist you in any way we can to allow God's will to be fulfilled in your lives.

Yours because of Him,

Pastor

5 / TO ASSOCIATE PASTOR ABOUT DISMISSALS

The time has now come for immediate action to be taken. By your continued constant devotion to your work for outside groups such as Right to Life, you have shown that you no longer desire to serve as full-time staff at First Church. Therefore, as of March 1, 19XX, you are relieved of your position of minister of Christian Education and youth work.

I regret having to take this step, but you have left me little choice. We simply cannot continue to pay you full salary while the responsibilities which go with that are unfulfilled. Perhaps you should consider the possibility of a job outside the ministry, in order to have the time you wish to spend on your volunteer efforts.

If I can help you in any way during this process of moving into a different position, don't hesitate to contact me. I am sorry that our working relationship must end this way, but I have every confidence that you will continue to go on to minister for God in a mighty way. May He bless and guide you.

Sincerely,

Pastor

6 / TO ASSOCIATE PASTOR ABOUT DISCIPLINARY ACTION—PERSONAL BEHAVIOR

Writing this letter is not something I relish doing, but unfortunately it is necessary. As you know, we have discussed in the past the problem you have been having of devoting too much time to causes outside church business, at the expense of your job here. I believed we had agreed that you were going to cut back on some of the outside efforts. However, at this point, I still have not seen any improvement.

I continue to feel that the work you are involved in for Right to Life, Community Food Pantry, and the Suicide Crisis Center are important and valuable. But your first responsibility must be to the ministry you have assumed at the church. You simply cannot handle what is meant to be a full-time commitment in Christian Education and youth work when you are here only part-time hours. Furthermore, when you overextend yourself, you cannot do your best at anything. We need your best here at First Church.

The bottom line is that you have two more weeks to prove to me that you wish to continue working in your current position in the church. If by then you have not cut back significantly in the amount of time you are devoting to these outside causes, I will be forced to dismiss you.

Please believe me that it is not my wish to take this step, but in all fairness to the church things cannot continue in their present vein. I very much hope that you will be able to cut back, so that we may keep on ministering together for Christ to the congregation here.

In His love,

Pastor

7 / TO ASSOCIATE PASTOR ABOUT EVALUATION—OF HIS OR HER WORK

You probably realize it is again time to evaluate the progress you have made in the past three months towards your job-related goals. Shall we plan on getting together sometime in the next week to discuss them?

As before, we will be going over the list of goals you set for yourself in March and determining what worked well and what didn't, as well as why it did or didn't meet our expectations. Then we can proceed to establish new goals for the upcoming quarter.

This system has worked well for me, and I'm hopeful that you agree. However, we can also talk about it if you are not satisfied, and look at other possibilities.

I look forward to spending several hours with you in the near future.

Serving Christ,

Pastor

8 / TO ASSOCIATE PASTOR ABOUT INSTRUCTIONS— UPON UNEXPECTED ABSENCE OF SENIOR PASTOR

I regret having to leave without telling you, but the critical illness of my father necessitated it. His condition has stabilized somewhat, yet I have no idea how much longer I will be here. He could be gone today or live for another couple of months. Hopefully by the end of the week I will know more; I will then contact you again.

In the meantime, the following are items I left unfinished that need to be cared for as soon as possible:

1. Visit Katherine Baker in the hospital before her surgery Thursday.

2. Counseling session (premarital) for Bob Ortiz and Joyce Main. Set for Wednesday; must be done then since wedding date is only two weeks away and they need two more sessions.

3. Stress at Church Council meeting the importance of the Food Pantry for needy families in the area and the small amount of money in the budget allotted for it. I would like to see twice the funds available for this work.

4. Postpone for me meeting with Harvey and Judy Kieffer (potential new members). I can see them whenever I get back.

There may be other things I am forgetting; check my calendar in my office. If you have any questions, please call. My parents number is (number). I appreciate your help during this difficult time.

In Him,

Pastor

9 / TO ASSOCIATE PASTOR ABOUT JOB DESCRIPTION

We are pleased to know that you have accepted our offer to serve as associate pastor (Minister of Growth and Mission) at First Church. You job description is as follows:

1. Serves under the direct supervision of the pastor.
2. Is responsible for the total evangelism program as it functions to invite individuals to learn about and accept Jesus Christ as Lord and Savior, as it invites and prepares individuals to become members of First Church, as it guides and nurtures new members in their spiritual growth and church involvement, and as it seeks to identify and reactivate those members who have become inactive.
3. Serves as staff resource for the Evangelism Committee.
4. Is responsible for the mission program of the church as it functions both locally as well as on the wider areas of community and world.
5. Participates in the worship services, preaching and teaching as scheduled by the pastor.
6. Assumes leadership role for the yoked ministry with West Second Avenue First Church.
7. Provides guidance and leadership along with the pastor for Positive Christian Singles, Christian Partners, Women's Association, Men's Fellowship, and any other organizations which need the support of church staff.
8. Participates in community, district, and conference activities as requested and as will benefit the total Church of Jesus Christ as well as the ministry of First Church.
9. Fulfills any other responsibilities and duties which will assist the pastor and strengthen the total church program.

I am looking forward to having you as part of the staff. If you have any questions about this or any other matter between now and when your new duties begin on May 1, please don't hesitate to call me.

In His service,

Pastor

10 / TO ASSOCIATE PASTOR ABOUT MEETINGS— REQUEST TO TAKE PLACE AT

Due to the support and funding that St. Mary's has given the Westcott County Shelter for Battered Wives, I have been invited to attend the annual fund-raising banquet for the shelter on Thursday, April 18.

However, since accepting the invitation I have found out that I will be out of town that evening on parish business. Would it be possible for you to attend the event in my place? It begins with a ham dinner at 7 P.M. followed by a program on "Domestic Violence—Can the

Cycle Be Broken?" by Susan Miller, a social worker from Detroit. The evening is scheduled to end by 9:30 P.M.

Please let me know as soon as possible whether or not you can go. Thank you.

Sincerely,

Father
St. Mary's Church

11 / TO ASSOCIATE PASTOR ABOUT PROBLEMS— CONCERNING ASSOCIATE'S BEHAVIOR

I regret to inform you that recently I have had several complaints from members of the congregation about your smoking; specifically, you lighting up a cigarette in the church immediately following morning worship.

You already know how I feel about smoking. I find it a disagreeable habit which wastes money as well as risks your health. However, I believe that it is a private matter between yourself and God, and I will not order you to stop.

However, I must ask you not to do it at the church on Sundays. As some parents have pointed out, it is a poor example, especially to the youth. As the spiritual leaders of the church, we have a responsibility to point people in the direction of the Savior, often at the expense of our own personal life.

If you feel you would like to break the smoking habit and are unable to do so, I am certain the church would be happy to finance a stop-smoking program, such as the one run by the hospital in town. Please let me know if this is your desire.

In the meantime, I appreciate your cooperation in limiting your cigarettes to times when the congregation at large will not see you.

In His love,

Pastor

12 / TO ASSOCIATE PASTOR ABOUT QUESTIONNAIRES—REQUEST TO COMPLETE

Enclosed you will find a questionnaire concerning current youth programs taking place within the First Church, which has been sent to us from denominational headquarters. They are compiling a list of youth resources and would like our help. Please complete the questionnaire and return it as soon as possible.

Thank you.

In Him,

Pastor

13 / TO ASSOCIATE PASTOR ABOUT RESIGNATION—OF SENIOR PASTOR

I regret to inform you that as of September 1, I will no longer hold the position of senior pastor. For several years, I have felt that it was time for me to move on to another church, but circumstances didn't work out for me to do it. However, now that my youngest son has graduated from high school, I have approached the bishop about this matter. He has agreed, and I have been assigned to (name of church) in (town). My wife and I will be relocating there.

While I am looking forward to the challenge of the new church, I also find myself reluctant to leave First Church. The past ten years which I have spent here have been the best years of my ministry, and I will truly miss the people who have been under my leadership.

It is especially hard for me to end the partnership which you and I have shared for the past three years. While we have not always agreed on everything, I have been confident that things would work out. My assurance was because you are a man of God, first seeking Him in every situation. You have challenged my own faith.

I wish you the Lord's best, wherever and whatever He has you doing. Should you remain at First Church, I know you will work with the new pastor to continue to minister Christ's love to the community.

With warmest regards,

Pastor

14 / TO ASSOCIATE PASTOR ABOUT SALARIES— INCREASE

I'm delighted to inform you that at the recent Board meeting, a salary increase of $0000.00 was approved for you. Effective January 1, it will raise your annual earnings to $00000.00.

Your faithful service to the church over this past year has been a blessing to me personally, and it pleases me to see this action. I am confident that as you continue to minister as associate pastor in the new year, you will be even more valuable to me, as well as to the congregation.

May God shower you with all the best!

Sincerely in Him,

Pastor

15 / TO ASSOCIATE PASTOR ABOUT SCHEDULES

Enclosed you will find a tentative schedule for preaching at morning worship during the summer months. Please check it over and let me know right away if there are any dates I have assigned to you which you are unable to take.

Notice that I have you down for August 1 and 8, during which time I will be on vacation.

Also, on June 22, I will be at a conference on time management for pastors. The other Sundays are negotiable.

Thanks for your assistance—knowing you can take some of the responsibility for preparing a message every week is a great help!

Serving Him Together,

Pastor

16 / TO ASSOCIATE PASTOR ABOUT SPECIAL EVENTS

I recently received the enclosed information about a conference for youth pastors in Columbia, South Carolina. As I read it over, I felt it would be especially helpful for you to attend such a gathering. In the two years that you've been here, you haven't gone to anything like this, and I think the board would be agreeable to financing the trip.

While it would be difficult to have you gone for a week, I am willing to sacrifice you if you feel the time would be well spent. Look over the brochure, and let me know what you think. Or perhaps you have heard of other similar conferences in which you might be more interested. Either way, I believe it would be a worthy goal for the church to send you to such a conference this year.

When I find out your feelings, I will be more than happy to approach the board on your behalf about this matter.

Sincerely,

Pastor

17 / TO BOARD MEMBERS ABOUT ACKNOWLEDGMENTS—OF REQUEST

This is to acknowledge your request to discuss at the next board meeting the possibility of hiring an associate pastor. I believe it would be extremely helpful for me to have someone in charge of the youth and singles programs, which, while strong, could be improved. I will put this issue on the agenda for the April 13 meeting, as the first new business with which we will deal.

I will be interested to see how other board members feel about this topic, and I thank you again for bringing the matter to my attention.

In Him,

Pastor

18 / TO BOARD MEMBERS ABOUT AGENDAS—ADDITION

Take note: to be added to the agenda for the April 13 board meeting is the question of whether or not this is the time to consider hiring an associate pastor, to be in charge of the youth and singles ministry.

Dick Wilson brought up the idea as one the board should discuss at this point in time. Personally, I believe an associate pastor would be an excellent investment, especially now that we are attempting to build our programs in those two areas.

I would ask that you prayerfully think about the possibility in order that we may talk about it at the meeting. I have listed it first under new business, and I am looking forward to hearing your opinion.

Sincerely,

Pastor

19 / TO BOARD MEMBERS ABOUT ANNOUNCEMENTS—OF PASTOR'S ENGAGEMENT

Because I have worked so closely with you, my brothers and sisters in Christ, I wanted you to be among the first to know that (name) and I have decided to marry. We haven't set an exact date yet, but we are thinking about sometime in the spring. Most of you will probably not be surprised by this news, since we have been dating for a year now.

Marriage is a great challenge, and it will mean adjustments for both of us. I'm so thankful that I can count on your continued support and encouragement both before and after the wedding. Do keep (name) and I in your prayers. We begin our engagement with a little apprehension, but also with great excitement that God has called us to unite.

Sincerely,

Pastor

20 / TO BOARD MEMBERS ABOUT APPOINTMENTS—REQUEST FOR THOSE WHO COULD ACCOMPANY PASTOR

I have just talked to the architect and found out that he will be unable to attend the March 10 meeting of the parish council, as he had planned. Therefore, I have set up an appointment with him for 10 A.M., March 8, to go over the blueprints for the new building. I expect it to take about an hour.

Since design is not my strong point, I would like to have at least one council member, and preferably two, accompany me to the architect's office. If you would be able to take off from work during that time, please contact me at once.

Of course, I would have preferred to have Mr. Johnson come to our meting, so that the entire council could have seen the latest plans and heard about the problems he is expecting. But since that is not possible, I feel this appointment will at least give us the basic knowledge we need at this time.

Sincerely,

Father
St. Mary's Church

21 / TO BOARD MEMBERS ABOUT BENEFITS— REQUEST FOR INCREASE

Asking for something for oneself can be awkward. In this example, the letter writer shows appreciation for what he already has, points out what others have provided for their clergy, and requests consideration of the same. Nevertheless, he makes it clear that he will graciously accept whatever the board decides.

It has always been a source of pride to me that First Church takes such good care of its pastors. Especially in the area of benefits, you have been more than generous in providing excellent insurance coverage. This provides important peace of mind for my family and myself.

However, lately it has come to my attention that a number of churches within our denomination are choosing to provide additional insurance to their pastors in the form of full dental coverage. The bishop has sent me a brochure about it, which I will share at the board meeting next week.

As you may know, our family has had significant expense in this area during the past few years. Obviously, then, dental coverage would be a big help to us. In light of this, I would like to discuss the possibility of First Church taking such a step, which will cost about $XXXX per year.

Naturally, I realize that the church has many expenses now which are much more important than this additional insurance. Perhaps, at this time, the budget cannot be stretched any more. If that is the board's decision, there is no problem; it can be considered again at a later date. I am confident of your ability to seek God's wisdom and make the right choice.

Thank you.

Because of Him,

Pastor

22 / TO BOARD MEMBERS ABOUT DISMISSALS— OF STAFF MEMBER

As you know, we have been having problems for some time with Marshall Nickles. Although his work as choir director is outstanding, he has persisted in unacceptable behavior such as smoking in the building; being harsh with choir members he did not want singing, to the point of getting them to quit; and using profane language.

I have discussed these issues with Marshall on a number of occasions, and he seemed willing to work to change. Yet I have seen no improvement. In addition, several girls in the youth choir have recently complained that he has made suggestive remarks to them. When I asked him about this, he said he was teasing.

But last week, he pinched one of the girls after practice. I'm sure you feel as I do; such behavior cannot be permitted to continue. I dismissed him, effective immediately. I enclose a copy of the letter I sent him.

According to the church bylaws, the pastor may dismiss any staff member guilty of this type of behavior. However, I would like your support. I will be asking for a vote of board members at the next meeting, and I would ask you to pray about this matter, in order that we might have the wisdom of the Lord.

Thank you.

Sincerely,

Pastor

23 / TO BOARD MEMBERS ABOUT DISCIPLINARY ACTIONS—AS A RESULT OF RECIPIENT'S BEHAVIOR

I dislike having to write this letter, but I have no other choice at this point. Effective immediately, you have been relieved of your position on the parish council.

In the past six months, your behavior has become unacceptable for a person carrying out the responsibilities of a council member. I have spoken to you a number of times about living openly with a woman to which you are not married, but you continue to do so. As I told you, this is a poor example to the people in the parish whom you profess to serve. It will not be permitted to go on any longer.

I hope that you know what you are doing is wrong, and that you will desire to change. In hopes of that, no further action will be taken at this time. However, if you remain in this same situation for much longer, I will be forced to take additional steps.

As always, I am willing to talk at any time, should you feel the need. May God have mercy on you and show you the error of your ways.

Sincerely,

Father
St. Mary's Church

24 / TO BOARD MEMBERS ABOUT ENCOURAGEMENT—IN MIDST OF BUILDING PROJECT

A new building (or the remodeling or addition of one) creates a sufficient amount of stress throughout the church or synagogue. Especially prone to stress are board members who are making project decisions which may not find universal acceptance. A letter to reassure such people of your support and appreciation can help.

The process we are undergoing—that of buying a new building and remodeling it to fit the needs of our congregation—must be a heavy burden at times. As the Church Council, you have the ultimate responsibility for many decisions concerning the building. You have to choose the best direction in everything form the amount of fund-raising that should be done to the type of pews to purchase. Even though you have the recommendations of the building committee, you still have to decide. I am certain that each one of you have spent many hours in prayer in order to have the Lord's wisdom in these matters.

I would just like to encourage you that even though there may be setbacks and it may seem like we'll never be in the new building, progress is being made. The months will pass, and very soon the time for decisions will be over as we move into our longed-for facility. Then you can sit back and relax, knowing that you have had a big part in the progress to this goal.

So keep on attending those late-night meetings, praying for God's wisdom, and making the decisions that will affect First Church for many days to come. And know that you have the appreciation of myself and the entire congregation.

May God bless you as you work for Him.

Sincerely,

Pastor

25 / TO BOARD MEMBERS ABOUT ELECTIONS— RESULTS

As a result of the elections held on November 16, the following will join the Board, effective January 1: (names)

We appreciate the willingness of these people to serve God and First Church in this way, and I'm confident that you will do all in your power to welcome them to their new positions. They will need to call on your expertise as they learn their new responsibilities, and I am personally grateful for your cooperation.

We have a tremendous job in front of us, as we seek to minister in the name of Jesus Christ. But with board members like you who are committed to working together, the task is considerably easier.

May God bless you,

Pastor

26 / TO BOARD MEMBERS ABOUT EVALUATION—RESULTS

For your information, I have enclosed a copy of the recent evaluation of the Sunday school department. You will remember that we sent out evaluation sheets to all of the teachers and students involved. Of 172 distributed, 73 percent were returned upon completion. I feel this is an excellent response, even though we did have to beg, threaten, and intimidate some people in order to persuade them to cooperate!

Looking over the forms, I was encouraged to see the overall positive response. The majority of the respondents felt the Sunday school program was one of the strengths of the church. They were pleased with the commitment of the teachers, and with the emphasis on a personal relationship with Christ and on growing in that relationship. Overall, the classes seem to be meeting the needs of our congregation.

Naturally, there are some weaknesses. A number of people would like to see more Scripture memorization. A request from the adult classes was for more discussion time, and some asked for more discipline in children's classes which have been disrupted by unruly students. I am meeting with the Sunday school superintendent to discuss these issues, and we will be having a meeting with the teachers in the near future.

If you desire, we can talk about the evaluation at greater length during the next board meeting. Please let me know your feelings on this.

In the meantime, you can take pride in the knowledge that our Sunday school department is progressing. May God continue to bless it.

Because of Jesus,

Pastor

27 / TO BOARD MEMBERS ABOUT INSTRUCTIONS

As you know, it is again time to begin planning the annual St. Mary's Festival. At the next meeting of the parish council, I would like to see the following done: a date set for the festival, a chairperson selected, and a budget established.

Please be thinking about who might be willing serve as chairperson, as well as how much we need to increase the budget from last years' figure of $XXXX. In order for the festival to be off to a good start, we need to start by doing our part now.

Thank you.

Sincerely,

Father
St. Mary's Church

28 / TO BOARD MEMBERS ABOUT MEETINGS

The regular meeting of the board will be held on Tuesday, October 1, at 7 P.M. in the library. Please make every effort to attend. In order to minister in the most effective manner, we need the input of each member; besides, we miss you when you can't make it!

I realize that being a part of the board demands a certain amount of sacrifice, often at the cost of other priorities such as your spouse or children. Thank you for your willingness to serve in this manner. May the Lord bless you abundantly!

See you on the 1st,

Pastor

29 / TO BOARD MEMBERS ABOUT PURCHASES— SUGGESTED BY PASTOR

A request for a major purchase can be met with resistance. Note here how the pastor begins with a lighthearted touch, and goes on to state clearly how the computer could be used and gives details of one available.

What is more powerful than a locomotive? Faster-thinking than a speeding bullet? Able to handle a multitude of tasks with the push of a button? You might have guessed—a computer.

I have recently been looking at some of these remarkable machines, and I have become convinced that the church would benefit immensely by the purchase of one. Not only would it be a great timesaver for myself and the secretary, but it would simplify many tasks, allowing more opportunities for personal ministry. The mailing list could be put on it, as well as record keeping, correspondence, budgets, and many other things.

While investigating this, I have found out about a used computer, a Kaypro 2, which is being sold by Memorial Church in Memphis. They have had it for two years and are now replacing it with a larger unit. Although they paid over $2,500 for it (including printer and software), they are willing to sell it to us for $800. I believe this is an excellent deal and I would like the board to seriously consider such a purchase.

I will have more information about this unit at the March meeting. In the meantime, I would like to encourage you to pray about such a decision. At this price, the computer from Memorial will not be available for long. Of course, we should not feel pressured to buy this particular one just because it is reasonably priced. If necessary, we can find another used computer from a different source. But I am convinced that the church needs to take this step at some point.

Thank you for your consideration.

In Him,

Pastor

30 / TO BOARD MEMBERS ABOUT RESIGNATION—OF PASTOR

At this time, I would like to submit to your my resignation as pastor of First Church, effective May 1, 19XX. I have accepted a position at Memorial Church in Lexington.

It is always difficult to make a decision such as this. In the five years I have served here, I have enjoyed many opportunities for ministry. My family and I have made close friends, and we have seen the church grow in a number of areas. I have come to know the Lord in deeper ways, and I will always treasure the time I spent here.

However, it seems that God is directing us to take on a new situation. As you know, it has been difficult for my wife to adjust to a rural area, and she has been unable to find employment in her field. She has willingly put that aside during the past years, but now she is ready to resume working outside the home. This is a major consideration in our decision.

In addition, a minister can lose his effectiveness after so many years in the same church. I feel this is beginning to happen, and rather than risking problems in the congregation, I would like to step aside to permit a new pastor to come in and continue the momentum.

I am sure that you can understand and accept my feelings. You have always been a support to me, and I appreciate the long hours you have spent working with me. I know you will continue to do so with the new pastor.

May God bless each of you.

Sincerely,

Pastor

31 / TO BOARD MEMBERS ABOUT SALARIES— REQUEST FOR INCREASE OF ASSOCIATE'S

I'm sure you would not hesitate to agree with me that hiring Jeff Rivers as assistant pastor here was an excellent decision. In his two years on staff with me, he has been a great asset to the church. I especially appreciate his cooperativeness and his example of a life in which Jesus Christ is in control. His work with the youth and the singles has been outstanding; as you know, both programs have increased at least 50 percent since he took over.

In light of Jeff's performance, I think it only appropriate to ask you to prayerfully consider a salary raise for him at this time. While he has never approached me concerning his financial needs, I know that it is difficult living on what he makes, particularly now that his first child has arrived. Yet his wife has felt God's call to stay home to raise their son. Can we do any less than support this young couple as they sacrifice to follow the Lord's leading?

Jeff currently makes $XXXXX annually, and I would recommend a X percent raise, effective immediately. First Church is known for its generosity, and it is only right that it should begin with the staff.

I realize that this is perhaps not the best time to be making this appeal. We are in the midst of repairing the church roof, and several families are facing unemployment, both of which affect the weekly offering. Yet I believe that there will never be a day when we can honestly say we have excess money; there will always be some expense which will stretch church funds.

Over the past years that I have worked with you, you have shown me again and again your faithfulness in seeking God for wisdom in decisions such as this one. I ask you now to seriously go before Him about this matter. As always, I will accept your answer.

Thank you.

In His service,

Pastor

32 / TO BOARD MEMBERS ABOUT SCHEDULES— CHANGE OF

I have just found out that there is a meeting of the Sandusky County Mental Health Board, on which I serve, on Tuesday, April 1. Although that is the regularly scheduled meeting night for the parish council, I wondered if it might be possible to move the council meeting to another night that week.

I would be available either Monday or Thursday evening. Please let me know within the next few days which you would prefer. If necessary, we could also meet the following Tuesday, April 8, but I would rather meet the usual week if possible.

Thank you for your cooperation.

Sincerely,

Father
St. Mary's Church

33 / TO CHRISTIAN EDUCATION STAFF ABOUT AGENDAS

Where are you planning to be on Saturday, March 21? I hope your calendar is already marked on that date to be at First Church for the Christian Education staff meeting. This will be an important time together, as we will be going over the recent Sunday school evaluation.

Although overall the evaluation was favorable, there are always places which can be improved. We will be brainstorming ideas for improvements in areas which might be weak.

Also on the agenda for the meeting will be some preliminary looks at Vacation Bible School curriculum and also a presentation on in-class discipline by Marlene Maxson.

See you then!

In His service,

Pastor

34 / TO CHRISTIAN EDUCATION STAFF ABOUT ANNOUNCEMENTS—ADOPTION OF CHILD

To all staff members:

I am delighted to inform you that my wife and I will be adopting a child from Korea next week. She is five months old and will be arriving in Detroit on Thursday, May 8. Some of you know that Janice and I have been working on this for several years, and we are both thrilled that our dream is now so close to reality.

Naturally, we have a number of things to do to prepare for the arrival of our new daughter, and I have decided to take off from work next Wednesday through Saturday. Please do not contact me unless it is an emergency. Most problems or questions that arise can easily be handled by an elder, the lay leader, or the Director of Christian Education.

Thank you so much for your cooperation. I'm looking forward to you meeting the newest member of our family!

In Him,

Pastor

35 / TO CHRISTIAN EDUCATION STAFF ABOUT APPOINTMENTS—WHICH FILL A POSITION

It's my privilege to inform you that the appointment of Carol Matthews as Director of Christian Education has just been confirmed by the bishop. She will be assuming her new responsibilities as of February 15, and I know I can count on you to help her adjust to them.

We are blessed to have as talented and dedicated a person as Carol coming onto the staff, and she will surely appreciate the cooperative spirit of the teachers as she comes in to help us.

Please make her welcome; I plan on having a small reception for her and the teachers within the month in order for you to get to know her. I'm sure you will find her a warm caring individual who will be an asset to First Church.

In His service,

Pastor

36 / TO CHRISTIAN EDUCATION STAFF ABOUT ENCOURAGEMENT—DURING A SLUMP IN SUNDAY SCHOOL ATTENDANCE

A drop in attendance can be demoralizing, especially to the teachers who are affected. The letter writer here points out some benefits of the situation and attempts to raise spirits, with a warm tone which offer assurance that things will improve.

I couldn't help but notice some long faces around the Sunday school wing recently. With the low attendance we've had in the past month or so, that's understandable. It certainly is demoralizing when you've spent a good amount of time preparing a lesson, only to have very few students show up.

However, remember that even if just one boy or girl hears your lesson, it is worthwhile. What you taught that week could be exactly what he or she needed to hear. It might be the words that stick with that child for the rest of his or her life. You can never underestimate how much influence you could unknowingly have.

So I would encourage you to keep on preparing those lessons. Continue to pray for your class, that you would be sensitive to the needs of the children who do come. With smaller classes, you will have more opportunities for one-on-one ministry. And don't stop believing that God can send more students your way.

With this goal in mind, I am going to be meeting with the Christian Education staff on a regular basis. As we work together, I am confident we will again see larger numbers of children in our classes.

In the meantime, may God bless you in a special way as you devote time each week to teach. May His joy fill you to overflowing, even the midst of some bleak circumstances.

In Him,

Pastor

37 / TO CHRISTIAN EDUCATION STAFF ABOUT INFORMATION

On Sunday evening, December 19, the children of the congregation will be presenting their annual Christmas program. Therefore, on that morning, regular Sunday school classes for grades six and lower will not be held, in order that the children may practice their presentation.

Thank you for your cooperation with this matter. As always, the entire church is looking forward to seeing the youngsters; it is always a blessing to all of us.

In His service,

Pastor

38 / TO CHRISTIAN EDUCATION STAFF ABOUT INSTRUCTIONS

As your know, the twentieth anniversary of Juanita Kameron's teaching Sunday school at First Church is only a few weeks away. We have planned a surprise reception for her to be held at that time, and one of the things we would like to do at it is to read comments by some of her former students. Would you please take a few minutes during your class this Sunday to find out who her students were? Then ask them to write just a brief statement or two in her tribute. It can be something lasting that she taught them, how she helped in a specific situation, the effect she had on a life, etc. We are looking for responses from former students of all ages. In addition, if you have found that your life has been touched by her, write that down too. Perhaps she was able at some point to share a helpful teaching hint or an encouraging word when you needed it. Let us in on it!

Papers should be turned in to me by October 7. Remember Juanita is not to know anything about this. Thank you for your help. I'm sure it will mean a great deal to her.

Serving Jesus,

Pastor

39 / TO CHRISTIAN EDUCATION STAFF ABOUT JOB DESCRIPTION

Here is the job description you requested:

1. To be responsible, under the direct supervision of the pastor and in consultation with the Christian Education Committee, for the total Christian Education program and youth ministry.
2. To be responsible for the Sunday school program:
   a. Recommend curriculum to the Church Council through the Christian Education committee.
   b. Recruit and provide for the training of teachers.
   c. Supervise equipment and room use.
   d. Work with Administrative Assistant in ordering material and keeping records.
3. To be responsible for all adult Christian Education:
   a. Coordinate Bethel Bible study program.
   b. Develop educational and study opportunities using the ministers and lay people as teachers for classes at the church as well as for working within the framework of the Parish Program for in-home, short-term study, or growth groups.
   c. Plan and coordinate adult retreats.
4. To be responsible for all youth involvement, especially junior and senior high age groups:
   a. Develop program, recruit and train leadership, and be fully involved in youth fellowship activities.

   b. Plan and provide leadership for youth retreats, work camps, and special projects or events.
   c. Share with the Director of Music in providing leadership and direction for any youth shows or special ministries.
   d. Develop an evangelism program for the youth.
   e. Call on the youth who have been sick or inactive.

5. To be responsible for the cooperation and coordination with other groups such as Boy Scouts, Young Life, Fellowship of Christian Athletes, etc.

6. To be responsible for youth confirmation class.

7. To be responsible for the planning and operation of Vacation Bible School.

8. To participate in judicatory and youth-related community activities as appropriate to the church position and as time permits.

Thank you for your interest. We hope to receive your application soon or the position of Director of Christian Education at First Church.

Sincerely,

Pastor

40 / TO CHRISTIAN EDUCATION STAFF ABOUT MEETINGS

On Saturday, March 31, I will be meeting with the Christian Education staff at 10 A.M. in the senior high classroom. Please make every effort to be there. We will be discussing several important matters, including making a decision about what curriculum to use in this year's Vacation Bible School.

I'm sure that you share my burden for the children and youth of the church; you've indicated that by your faithful service in your position. I greatly appreciate all you've done. Together, we must continue to do what we can to guide the young people in making a firm commitment to Christ and then helping them grow in that relationship.

See you on the 31st,

Pastor

41 / TO CHRISTIAN EDUCATION STAFF ABOUT POLICIES—CONCERNING SUNDAY SCHOOL TEACHERS' TIME OFF

While welcomed by many, some people would not like being asked to step down from a teaching position, even only temporarily. This letter restates the policy and cites when the teacher took on her responsibilities, and then expresses appreciation for a job well-done. It also leaves the door open to resume teaching after the required time off.

As you know, it is the policy of the Sunday school Department here to have nine months on/three months off for teachers. According to our records, you have been teaching the third and fourth grades since June of last year. Therefore, it's time for you to have a well-deserved break of three months.

If you have someone in mind who might be willing to take over your class as of April 1, please let me know. Otherwise, I will be glad to call on one of the people on the substitute list.

When July 1 comes, you are welcome to resume teaching the same class, or you may choose to take on a different age level. Of course, if you prefer, you needn't teach at all.

Whatever you decide at that time, we want you to know how much we appreciate your dedicated service to the children in your class. I trust that these months off will be a period of spiritual refreshment for you.

May God bless you richly.

Sincerely,

Pastor

42 / TO CHRISTIAN EDUCATION STAFF ABOUT PURCHASES—REQUEST FOR HELP IN JUSTIFYING

Recently I have been investigating the possibility of using a computer here at the church, and I have become convinced that it would be extremely helpful in my work. I plan to present my views on this subject to the board at its November meeting.

It has occurred to me that perhaps such a unit would also prove helpful to you in some way. If you know anything about computers and feel they would prove to be an asset in the Sunday school department, please inform me in writing as soon as possible. I would especially appreciate any specifics on how a computer would assist you. If possible, it would also help for you to come to the board meeting to share your feelings.

Thank you for any assistance you can give me. I'm not certain that the church has funds at this point to pursue such an option, but I want to at least present it to the board.

Because of Him,

Pastor

43 / TO CHRISTIAN EDUCATION STAFF ABOUT QUESTIONNAIRES—REQUEST FOR INPUT IN ASSEMBLING

I am in the process of putting together a questionnaire to be filled out by those participating in our Sunday school program. The purpose is to determine the likes and dislikes of both the students and the teachers regarding a time of opening and/or closing for the entire department. As Director of Christian Education, you may be able to assist me.

In the past, we have all met together in Fellowship Hall for ten minutes of singing, readings, etc. before going to individual classes. This was discontinued several years ago. Recently, however, I have had a number of requests to begin such a time again, either at the start of the class or at the end.

In order to see how widespread this feeling is, I plan to distribute a questionnaire about it in several weeks. I enclose a copy of what I have been working on. Do you have any suggestions of other questions I could ask? Are there any other areas about which you would like to get opinions?

I look forward to your response.

Gratefully,

Pastor

44 / TO CHRISTIAN EDUCATION STAFF ABOUT RECOGNITION

It is a great joy for me to recognize Juanita Kameron's outstanding contribution to our Sunday school. On October 15, she will have taught twenty years, primarily in grades one and two.

As you can imagine, it takes a tremendous commitment to children and to Christ Himself to be willing to take a Sunday school week after week, year after year. I personally appreciate her sacrifices made on behalf of her students, and I encourage you to take her example to heart. Her faithfulness is an inspiration to us all, but especially to those of us who also teach Sunday school.

As the anniversary of her twenty years here draws nearer, we will make some special plans to honor Juanita. In the meantime, I am happy to recognize her as a part of our program of Christian Education.

Sincerely,

Pastor

45 / TO CHRISTIAN EDUCATION STAFF ABOUT SPECIAL EVENTS

Most teachers agree that discipline in Sunday school creates more problems than anything else. How do you control behavior problems while continuing to communicate God's unconditional love? Is it possible to deal with the class troublemaker in such a way that he/she is not disruptive but still feels like he/she is wanted?

For the answer to this and other questions, plan on attending the teacher training workshop on Saturday, October 3, from 10 A.M. until 4 P.M. Meeting in Fellowship Hall where the opening session will be held.

The leader of the workshop will be Harry Thomas, who has been in the field of Christian education for fifteen years. A professor at Calvary Bible School, he has written two books and numerous magazine articles. His practical approach to his subject will inform as well as entertain you.

Because of the great importance First Church places on the religious education of our children, youth, and adults, the board has decided to absorb the cost for the day. All you are asked to contribute is your presence at the workshop. An effective teacher is a trained one, and we know you won't want to miss this special opportunity to improve your teaching skills.

As a part of our Christian Education staff, you have a big responsibility, and we are grateful for your willingness to fulfill it. Our prayer is that the workshop will help you to carry out your job in the best possible way.

See you on the 3rd,

Pastor

46 / TO MUSIC STAFF ABOUT AGENDAS

As you may remember, an update of one of the various ministries or programs of the church is on the agenda of each board meeting. For the upcoming November meeting, it is again time to present the latest update about the music ministry.

Therefore, I would like to ask you to plan to attend. You will have approximately fifteen minutes to share how you feel that things are progressing for the music, including organ, choirs, bell choirs, cantatas, etc. This is also an excellent time to bring up your goals for the next year, as well as perhaps mentioning a future dream or two. Board members will be free to ask questions, so be prepared.

Music is a vital part of First Church, and I look forward to hearing your presentation.

See you then,

Pastor

47 / TO MUSIC STAFF ABOUT ANNOUNCEMENTS

As the youth have gone about planning the worship service for May 19, they have decided to try several different things. One of them is that they would like to have the entire service without organ music. Instead, they will be calling on members of the youth group to provide accompaniment through piano, guitar, and other instruments.

So it looks as if you won't need to sit at the organ at all that day; they even want to have just piano for the prelude and postlude. Consider it a day off for you. But remember, we'll be looking forward to having you back at the organ the following Sunday!

In His service,

Pastor

48 / TO MUSIC STAFF ABOUT APPOINTMENTS— SETTING UP A TIME

Though it still looks very much like winter outside, spring is not very far away, and it's time for us to get together to discuss plans for the upcoming months. Could we meet in my office on Wednesday morning at 9 A.M.?

I assume that you want to put on another Easter cantata this year, and we need to talk about that. Also, did you want to have charge of an evening service devoted to music by groups and individuals within the church? If so, a date needs to be selected for it.

I look forward to hearing your ideas about these things as well as anything else on your mind. If the scheduled time is inconvenient, let me know and we can work something else out.

In Him,

Pastor

49 / TO MUSIC STAFF ABOUT CONGRATULATIONS—ON RECEIVING AWARD

What an honor it is to have our senior high bell choir recognized as outstanding ringers of the day at the recent bell choir festival! As director of the group, you must be elated, and for good reason. Now it's public knowledge what we at First Church were already aware of: the youth bell choir is one talented, dedicated group.

Congratulations to you and to each member of the choir. We are proud of all of you and we ask God's richest blessings for the group as well as for each individual involved. May you continue to serve Him Who has given you the musical talents recognized at the festival.

Sincerely in Christ,

Pastor

50 / TO MUSIC STAFF ABOUT CONTRACTS AND AGREEMENTS

Please sign and return the enclosed contract within the week. Thank you.

This agreement made this _____ day of _____ 19_____, between First Church, first party, and _____, (position), second party, witnesseth:

First Party hereby employs second party for the calandar year of 19_____, at a salary of $_____, _____, payable in weekly installments of _____.

In consideration therefore, second party accepts said employment and salary and agrees to faithfully fulfill his/her duties, with the following terms:

Salary is subject to government withholding provisions, city and state tax.

Employee subscribes to and is in full agreement with "I believe the Bible to be the Word of God, the only infallible rule of faith and practice, and that it has been clearly and consistantly interpreted in the Church 'Statement of Faith.' "

Employee's inability to provide adequate service because of inefficiency, physical disability, or conduct detrimental to the school shall result in termination of this contract.

If either party shall default in any of the provisions of this contract as set forth, said contract shall be deemed terminated.

In witness whereof the parties hereto have set their signatures,

Date _____ Pastor _____ Employee _____

51 / TO MUSIC STAFF ABOUT ENCOURAGEMENT— AFTER POOR SHOWING IN CONTEST

On the way home from the recent choir festival, the mood on the bus must have been subdued. After all, you had worked hard to prepare for the festival, and you were confident that you would do well. Not receiving an award for your efforts must have been a shock as well as a disappointment.

Of course, you know that every participant cannot win, that what counts is that you tried, and that we at First Church still love you all and feel that you're the best, regardless of what anyone else says. All that is true, but it doesn't help take away the sting of knowing that your talents and hard work weren't acknowledged in public.

All I can tell you is to hang in there. There's another festival to go to next time, and you will be ready then to try again. May God reassure you today and every day of your value in His sight.

Sincerely,

Pastor

52 / TO MUSIC STAFF ABOUT EVALUATION—REQUEST FOR HELP IN DETERMINING HOW TO DO

From time to time, I feel it is wise to evaluate the various ministries and outreaches of the church. In doing so, we can become aware of the strengths and weaknesses of the programs, which in turn helps us seek solutions for the problems and continue to strive for even more strength in the areas in which we excel.

Therefore, I would like you to begin thinking about how you can be a part of this process in the music ministry. Perhaps an evaluation form can be made up and distributed to choir members, etc., or maybe even the entire congregation. It might allow us to determine how effective the program is, as well as find out worshippers' preferences as far as type of music, amount per service, and so on.

See what you can come up with, and plan on sharing it with me within the next two weeks.

Because of Jesus,

Pastor

53 / TO MUSIC STAFF ABOUT INFORMATION

I am delighted to inform you that the board has approved your request to begin a children's choir for grades one through four. The group, to be call the Cherub Choir, will sing during morning worship four to five times per year, and they will practice on Thursdays from 4–4:30 P.M., from September until May.

We pray that you will have wisdom and guidance as you begin this new ministry, and it is with great anticipation that we await the first appearance of the Cherub Choir in the sanctuary.

If I may be of any help to you as you set things up, don't hesitate to let me know.

Sincerely in Christ,

Pastor

54 / TO MUSIC STAFF ABOUT JOB DESCRIPTION

As you requested, here is a copy of your updated job description as Director of Music:

1. Be responsible for the development, nurture, scheduling, and direction of all choirs, vocal and handbell, utilizing volunteer leadership whenever possible and/or necessary.

2. Share with other staff members and volunteer advisors in the Youth Fellowship activities.

3. Work with the teachers to provide music—vocal and instrumental—in the Sunday school program.

4. Select appropriate music for all the choirs, share with the pastor in the scheduling of choirs and selection of hymns, and be responsible for any special musical services or choral vespers.

5. Be responsible for the maintenance of organ, piano, choir robes, and any other musical instruments or equipment, making recommendations to the church council when replacements are needed.

6. Give general supervision to the organist.

7. Be responsible for the accompanist at all services, including weddings and funerals, making arrangements for a substitute organist if the church organist is not available.

8. Develop and provide soloists for regular services as well as for special occasions. Also serve as contact person and coordinator for visiting musicians or musical groups.

9. Work with choir members on an individual basis, making calls when there have been problems, sicknesses, or absences.

10. Be responsible to and supportive of the pastor in all phases of the church program.

11. Make initial calling on prospective choir members

Contact me if you have any questions.

In Him,

Pastor

55 / TO MUSIC STAFF ABOUT POLICIES— CONCERNING USE OF ORGAN

Recently, some questions have arisen about church policy for use of the organ during weddings. For your information, the policy is that no one is permitted to play it except our own church organists. However, should a bride or groom have a family member who is qualified, they may ask the board to make an exception. It will usually be granted, providing that the person who will be playing is willing to meet with one of the church organists first to practice and to find out the instrument's unique characteristics.

If such a person is not available, the bride or groom must make their own arrangements with one of the church organists; the pastor does not handle this himself.

We have a beautiful and expensive organ which is an important part of worship at First Church. This policy is not meant to inconvenience anyone, but to uphold our responsibility in caring for the organ. Thank you for your cooperation.

Because of Him,

Pastor

56 / TO MUSIC STAFF ABOUT PROBLEMS— CONCERNING CHOIR MEMBERS LEAVING CHILDREN UNSUPERVISED

It has come to my attention that recently, during adult choir practice, problems have been occurring with unsupervised children in the church. As I understand it, several of the choir members are bringing their preschoolers to the church and leaving them on their own while the rehearsal takes place. On at least two occasions of which I am aware, these youngsters have been found in rooms they should not be in, such as the library and the kitchen.

I'm certain that you share my concern for the children's welfare and safety. Naturally, we would be horrified if anything happened to harm them, and it would surely be a source of embarrassment to their parents if the children unintentionally caused damage to any church property.

Because of this, I'm asking that you instruct your choir members to leave the young ones at home or obtain a babysitter to take care of them in the church nursery. I am aware that sometimes circumstances arise which cannot be controlled, perhaps resulting in parents being forced to bring their children to choir practice. But these situations should occur rarely, and even then someone must stay with the children.

I am confident that I can count on your cooperation in dealing with this problem.

In His service,

Pastor

57 / TO MUSIC STAFF ABOUT PURCHASES— SUGGESTED BY STAFF

Situations arise in which someone besides the pastor requests a major purchase, one that the clergy may not entirely approve of. In the following letter, the pastor agrees to present the matter to the board instead of coming out against it. Nevertheless, he points out reasons why it may be turned down and even goes a step further in suggesting possibilities which may help.

Thank you for your recent letter expressing the need for new robes for the youth choir. I certainly agree with your reasoning about why they are necessary now.

As your requested, I will bring the matter up at the next board meeting. However, with the new building program, it is very possible that the board will not be able to designate much if any funds at this time.

Nevertheless, you are welcome to attend the meeting if you choose. It will be at 7 P.M. on Monday, March 29. If you could bring samples or pictures of the robes, that would be helpful. In addition, the board might be more open to the subject if you have some sort of plan to have the choir itself raise a percentage of the cash needed. Perhaps if you can show exactly how much money is required and offer to do car washes, dinners, etc. for the purpose of earning part of it, the board would reciprocate by offering you a portion of the funding. Naturally, I cannot guarantee this, but I think it is a possibility.

As I mentioned, I am behind you in this and I will do anything I can to help.

Sincerely,

Pastor

58 / TO MUSIC STAFF ABOUT RECOGNITION

"Well done, thou good and faithful servant."

After the Easter cantata last Sunday, God will certainly be saying such praise to you. The message was convicting; the presentation professional in every aspect. I can only say thank you for all the hard work put in by you and by the choir. It was well worth your time and effort. My sentiments have been echoed by a number of others in the congregation.

In short, I am very proud to have you as music minister at First Church. Your talent, your servant's heart, and your dedication to the church are obvious, and I believe they should not go unrecognized.

May God bless you in every way.

In His service,

Pastor

59 / TO MUSIC STAFF ABOUT SALARIES— DENIAL OF INCREASES

As you know, the subject of your salary was discussed at the board meeting last night. I regret to inform you that at this time, First Church is unable to offer you any increase from the $XX you are currently receiving per Sunday for serving as organist.

Please understand that this in no way reflects how the board views your job performance. We are all grateful for the hard work you do and the dedication you have shown to Christ, both personally and professionally. We cannot even offer any suggestions for improvement.

But the finances on the church are not in the place where we would want them. Offerings have been down, and with the recent roof repair, the funds are limited. Unfortunately, it appears that this is not a short-term problem. Strictly on this basis, the church cannot afford to increase any staff salary this year.

Believe me, none of us like this decision. It doesn't seem fair to you; you deserve more. Yet there is really nothing else we can do. However, I can promise you that I will bring up the matter again, should the finances improve significantly.

Under the circumstances, you are certainly free to look into other organist jobs which might be able to pay you more. We would understand if you chose to take one, but I know I speak for the board and the congregation in saying I hope you will decide to remain at First Church. You are an important part of things here, and we would hate to lose you.

May God bless you in every way.

Sincerely,

Pastor

60 / TO OTHER EMPLOYEES ABOUT ACKNOWLEDGMENTS—OF REQUEST FOR VACATION TIME

This is to acknowledge your request for the week of June 4–11 off for vacation. I will present it to the board at the next meeting for its decision, but I foresee no problem with you being on vacation that week.

As you know, now that you have been employed here for a year you are entitled to two weeks of paid vacation per twelve-month period. I prefer at least a month's notice before a vacation, as I have to enlist someone else (usually my wife!) to serve as secretary while you are out of the office. Thanks for your cooperation in this matter.

I will inform you of the board's decision as soon as possible, yet I'm sure you're safe to go ahead and make plans for your trip. While you're gone, I will miss your efficiency, but it helps knowing you'll be back to help me in a week!

In Him,

Pastor

61 / TO OTHER EMPLOYEES ABOUT AGENDAS

On the agenda for the March meeting of the Church Council is a discussion about the possibility of hiring another secretary. Therefore, I would like you to plan on being present. By sharing information about how heavy your work load is and explaining exactly the tasks for which your are responsible, you will be much more convincing than I could be about the necessity of employing more secretarial help.

If there is any reason why you cannot attend the 8 P.M. meeting on March 6, please contact me at once. Otherwise, I will look forward to seeing you there. The discussion will be the first thing on the agenda, so you can be prepared to speak to the council for maybe five or ten minutes, answer any questions, and be able to leave by around 8:30 P.M.

Thank you for your cooperation. I know you join me in hoping that the council will see how urgent it is that we have another secretary and appropriate the funding as soon as possible.

In Him,

Pastor

62 / TO OTHER EMPLOYEES ABOUT APPOINTMENTS— CANCELLATION OF MEETING

I have an appointment with David Masters for 10 A.M. next Friday to interview him for a janitor position. Would you please contact him and cancel the meeting? Inform him that the current janitor has changed his mind and decided to stay, so we are no longer in need of new applicants. However, we will keep his name on file, and when another opening does occur, he will be notified. We appreciate his interest.

Thanks for taking care of this for me!

Sincerely,

Pastor

63 / TO OTHER EMPLOYEES ABOUT DISMISSAL— OF SECRETARY

In the serious case of a dismissal, the tone of the letter is rather formal. But the clergy here lessens the blow with a personal note of concern for the employee, while making it clear that the decision to terminate will not be reconsidered.

We regret to inform you that your employment as a secretary for First Church will be terminated at the end of the working day on Friday, April 16, 19XX.

During your six months of employment, we have found it necessary to reprimand you on nine separate occasions. You have been notified about your frequent lateness, and the general poor quality of your work. More serious, you have carried confidential information learned on the job outside the church on at least two occasions.

Last month, you were informed that continued problems in these areas would result in reappraisal of your employment. To date, no improvement has manifested itself, and recently your attitude has been extremely hostile toward the people in which you have come in contact. When I have repeatedly asked if a personal matter (or a matter concerning the church) was interfering with your job performance, you have refused to discuss it or seek help.

Therefore, your dismissal seems more than warranted. You will receive your final paycheck in the mail on Friday, April 23, 19XX.

It grieves me to reach this point, and I want you to know that even though our professional relationship must end, I am always available to assist you in any way possible. God loves you, and whatever may be causing you to act in this way, He wants to help. Please let Him do it.

My prayer is for your happiness and health.

Sincerely,

Pastor

64 / TO OTHER EMPLOYEES ABOUT DISCIPLINARY ACTION

I'm sure you are aware that yesterday you were again late coming to work. Unfortunately, the talk which we had last week about the importance of arriving at your desk on time seems to have had little effect. As I told you then, you have an important responsibility as my secretary to be in the office in order to answer the telephone for me, as well as to complete the duties of correspondence, filing, etc. I have tried to be reasonable about this; I realize that with families, things do occasionally come up at the last moment which can make one late. But in your case, you have been arriving from a half hour to an hour and a half late approximately three days a week.

It's my unfortunate duty to inform you that this must not continue. Effectively immediately, your pay will be docked $XX each time you are more than fifteen minutes late, unless you have proof of an emergency.

I regret very much having to take this step, and I hope that it will prove unnecessary. But I simply cannot and will not tolerate any more of what has turned into a very bad habit.

In almost every other area, you are a highly efficient worker and an asset to the church. I appreciate the many things you do to help me; if you can just stop this tardiness, you will find you have virtually no problems.

I look forward to working out this situation favorably for both of us.

Sincerely,

Pastor

65 / TO OTHER EMPLOYEES ABOUT ENCOURAGEMENT—OF NEW SECRETARY

How often do you find yourself quick to criticize but slow to offer praise? It's a frequent problem. The recipient of this letter is sure to glow for a week after getting such a warm (and probably most unexpected!) note.

Now that you have been employed by First Church for a month, I wanted to take this opportunity to tell you that I'm pleased with your work. Adjusting to a new job is never easy, and in addition to learning the way we do things here, you have had to deal with some people who are not as pleasant as they could be. Yet you have consistently handled your responsibilities well while maintaining a positive and uplifting attitude. Since you represent both First Church and the Lord Jesus Christ, this is vitally important.

When you have completed three months employment, your job performance will be officially reviewed. But in the meantime, be assured that you're doing great! If your have any questions or concerns, don't hesitate to ask me about them.

Blessings,

Pastor

66 / TO OTHER EMPLOYEES ABOUT INFORMATION— REQUEST FOR HELP IN ASSEMBLING

In honor of the fortieth anniversary of the establishment of First Church, we have planned to put together a booklet covering the past and present ministry. A committee of Violet Rogers, George Adams, and Mary Ingram will be in charge of assembling the booklet, which will be distributed to the congregation as well as to any past members who are interested.

In light of this, the committee will need information about the pastors who have served here. Would you please look through the church records to find anything which might help them in writing a brief summary of each pastor? They will be responsible for organizing the material, but if you could gather it together for them, it would be a great help.

Someone from the committee will be talking to you soon about this project and when the information is needed. In the meantime, you might want to begin looking around for it. There's no telling how good (or bad!) the records were from years ago; it might be an easy task for you or it might require an extensive amount of time. But as efficient a secretary as you are, I'm confident you can handle it. Thanks!

Sincerely,

Pastor

67 / TO OTHER EMPLOYEES ABOUT INSTRUCTIONS

The company who will be repaving the parking lot has finally set Tuesday, May 1, as the date for the work to begin, if the weather cooperates. Therefore, plan on parking on the street that day. And be careful to avoid the blacktop until it has fully dried, which should take several days.

In addition, if you talk on the phone or see others who plan to come to church that day, warn them to park elsewhere.

Thanks for your cooperation in this matter. I'm anxious to once again have a beautiful, rut-free parking lot!

Sincerely,

Pastor
St. Mary's Church

68 / TO OTHER EMPLOYEES ABOUT MEETING

We have just arranged that a newly formed Weight Watchers group will meet in the church on Thursday evenings from 7 to 9 P.M. They will be using the cafeteria. Therefore, you will be needed to clean that room following the meeting and lock up the building in the evening. The group is to notify the church if it won't be getting together, such as for holidays, bad weather, etc., and we will contact you if this happens.

Thanks for your extra help.

Sincerely,

Father
St. Mary's Church

69 / TO OTHER EMPLOYEES ABOUT POLICIES— CONCERNING JANITOR'S SUPPLIES

In the past, it has been the policy of the church to order cleaning supplies for the janitor's use on an as-needed basis. However, in recent weeks, I have noticed that the supplies in the cleaning closets are not being used up. Since I know you are doing the work, I can only assume that you are bringing supplies from home.

This is not necessary. If you prefer to use other supplies than the ones available, please inform me and we will order the ones you want. Or, if you wish, buy what you will use and submit the bills to me for reimbursement. In this matter, it is no problem at all to change the church policy to suit you.

Please let me know your preference in this. No one expects you to pay for the supplies you use at the church, and I would like to get this matter resolved as soon as possible.

May God bless you for your hard work on our behalf.

Sincerely,

Pastor

70 / TO OTHER EMPLOYEES ABOUT PROBLEMS— JANITOR'S NEGLECT OF DUTY

For the past few weeks, I have noticed that the interior of the church has not been cleaned to the extent to which it is supposed to be. The floor in the back foyer was obviously not mopped, the kitchen was not cleaned, and at least several Sunday school classrooms were left in a state of disarray.

I believe the weekly responsibilities of the janitor are spelled out clearly in your job description. Therefore, you must know that you are currently not doing all that you have been hired to do.

The question which remains is, why isn't the work getting done? If there is some sort of problem which is affecting your work, I would like to know about it. Perhaps something can be worked out. Should you want to talk about anything, please contact me at once.

If I don't hear from you, I will assume that whatever has been causing the poor job performance lately has been resolved, and that our church will again be cleaned as specified in the janitor's job description. The condition of the building reflects what the congregation thinks of God as well as of His house, and we simply cannot have anything less than an efficient job. Therefore, I am confident that this problem will not continue.

Thank you.

Sincerely,

Pastor

71 / TO OTHER EMPLOYEES ABOUT PURCHASES— ACKNOWLEDGMENT OF REQUEST FOR

Thank you for the list of cleaning supplies you need. I will order them this week, and they should be in by the end of the month.

As I told you before, you are welcome to request anything that you need to keep the church clean. Don't hesitate to let me know if there is anything else you want.

I appreciate the fine job you are doing; may God bless you for your hard work.

Sincerely,

Father
St. Mary's Church

72 / TO OTHER EMPLOYEES ABOUT RECOGNITION

It gives me great pleasure to recognize the fifteenth anniversary of the day you began here as my secretary. In all those years, I have come to depend on you in many ways. Your cheerful smile has lifted my spirits on a number of occasions, and your dependability, attention to details, and organization skills have made my job easier. In addition, you are an asset to the church staff in the easy, warm manner in which you relate to other staff, church members, and visitors.

I hope that you have been equally satisfied with your employment at First Church and that you will continue with us for another fifteen (or more!) years. You are appreciated more than you know.

With warm regards,

Pastor

73 / TO OTHER EMPLOYEES ABOUT RESIGNATION—OF PASTOR

As of January 1, 19XX, I will no longer be senior pastor at First Church. My family and I will be moving to (name of town), where I have accepted a position as professor of New Testament at Trinity Bible College.

While I am greatly looking forward to the new challenges that await me as I return to full-time teaching, I regret leaving many good friends and colleagues. You are among them. During the five years which you have served as my secretary, you have done an outstanding job. Your office duties have been handled correctly and on time, and your smile and pleasant personality have brightened my day many times. I only hope that my secretary at Bible school will be half the help you have been.

As the new pastor adjusts to First Church, I am confident that you will do everything in your power to assist him. My prayer for you is that God will continue to bless you abundantly in every area of your life.

With warmest regards,

Pastor

74 / TO OTHER EMPLOYEES ABOUT SALARIES— ACKNOWLEGMENT OF REQUEST FOR INCREASE

Thank you for your recent request asking about the possibility of a salary increase. I certainly agree with you that it is time to look into the matter, and I will present your proposal to the board at the September meeting next week.

In the two years in which you've been my secretary, I have been more than pleased with your performance, and I have every reason to expect the board to accept my recommendation of a raise for you. I'm just sorry that I didn't think of asking for it before your letter!

I will let you know what happens as soon as I can. In the meantime, keep up the good work.

In the Master's service,

Pastor

75 / TO PRIVATE SCHOOL STAFF ABOUT ACKNOWLEDGMENTS—OF CHANGE IN CONFERENCE DATES

Thank you for your letter of (date), informing me that parent/teacher conferences have been moved from Tuesday, March 21, as was planned, to Thursday, March 23. I certainly understand that parents, students, and staff will want to attend the tournament basketball game in which our own team is playing. (I plan on being there too!) Having regular classes in the morning and then dismissing school at 1 P.M. in order for everyone to have time to drive to the game sounds fine. Then on Thursday, we'll expect to have the conferences. Since nothing special is scheduled at the church on that day, I see no problem with the change in dates.

I appreciate you keeping me posted on what is happening at the school, and I'm looking forward to seeing some outstanding basketball!

Sincerely,

Pastor

76 / TO PRIVATE SCHOOL STAFF ABOUT ANNOUNCEMENTS—OF CHURCH ANNIVERSARY

Perhaps you are aware that 19XX is the fortieth anniversary of the establishment of St. Mary's Church. Therefore, we are already in the process of planning special events in honor of the occasion. Possibilities include a commemorative booklet, a new car raffle, inviting priests who formerly served the parish to return for a visit, etc.

I am certain that you will also want the school to take part in the anniversary celebration. I had thought that the children might complete in a contest to design a poster for it, or maybe they could write brief essays on what attending a parochial school means to them. No doubt you have other ideas and can generate even more suggestions from your teachers.

I look forward to hearing what you would like to do, and I am confident that together, we will have an unforgettable anniversary.

Sincerely,

Father
St. Mary's Church

77 / TO PRIVATE SCHOOL STAFF ABOUT CONGRATULATIONS—ON COMPLETION OF SUCCESSFUL FUND-RAISING DRIVE

It gave me great pleasure to hear about the school's recent completion of the campaign to raise money for new audiovisual equipment. As you know, earning over $XXXX is no small feat, and I am quite impressed at the dedication and hard work shown by our staff and students in pursuing this worthy goal. Congratulations to all of you!

And yet, perhaps it is to so surprising what was accomplished. Our school has always proven itself to be outstanding in every area; once a goal has been set, it has been reached. Only top-notch faculty and students can consistently do that!

I am confident that the new equipment will be put to good use within our classrooms, and I again congratulate each person who contributed time, effort, or money to the project.

In Him,

Pastor

78 / TO PRIVATE SCHOOL STAFF ABOUT CONTRACTS AND AGREEMENTS

To: (Name)
Position: Teacher
Standard Work Schedule: Daily _____
                                        Weekly _____
    Reports to: Principal
    We are confirming your salary for the 19XX-XX school year. Please immediately advise if these figures are incorrect. Otherwise, simply initial and return to the office by (date).

Salary Index _____	Salary _____
Supplemental Assignment _____	Salary _____
_____	Salary _____
Total	Salary _____

Thank you.

Sincerely,

Pastor

79 / TO PRIVATE SCHOOL STAFF ABOUT ENCOURAGEMENT—AS NEW SCHOOL YEAR BEGINS

As another school year begins, I sense excitement in the air. And why not? Enrollment is significantly up, we have several new faculty members who upgrade our already outstanding staff, and we are expecting to become accredited this fall. Overall, we are in store for a wonderful year.

I hope that you share my feelings and are prepared to resume your teaching duties. As a staff member of Southwest Christian Academy, you have a great privilege as well as a big responsibility. Parents from our church and community are entrusting their children to your care, not only in order for them to learn the academics in which you can instruct them, but also for the caring personal touch you add and the witness of your own commitment to Christ.

I am confident that you are able to meet this challenge, and I thank you in advance for the hard work and dedication which you will give this year. Perhaps the rewards will not be obvious at first, but remember, you are directly affecting the lives of the future leaders of our churches and communities.

So as you begin teaching this fall, go often to the Lord for His strength and wisdom. Give all you can to your students. Don't always settle for the same way of doing things. Then you can be assured that your reward—in Heaven, if not on earth—will come. May God bless you with a productive year.

Sincerely,

Pastor

80 / TO PRIVATE SCHOOL STAFF ABOUT EVALUATION—UPON RECEIVING A FAVORABLE ONE

Thank you for the recently submitted results of student achievement tests. I was pleased to see how high a number of our students scored, particularly in reading and writing, both of which are important skills to master. The slightly lower scores in math indicate to me that perhaps the subject should be stressed a little more than it has been, but obviously, since the scores were far above the state or national average, it is not a matter of great concern.

Excellent results in uniform testing such as what the students have taken not only shows what they have accomplished; it also reveals a good bit about how the faculty is doing its job. Most students don't learn unless they have a teacher who is communicating the information to them in a way in which they can understand. Scores such as what I have before me say that our teachers are doing their jobs well.

Overall, I am greatly encouraged by the scores. I will be presenting them to the Church Council at the next meeting.

Keep up the good work!

Because of Jesus,

Pastor

81 / TO PRIVATE SCHOOL STAFF ABOUT INSTRUCTIONS

As you know, throughout the winter we have had ongoing problems with the furnace. Therefore, we have arranged for a repairman to come on Thursday, February 1, to check over the entire system and recommend a course of action (a new system needed or repairs made.)

In order for this to take place, the heat will need to be off during the time the repairman is here. Please inform your staff that school will not be in session that day, and have them send a note home with the students to their parents. Since we don't know exactly what time the repairman will arrive or how long it will take for him to complete his work, it has been decided that classes should not be held all day.

Thank you for your cooperation in this matter. I sincerely hope that this will clear up the problem with the heat, so that your staff and students will not have to put up with the extremes of temperature that have occurred in the classrooms lately.

In His service,

Pastor

82 / TO PRIVATE SCHOOL STAFF ABOUT JOB DESCRIPTION

Enclosed you will find the updated job description for teachers at Lakeland Christian Academy:

1. Duties (Direct)
   a. Planning
      Recognize need to plan with specific objectives in mind. Provide detailed plans for substitutes. Be flexible enough to change plans if necessary.
   b. Understand Students
      Accept each one for who he/she is and offer assistance in reaching highest potential. Show respect for student, but be impartial. Recognize individual differences between students and make called-for adjustments. Provide extra help when needed.
   c. Classroom Control
      Maintain atmosphere condusive to learning. Develop self-discipline in students. Establish teacher as authority figure.
   d. Teaching Method
      Instruction methods to be compatible with school objectives. Use educational aids, such as tapes and radio, when possible. Encourage students participation. Prompt evaluation of pupils.
2. Duties (Indirect)
   a. In-Service Education

Find opportunities to increase knowledge and qualifications as teacher, such as graduate studies, workshops, research, etc.

b. Relationships with Other Staff Members

Openness in exchanging information with others. Demonstrate respect for other teachers and work with them as part of the team.

c. Dealing with Administration

Cooperate with policies and procedures; respect the authority. If a problem arises, seek God's direction, then see principal, then see superintendent. If still not satisfied, may bring it before school board.

d. Parent Relationships

Become a part of PTF. Hold parent conferences and look for opportunities in community to discuss school. Encourage visitation.

e. Personal Qualities

Dress tastefully; speak as an educated person should. Behavior inside and outside of school to be dignified. Make every effort to maintain good health.

I appreciate your cooperation.

Sincerely,

Pastor

83 / TO PRIVATE SCHOOL STAFF ABOUT MEETINGS

You are cordially invited to attend First Church's annual meeting, to be held on Sunday, January 10, in Fellowship Hall. Following a potluck dinner at 5:30 P.M. we will move to the sanctuary, where progress reports about each of the various ministries in the church will be presented. The principal will be sharing about the school, but after her remarks there will be an opportunity to recognize new teachers.

Because you became a part of the school staff this year, at that point we would like to introduce you to those of the congregation who have not yet made your acquaintance. We consider the school's faculty a part of our church family, even if faculty members choose not to worship with our fellowship on Sundays.

I hope you will be able to join us on January 10. May God bless you in your teaching endeavors.

Sincerely,

Pastor

84 / TO PRIVATE SCHOOL STAFF ABOUT POLICIES— CONCERNING FIELD TRIPS

In the past, the policy of the Southwest Christian Academy concerning school-sponsored trips has been to have each student's parents fill out a new permission slip every time such an outing is planned. The slip was to include the destination of the trip, the approximate times of leaving and returning to the school, the cost per child (if any), and the statement "I hereby relieve the Southwest Christian Academy of all responsibility beyond that of normal supervision."

However, at the last meetings of the parent/teacher organization, it was decided to have one blanket permission slip sent out to parents in the beginning of fall. It would cover responsibility for any field trips taken during that school year.

To keep parents informed, teachers would still be responsible for sending out information sheets with the details of each individual trip a minimum of two days before the trip is taken. These would not need to be signed and returned.

In planning your field trips of the upcoming year, please keep in mind the new policy. A copy of it will be sent to the parents, along with the blanket permission slip during the first week of classes.

Sincerely,

Pastor

85 / TO PRIVATE SCHOOL STAFF ABOUT PROBLEMS— ACKNOWLEDGMENT OF AND ASSURANCE OF COMING IMPROVEMENT

Thank you for the recent concerns which have been voiced over the use of school learning aids by children attending Sunday school classes. I certainly understand the frustration you would feel upon coming into your classroom on Monday morning, only to find your supplies used, your materials out of place, etc.

Unfortunately, this is one of the problems which occurs when a private school holds classes in a church. Because you do have to use the same rooms in which Sunday school takes place, you do run the risk of this happening, even though the Sunday school teachers are urged to keep their students away from your things.

However, because of the high number of complaints I have received, I am recommending that the church purchase locked cabinets in which you can store your supplies, with confidence that they will not be disturbed. I hope to have these installed within a month.

In the meantime, please bear with me. The situation will improve!

Sincerely,

Pastor

86 / TO PRIVATE SCHOOL STAFF ABOUT QUESTIONNAIRES

As you may know, the Church Council has began talking about beginning the next phase of the building program, possibly in the spring. A large part of it involves expanding the present school facilities by about one-third. While we do have blueprints for the project which were made at the time of constructing the first phase of the church, we value the opinions of our staff. Therefore, I would like to ask each staff member to complete and return the enclosed questionnaire concerning preferences for the new part of the school.

Naturally, we will not be able to act upon everyone's suggestions, but I know it will prove helpful for the council to find out what the teachers would like, if there are options available.

Please make sure your questionnaire is retuned to me by September 30. I will keep you informed about the progress being made. Your help is appreciated!

Serving Christ,

Pastor

87 / TO PRIVATE SCHOOL STAFF ABOUT SCHEDULES

Thank you for the proposed schedule for the upcoming year of school. In looking it over and comparing it with events the church will be holding, I see no reason why the schedule cannot be approved as it stands.

As always, when it is officially adopted, please make sure my secretary has a copy, so that significant dates may be listed on the church calendar section of the monthly newsletter.

I'm looking forward to another good year for Southwest Christian Academy, as you continue to excel in your position of principal.

Sincerely,

Pastor

88 / TO PRIVATE SCHOOL STAFF ABOUT SPECIAL EVENTS

This is to inform you that on Friday, October 24, St. Mary's Church will be holding a one-day seminar for senior citizens in the parish. It will take place from 9 A.M. until 3 P.M. in the auditorium. I have already asked the principal to move any regularly scheduled events to another location, but I want to be sure that you know not to plan to use it for any other purpose on that day.

Thank you for your cooperation.

Yours in Christ,

Father
St. Mary's Church

89 / TO SPECIAL GROUP LEADERS ABOUT APPOINTMENTS—REMINDER TO ATTEND

This is to remind you of our appointment for Thursday, August 23, to discuss the possibility of a Weight Watchers group being held in the church this fall. God expects us to care for our bodies, as well as our souls and spirits, and I am very interested in hearing about your program. I feel it could give a great deal of help to those within our church and community who are struggling with a weight problem.

I look forward to seeing you in my office at 10 A.M. on the 23rd. I am certain we will be able to work something out to the advantage of both the church and your group.

Sincerely,

Pastor

90 / TO SPECIAL GROUP LEADERS ABOUT CONGRATULATIONS—UPON STUDENTS' COMPLETION OF COURSE

Congratulations! All fourteen of the Stephen Ministry trainees whom you have been supervising have completed phase one of the program. After interviewing each one individually, I am convinced that he/she is capable of ministering in crisis situations involving church or community members. I was impressed with the insight and compassion shown by each, and I feel it is time for the next phase: actually beginning counseling those in need, under your supervision or mine.

You can take pride in knowing that your many hours of teaching the trainees about crisis theory and intervention, as well as specifics in the areas of depression, grief, etc., have paid off. Your efforts will benefit many people in the years to come as the Stephen Ministry begins to reach out to hurting individuals in all walks of life.

Again, congratulations for a job well done. I look forward to the next phase of the program!

Serving Christ,

Pastor

91 / TO SPECIAL GROUP LEADERS ABOUT DISMISSALS—FOLLOW-UP

In this situation, a former head usher made his discontent obvious after he received a note of dismissal. Notice how the letter writer, in this second letter, attempts to smooth over hurt feelings by expressing concern for the individual instead of anger at his reaction. Nevertheless, he stands by the initial decision.

I was sorry to hear that you were upset by the recent letter I sent you concerning your dismissal as head usher. Your feelings are certainly understandable, but I must again ask you to consider my viewpoint.

As I stated before, I do not think it is fair for you to continue in your position, given the number of times you have shown up late or not at all for services. I have brought this to your attention more than a few times, and while you have indicated you will change, I have seen little if any improvement.

I have discussed this situation with the Church Council, and it is in agreement with me; therefore, the decision to relieve you of your duties stands.

As before, there is always the possibility that you may return to your position, if there is significant reason to believe that things have changed for the better.

Keep in mind that this is in no way a rejection of you as an individual; you are loved as you have always been here. But it is the opinion of the council as well as myself that your irresponsibility in your service may mean a deeper problem in your life which needs to be dealt with. Should you wish to talk, I am available.

Sincerely,

Pastor

92 / TO SPECIAL GROUP LEADERS ABOUT DISCIPLINARY ACTION

It is with regret that I must inform you that Cub Scout Troop 335 may no longer meet at First Church. Over the past several months, you have been warned a number of times about the boys' behavior before and after meetings. Yet church property continues to be broken or missing, outside doors are left open, and the rooms in which you meet are found in disorder. Last week it was discovered that someone had written on the mens' room walls during the time your group was at the church.

Although you have seemed willing to work harder to control the boys, we have seen no changes. Indeed, with the passing of the weeks, the problems have seemed to increase. Therefore, I find myself in the difficult position of having to do something to stop what has been happening.

Believe me, I do not like having to take this step, but at this point I can see no other options. If, after a period of three months from now, you feel you have adequate control of the scouts to prevent the problems from recurring, I will consider again letting you meet in our facilities. But until that time, you will have to find some other place in which to hold your meetings. Thank you.

Sincerely,

Pastor

93 / TO SPECIAL GROUP LEADERS ABOUT ENCOURAGEMENT—UPON DECLINING ATTENDANCE

I understand that recently the attendance at the "Fit for the King" programs has dropped off significantly. While this may seem quite discouraging, I would like to urge you to keep your spirits up. What you are doing is important work, and even if only a small group of women is now taking advantage of your programs, it is worth doing. We have a responsibility to the Lord to keep our bodies in good physical health, and an exercise program such as yours is an excellent way to help do that.

Perhaps many of the women who used to come are involved with preparations for the upcoming holidays. In January, they may be anxious to return to the sessions. But if not, you still have a valuable outreach, even if not many choose to utilize it.

Again, remember that you are doing a good work for God, and He would encourage you to continue in it faithfully, no matter what happens. May He bless you in every way!

Sincerely,

Pastor

94 / TO SPECIAL GROUP LEADERS ABOUT INFORMATION

Prepare for a full church Sunday! In addition to receiving the youth confirmation class, we will be partaking in the sacrament of Infant Baptism.

You might want to ask your ushers to be at the church extra early, and it might also be appropriate to find some of our teenage boys to serve as parking attendants. I have already instructed the secretary to run off extra bulletins, and the janitor will be bringing folding chairs to the back foyer, in case they are needed.

Of course, the congregation may number about what it usually does, but with both extra events taking place in the same service, I anticipate more. And I wanted you, as head usher, to know, in order that any additional preparations may be made.

Thanks for all your help—you are appreciated!

In Him,

Pastor

95 / TO SPECIAL GROUP LEADERS ABOUT MEETINGS—DENIAL OF REQUEST FOR USE OF BUILDING

Thank you for your recent request to use the church on Saturday, May 17, for an all-day district Boy Scout rally, in place of your regular meeting on Tuesday evening of that week. While we would like to accommodate you, it is not possible. Two weddings have already been scheduled for that date.

However, the Saturday before, May 10, the church would be available for your use. If you could change your date and would like the facilities then, please contact us. We will be happy to oblige you.

Sincerely,

Father
St. Mary's Church

96 / TO SPECIAL GROUP LEADERS ABOUT QUESTIONNAIRES—UPON RECEIVING RESULTS OF

Thank you for sharing with me the results of the questionnaires recently completed by the Stephen Ministry trainees for which you are responsible. I was pleased to see that they approve of the training they are undergoing to prepare them to minister to those in the congregation experiencing trauma. Some of the suggestions made concerning future topics to cover were excellent, and I'm sure you will be utilizing them.

I also agreed with the comment made that this specialized training should be undertaken only by those who have their own lives in order. From the first, we attempted to do that, but it is valuable to continue to make sure that those in the program are not in the midst of personal crisis.

Again, I appreciate all the efforts you have made in helping develop this new program in the church, I am certain there is a great need for this type of ministry, far more than what I can handle myself in counseling situations. I look forward to the day when the trainees have completed their preparations and are ready to help in this important ministry.

Sincerely,

Pastor

97 / TO SPECIAL GROUP LEADERS ABOUT RESIGNATIONS—OF OTHER STAFF

I was sorry to hear that Ed James will no longer be able to serve as cameraman for the TV Ministry. We will certainly miss his expertise as well as his obvious dedication to the ministry, but his decision to resign so as to devote more time to his duties as home Bible Study leader is understandable. I also appreciate his willingness to help in training someone to fill his spot.

Have you someone in mind to take Ed's place? If not, I may know of several who may want to check it out. Or, if you wish, I can have something put in the bulletin, asking those who might be interested to contact you. Let me know your preference.

While Ed's leaving will leave a hole in the TV crew, I am confident that God will soon raise up the person He has in mind for this.

In His service,

Pastor

98 / TO SPECIAL GROUP LEADERS ABOUT SCHEDULES

I have just talked with Dr. Harold Jones, and I mentioned to him the possibility of our interviewing him on the TV program while he is in Denver on April 18. He was quite receptive to the idea, but he is on a extremely tight schedule. The only hours he has free are between 8 and 9 A.M. on the 18th, or between 4:30 and 5:30 that evening. Would it be possible for you to get together a TV crew for either of those times?

I feel that an interview with an outstanding speaker like Dr. Jones would be a big addition to the program, and well worth the inconvenience of shooting the film at a different time and location. If at all possible, I would like to work this out in order to take advantage of his willingness to fit us into his schedule.

Therefore, please let me know as soon as you can whether or not you can work out the schedule to have a TV crew available at one of the aforementioned times. I am anxious to have Dr. Jones share his wisdom with our TV audience.

Thanks!

In Christ,

Pastor

99 / TO SPECIAL GROUP LEADERS ABOUT SPECIAL EVENTS

I was pleased to hear that you and the entire TV Ministry crew were able to attend the recent seminar in St. Louis. The in-depth workshops on everything from camera techniques to conducting an interview will certainly prove helpful as you apply what you have learned to our television outreach program. We have before us a constant challenge to improve the quality of it, both in the type of program we put together and in the technical method in which it is done.

Naturally, the goal we strive for is not just in the production of a "great" program, but it is that what we do put out would be a tool used by God to minister. This is what must always be before our eyes: how can we reach out most effectively to those who need a personal relationship with Him and to those who desire to grow in Him?

By making attending the seminar a priority, you have shown that you share this commitment to making First Church's TV ministry one that makes a difference for Him. May God bless you as you continue to lead the TV ministry team.

Because of Jesus,

Pastor

CHAPTER 5

Letters to the Community

An important part of a church's community outreach revolves around the pastor's involvement in various community organizations, the church's dealings with local government and with business, and the use of the church's facilities by responsible community groups.

The effective minister is careful to be a good steward of the church property and resources, and will want to communicate a positive and responsible image to government, civic, and business personnel.

The letters in this chapter deal with zoning and building permits, rules for building use, notification of services available to the community, and more. This section will prove invaluable to the responsible minister's role as business administrator.

1 / TO BUSINESS LEADERS ABOUT INQUIRIES AND REQUESTS—INFORMATION

As the holiday season again approaches, we were wondering if this year the Businessmens' Association is going to hold a contest for the best outdoor Christmas decorations on homes and businesses. The contest last year was certainly well-received, and an asset for the community.

Hopefully you will be sponsoring the contest. If so, we would like to remind you to have the judges drive down our road, White Creek Blvd. Because it is a dead-end street with few buildings on it, it was passed by last time. Since St. Mary's very much wants to be part of the festivities, please make sure we are included! Christmas is an important occasion for us, and we make every effort to make the outside of our church reflect our celebratory spirit.

Thank you, and we applaud you for the good work the Businessmens' Association is doing.

Sincerely,

Father
St. Mary's Church

2 / TO BUSINESS LEADERS ABOUT PUBLIC AVAILABILITY OF CHURCH FACILITIES

In light of the recent earthquake in Mexico, a number of people in our community have indicated an interest in donating nonperishable food, clothing, household items, etc. to help those in need. This is certainly a valid concern.

As I understand it, the Businessmens' Association is also organizing a campaign to collect necessities for this cause. I wanted to make sure you knew that First Church has already begun such a drive; supplies are being stored in the church basement until there are enough to send to Mexico.

It has occurred to me that combining the resources of the church, local businesses, and concerned individuals might be in the best interests of all involved. Therefore, I would like to extend our facilities to you as a location to gather the donations and prepare them for shipping. We have a great deal of space, and someone is around the church during the day and most evenings.

If this is agreeable to you, please be in touch. Thank you.

Sincerely,

Pastor

3 / TO BUSINESS LEADERS ABOUT SCHOOL POLICIES—CONCERNING STUDENTS OFF CAMPUS

It has recently come to my attention that some students from St. Mary's School have been leaving our grounds during the lunch hour to walk downtown. I have not heard of any problems that these young people are causing to local businesses; however, our policy has always been that students are not permitted to leave the school grounds at any time during the day. The only exception to this rule is if they are in the company of their parent or guardian and have a written pass from the school office.

Therefore, I would ask for your cooperation. Please inform your employees that if they see any of our students in or near your business location during school hours, they should call our office, 446-8091. If possible, they should be able to supply the names of the students observed.

Thank you very much for your help in this matter.

Yours in Christ,

Father
St. Mary's School

4 / TO CITY OFFICIALS ABOUT BUILDING CODE REGULATIONS

Beth-El Congregation is in the process of planning to build a new synagogue at 1515 N. Wilson Bridge Road, Columbus, of approximately XXXXX square feet. Please advise us on the new building code regulations which recently were passed by the state. Our architect is Miller, Hielman, and Associates, of Columbus. Naturally, we are committed to following the building code in its entirety.

Thank You.

Sincerely,

Rabbi,
Beth-El Congregation

5 / TO CITY OFFICIALS ABOUT EXTENDING HELP— IN TIME OF LOCAL EMERGENCY

In light of the tornado last month which damaged a number of residences in (name of city), we at First Church would like to inform you about ways in which we can aid the victims currently being resettled in their homes.

We operate a food pantry and a clothes bank, both of which are available to those who need assistance at this time. In addition, several members of our congregation have used furniture which they would like to donate, including some large appliances.

We would greatly appreciate it if you could inform the victims of these resources available to them. We have notified the newspaper about them, but some people may not have seen the announcement there.

If anyone is interested, have him/her contact the church office, which will have the specifics of the services we can offer.

Thank you very much, and don't hesitate to call me if I can be of any other help to you or to the victims of the recent tragedy. I am confident that our city will soon be restored to the place of beauty and tranquility which it has always been.

Serving because of Christ,

Pastor

6 / TO CITY OFFICIALS ABOUT INQUIRIES AND REQUESTS—FOR ASSISTANCE

When asking for the cooperation of those in positions of responsibility, be clear as to what is wanted and be specific. (Note the clergy's enclosing a map showing exactly what parts of the streets will be affected). In addition, keep the letter brief.

Easter—for us at First Church, this holiday is the remembrance of the glorious victory over death of our Lord Jesus Christ.

This year, as part of our celebration, we would like to lead a live donkey, escorted by members of the congregation waving palm branches, through several streets near the church. This recreation of Jesus' entry to Jerusalem nearly 2,000 years ago would take place on Sunday, April 11, beginning at the church at 8:30 A.M. Approximately XX worshippers would be involved.

I enclose a map marked with the proposed route of the participants. Would it be possible for the streets to be closed to traffic until the march is completed (about one-half hour)?

We are anticipating a great amount of excitement at this novel way to observe Palm Sunday and are hopeful that you will be able to cooperate with our efforts.

Thank you very much, and may God bless you.

Sincerely,

Pastor

7 / TO COMMUNITY LEADERS ABOUT EXTENDING HELP—DURING LOCAL EMERGENCY

In the aftermath of the recent tragic train wreck in our area, many people are dealing with feelings of grief, guilt, and shock. If not dealt with, these emotions can have far-reaching consequences such as depression, substance abuse, and suicide. Therefore, how the survivors and families of victims cope concerns all of us in this locality.

We at First Church would like to extend a caring arm to those in need of help in handling potentially harmful feelings. For those who want it, a support group has been formed under my leadership. It will meet on Thursday evenings from 7 to 9 P.M. and is open to the community. In this group we will discuss the tragedy and the emotions generated by it, as well as how to cope with them. It will continue for as many weeks as there is interest.

In addition, for those who are experiencing severe difficulties, personal counseling is available from trained workers, including myself and two members of our congregation who are licensed social workers. Persons interested should call the church for appointments. There is no charge for this service.

We would appreciate it if you could help get the word out about these programs. Having been a part of a tragedy like what happened in our area is something one will never forget, but we want to do our part to help people be able to live with it.

Thank you.

In His service,

Pastor

8 / TO COMMUNITY LEADERS ABOUT PUBLIC AVAILABILITY OF CHURCH FACILITIES

Thank you for your recent letter concerning the community summer concert series to be held on the second Saturday of the month beginning June 13. We would be delighted to have our facilities as a back-up location in case bad weather makes the outside park site unavailable.

Hopefully our sanctuary will not be needed, but we will set it aside, just in case, for the dates of June 5, July 11, and August 8.

We appreciate your thinking of us and we are glad to be able to help.

Sincerely,

Pastor

9 / TO COMMUNITY LEADERS ABOUT ZONING LAWS—REQUEST FOR HELP IN OPPOSING CHANGE

This rather lengthy letter explains not only the proposed zoning change, but exactly why the church is opposed and how the recipient can help. Before writing such a letter, the clergy needs a good understanding of how the zoning board operates.

I recently heard that an individual in our community has applied to the zoning board to change the area of the 1500 block of Monroe Street, west to Walker Street, from residential to commercial zoning. From what I understand, he plans to open a drive-through which would sell, among other things, beer and wine.

Since First Church is located in this area, we are very concerned about this matter. We do not feel this is in the best interests of our neighborhood—greater ease in obtaining alcoholic beverages would only lead to more problems with teenage substance abuse, drunk driving, violence, etc., none of which we desire to have in any larger numbers. In addition, if the zoning was changed to commercial, any other business, however unsavory, could also come into the area.

If you agree, please plan on attending the Zoning Board meeting on Monday, April 16, at 7:30 P.M. This is an open forum in which the individual wanting the drive-through, and anyone else, can voice their opinions.

After the open meeting, the Zoning Board considers the opinions aired in making its recommendation, which is then sent to the City Council for a final decision.

Let me assure you that the Board is heavily influenced by the public's desires, and that the Council almost always follows the recommendation of the Board. Therefore it is extremely important that the meeting have a good showing of people opposed to this zoning change, if we are to stop it.

I very much hope that you will join us in fighting to keep our locality what it is now—a decent, family oriented area of residences that is a good place to bring up children. See you on the 16th!

In His service,

Pastor

10 / TO COUNTY OFFICIALS ABOUT BUILDING CODE REGULATIONS

Thank you for the information you sent us concerning local building code regulations. At this point, we are ready to set up an appointment with you to discuss the materials needed to begin construction of our new addition. Our blueprints have been approved by the state and returned to our architects, Walters & Reed, and we are anxious to begin work.

Our building committee would be free to meet with you Thursday afternoons, Saturday mornings, or Tuesday or Thursday evenings. Please contact us with your preference.
Again, we appreciate your cooperation.

Sincerely,

Father
St. Mary's Church

11 / TO COUNTY OFFICIALS ABOUT LICENSES— REQUEST FOR INFORMATION

Now that Beth-El Synagogue has moved into our new location at 446 Main Street, we find ourselves with a kitchen for the first time. Please advise us of the procedure to obtain a food handler's license for this year. Naturally, we have every intention of abiding with county health department standards for our facility.
We look forward to hearing from you.

Sincerely,

Rabbi,
Beth-El Congregation

12 / TO COUNTY OFFICIALS ABOUT ZONING LAWS— EXPRESSING DISAPPROVAL OF SUGGESTED CHANGE

In this letter, the rabbi cites reasons having nothing to do with religion for why a zoning change should not occur. Since clergy are often expected to support or reject ideas based on their faith, it is usually more credible if other considerations can be used.

I understand that the Zoning Board recently decided to recommend that zoning be changed from residential to commercial in the area between Monroe and Walker Streets, and that this will be presented and discussed at your next meeting. May I urge you to rule against changing the zoning?
Since our synagogue is located within the area in question, we have been outspoken from the beginning in our opposition to this plan. Traffic is already too heavy on Monroe, and having a drive-through there would only increase the problem. Also, there are a number of children who live on Walker; more motor vehicles would significantly heighten the amount of danger to

them. This aspect was not mentioned last week at the open meeting held by the Zoning Board to get the public's opinion.

In short, we want our neighborhood to remain residential only. As township trustees, you have an obligation to do what is best for those within your jurisdiction. Permitting a change in zoning would not fulfill this responsibility.

Please vote against the zoning change for the Walker-Monroe Streets area. Thank you.

Sincerely,

Rabbi,
Beth-El Congregation

13 / TO HOSPITAL ABOUT EXTENDING HELP—OFFER OF VOLUNTEERS

At First Church, finding volunteers for positions such as Sunday school teachers and youth group leaders is not always easy. I imagine that you have the same problem.

If so, I have some good news for you. In our senior high youth group, there are four girls who have expressed an interest in doing volunteer work at the hospital on a regular basis. They are all extremely responsible young women, and I'm certain they would be a great help in whatever place you would put them. Although they are being encouraged to choose a community outreach in which to participate in their youth group curriculum, these girls want to be involved on a long-term basis, not just while the group is studying this unit.

I would greatly appreciate it if you would forward to me the name of the person these girls should contact to begin the process of applying for volunteer positions.

Thank you very much.

Sincerely,

Pastor

14 / TO HOSPITALS ABOUT INQUIRIES AND REQUESTS—TO RECONSIDER POSITION ON ISSUE

In the many times that I have visited patients in your hospital, I have been impressed by the caring attitudes of your staff, from doctors to cleaning personnel. I have always considered you to be a facility dedicated to providing quality and compassionate health care, with which I would entrust my own loved ones.

However, I have recently heard that abortions are performed routinely within your walls, something quite contrary to the high standards I've just expressed. I can understand that occasionally a pregnancy is a true threat to the mother's health, and that terminating it really is necessary. But the vast majority of abortions do not fit into that category, and to these others, you do a great disservice. It has been proven that abortion leads to higher incidence of miscarriage and infertility, as well as great emotional distress for the women, not to mention the very taking of life as experienced by the unborn baby.

I am sympathetic to the problems that may lead a woman to consider ending her pregnancy, but abortion is not the answer, especially when there are so many deserving couples waiting to adopt babies.

Please reconsider your position on this important issue. With your current policy, I cannot patronize your hospital, nor recommend it to my parishioners.

Yours in Christ,

Father
St. Mary's Church

15 / TO HOSPITALS ABOUT VISITATION—REQUEST FOR ONE-TIME CHANGE IN VISITATION RULES

A member of our congregation, Kathy Myers, has been a patient in your pediatric unit for several weeks now as she recovers from the injuries she received in a car accident. Might I ask for your cooperation in helping make her stay a little more pleasant?

Kathy's eighth birthday is April 2, and even before the accident she had been involved in planning a birthday party, to which her Sunday School class was to be invited. I realize that she has gone through a very traumatic experience, but I feel that holding a party for her at the hospital would be therapeutic. I would like to bring the eleven other children in her class (and several parents) to the hospital with me for this purpose.

I know that this is a number of youngsters, but I assure you that they will be well-behaved. Seeing her friends will be good for Kathy, as well as for the other children, who need to know that she is still their classmate, in spite of the visible injuries she received. We will plan on staying for one hour so as not to tire her too much.

We can have the party either in the afternoon or evening, whichever would be more convenient for your staff. Also, it could be on Saturday the 2nd or Sunday the 3rd. Please let me know your preference.

Thank you for your cooperation in this matter. I look forward to hearing from you soon in order to make plans for the party.

Sincerely,

Pastor

16 / TO ORGANIZATIONS ABOUT EXTENDING HELP—FOR FUND-RAISER

We were pleased to hear of your setting up a Walk-a-Thon to raise funds to open the House of Hope. Domestic violence is certainly a problem which must be dealt with, and having a shelter for abused women and their children is a step in the right direction.

Because of our concern for this issue, we at First Church would like to help in your efforts. Several ideas of ways in which we might be able to assist you occurred to me. Since our church is located centrally, you might want to consider using it as the starting and/or ending point for the Walk. We have room for participants to rest, lavatories, a place to serve refreshments, etc. We would also be willing to contact other local churches to enlist their support, either in recruiting participants or in donating funds.

Perhaps you have other needs of which I am not aware. If so, please contact me. As I said, we are very willing to work with you in this worthwhile project.

Because of Jesus,

Pastor

17 / TO ORGANIZATIONS ABOUT PUBLIC AVAILABILITY OF CHURCH FACILITIES

Thank you for your letter of May 29, requesting information about the possibility of your Lions Club meeting in our church. Normally, we do permit organizations such as yours to use our facilities for a minimal charge which covers the additional custodial services.

However, although we would like to grant you permission to gather here in the fall, we must refuse at this time. Your meeting nights, the first and third Thursdays of the month, conflict with previously scheduled church activities which utilize Fellowship Hall and the adjoining kitchen.

If you are willing to change to another weeknight, such as Monday or Friday, we would be happy to accommodate you. We applaud your numerous service projects which benefit the community.

Again, thank you for your interest, and do contact us again if we can be of any help to you.

Sincerely,

Pastor

18 / TO ORGANIZATIONS ABOUT VISITATION— ACCEPTANCE OF OFFER TO VISIT

Thank you for your recent offer for our youth fellowship to attend your October 17 meeting. We accept. The program on domestic violence sounds excellent, and will fit right in with the current themes the youth are studying.

We will be bringing approximately twenty-five youth and advisors, and we will plan to arrive by 6:45 P.M. at the school cafeteria where you meet.

Again, we appreciate your thinking of us, and we look forward to being your quests on Thursday the 17th.

In His service,

Pastor

19 / TO REGULATORY AGENCIES ABOUT LICENSES— REQUEST FOR INFORMATION

First Church is looking into the possibility of beginning a day-care center as a service to our members and the community. Therefore, please advise us of your procedure for obtaining a license, and also inform us of the necessary requirements in order to receive one. We have in mind starting with two teachers, two teachers aides, and approximately twenty-five children, ages two to five. If possible, we would like to open in the fall of 19XX.

Thank you for your assistance.

Sincerely,

Pastor

20 / TO REGULATORY AGENCIES ABOUT SCHOOL POLICIES—ACKNOWLEDGMENT OF NEW POLICY

Thank you for your recent communication concerning the State Board of Education's new policy on corporal punishment. However, for a number of years, it has been the policy of our school not to paddle students. Discipline is maintained by the use of other means, such as denial of privileges, which we have found to be very effective.

In light of our current policy, we will not need to make any adjustments to cooperate with the new state policy.

Sincerely,

Pastor

21 / TO REGULATORY AGENCIES ABOUT PROBLEMS— REGARDING GETTING APPROVAL FROM AGENCY

On July 29, 19XX, our bus successfully passed state vehicle inspection for the school year of 19XX-XX. We were informed that we would receive our license within thirty days. However, it has now been quite a bit longer than that, and no license has arrived. Now that our old license has expired, we cannot operate the bus without going against the law, which naturally we will not do. So the bus sits unused, while our programs, particularly the youth programs, try to manage with car pools and postponements.

As you can see, it is vital that we get our license as soon as possible. Would you please look into this situation and inform us as to what steps we should now take? Has the license been lost in the mail or is there some other problem? We would like to get our bus back on the road within the next week or so.

Thank you.

Sincerely,

Pastor

22 / TO SCHOOL OFFICIALS ABOUT INQUIRIES AND REQUESTS—CONCERNING POSSIBILITY OF ITEMS FOR SALE

I recently read in the newspaper that you have just replaced several typewriters used in your business classes with newer models, and I wondered if the old ones might be available for purchase by the public. Our secretary's typewriter has been in the repair shop more than out of it during the past few months, and at this point it appears that it is no longer fixable. Therefore, we are in the market for another one, hopefully without a high price tag. It occurred to me that you might be able to help.

Please inform me whether any of your old typewriters are for sale and, if so, what models you have and what you are asking for them.

I look forward to hearing from you.

Sincerely,

Rabbi,
Beth-El Congregation

23 / TO SCHOOL OFFICIALS ABOUT PROBLEMS— REQUEST FOR COOPERATION IN SOLVING STUDENTS' TRESPASSING

It has recently come to my attention that a problem has arisen of which I'm sure you would wish to be aware. During the lunch hour, a number of our students are coming over to First Church's back parking lot, apparently feeling that there, they may break school rules concerning smoking, etc. Since several of our nursery school classrooms overlook the parking lot, we feel this is unacceptable.

I am certain that you share my concern for the students, and that action will be taken to work out the problem. Please contact my office if this matter needs to be discussed further; I have every desire to cooperate fully with you in any way in which I can.

Sincerely,

Pastor

24 / TO SCHOOL OFFICIALS ABOUT PUBLIC AVAILABILITY OF CHURCH FACILITIES

Thank you for your letter of September 15, 19XX, asking about the possibility of renting the gymnasium of First Church on a regular basis. We certainly understand your need to have a location easily accessible to the school in which the girls' junior high basketball team can practice.

The board's policy is that groups outside of the church may rent facilities for a charge of $XX per occasion, which covers the cost of the janitor's services. We would be happy to have you use the gymnasium under these conditions.

Please contact my office so that we may set a time to discuss the specifics, such as the days and hours in which you would be interested, which would not interfere with the programs we are operating.

Working together with the school system has always been a pleasure, and I look forward to continuing that cooperation.

Sincerely,

Pastor

CHAPTER 6

Letters to the Media

Most churches offer a variety of programs open to the community, ranging from seminars on childcare, to concerts, to vacation Bible school, to distributing food and clothing to the needy. Yet, unless the community is aware of these programs and services, they are not put to good use.

It is vitally important that the successful minister maintain good relations with the media in the community and share the good news of what the church is doing. These letters are addressed to this crucial need for good public relations.

Also, from time to time, the minister will find it necessary to express an opinion, or to state the church's position on an issue. Examples of these kinds of communication are also provided in this chapter, and are aimed at concerned ministers who go beyond speaking the truth and actually take a stand on truth.

1 / TO MAGAZINES ABOUT ADVERTISEMENTS

Please run the following in your classified advertisement section for the next two issues of your magazine:

Church seeks Director of Christian Education. Must be experienced and have degree. Large congregation, excellent salary and benefits. Send resume to First Church, (address), attention: Pastor.

Enclosed you will find payment as specified on your classified ad page. If you need further information, contact me at the above address.

Thank you.

Sincerely,

Pastor

2 / TO MAGAZINES ABOUT ARTICLES— REACTION TO PUBLISHED ARTICLE

Often, magazine articles generate strong emotion, and editors hope that readers will respond by writing to them. Here the pastor refers to the offensive piece by title and date, gives evidence to support his viewpoint, and suggests a way to make the story less one-sided.

I read with interest your article, "Church Growth: Dropping Off at Record Rates" (May, 19XX issue). While I am sure that the experts you quoted told you the truth, I don't believe that the whole story was told. For example, within our denomination, attendance in the United States has increased 23 percent in the last five years, giving has gone up to 16 percent in that time, and our missionaries overseas have grown from 69 in 1970 to 193 now. Hardly the dismal picture painted in your article.

In light of this, I would like to suggest that you run another piece on church growth in a future issue, this time from the standpoint of evangelical churches such as ours. If you need statistics such as I mentioned, contact me or my denominational headquarters, at (address).

I know you pride yourselves on unbiased, accurate journalism. Therefore, you will want to make every effort to present a true portrait of an important subject like church growth.

Thank you.

Sincerely,

Pastor

3 / TO MAGAZINES ABOUT EDITORIALS— NEGATIVE REACTION TO

Each month I enjoy reading Editor Mike Reese's editorial. Seldom have I been disappointed by his insights and humor.

But this month's editorial was another matter. I can only hope that his mind was "out to lunch" when he wrote his supposedly humorous look at the church today. Referring to clergy as "fat cats" who twist peoples' arms to donate, only to have the funds end up in expensive three-piece suits and Cadillacs for the men who are pretending to be putting God first, is an unfair blow to the many pastors in this country who have for years devoted their lives to their congregations. I, for one, know very few ministers who have anything close to the material riches described in the editorial.

Suffice it to say that I am extremely disappointed that Mike would write such a piece, and equally sad that your publication had the poor taste to print it. I think that you owe an apology to clergy everywhere.

Sincerely,

Pastor

4 / TO MAGAZINES ABOUT INQUIRIES AND REQUESTS—DESIRE FOR CONTACT WITH AUTHOR OF ARTICLE

Writers are usually pleased to be of further help to readers. However, many magazines have a policy of forwarding a letter like this to the author and allowing him/her to decide if he/she wants to make contact, instead of giving a reader the writer's address.

I was intrigued by your article, "Fighting Pornography in Your City: You Can Win!" in the October 19XX issue of (name of magazine). The author, David Howe, had some excellent suggestions on dealing with this problem.

However, I found that after completing the article, I had some additional questions about how some of his ideas could be implemented. Therefore, I wondered if it might be possible for me to have direct contact with him, in order that he might explain further.

If it goes against your policy to send me his address, please forward this letter to him so that he can write to me. I am excited about trying several of his concepts in our city, and I am hopeful that he will respond to my request.

Thank you.

Sincerely,

Rabbi,
Beth-El Congregation

5 / TO NEWSPAPERS ABOUT ADVERTISEMENTS

We are interested in buying a display ad in your newspaper to publicize our annual St. Mary's Festival. The ad is to run on Monday, May 21; Wednesday, the 23; Friday, the 25; Monday, the 28; Wednesday, the 30; Thursday, May 31; Friday, the 1; and Saturday, the 2. The two-inch by three-inch ad should say the following:

Annual St. Mary's Festival
Friday and Saturday, June 1-2
10 A.M. to midnight
Games, Food, Bingo, Kiddie Rides
New Car Raffle
Everyone Welcome

Please bill the church, and if you need more information, contact my office.

Sincerely,

Father
St. Mary's Church

6 / TO NEWSPAPER ABOUT ANNOUNCEMENTS— CHANGE OF LOCATION

This is to inform you that as of October 15, 19XX, First Church will be meeting at a new location, (address). Please correct the listing for us on your religion page. Service times will continue to remain the same; only the address has moved.

Thank you very much for your cooperation. We appreciate (name of city's) various places of worship being included each week with the religion news. This is a valuable resource for your readers.

Sincerely,

Pastor

7 / TO NEWSPAPER ABOUT ARTICLES—SUGGESTIONS FOR POSSIBLE STORIES

Most newspapers are constantly looking for interesting feature stories. In this example, the letter writer shows familiarity with the newspaper by even suggesting the section in which the article might appear.

Is finding subjects for feature stories sometimes a headache? First Church may be able to help.

Among our members, we have several who may prove to be interesting people to your readers. Helen Comer, eighty-six years old, has a collection of antique and rare Bibles, containing over sixty volumes. Her interest in them began when as a young woman, she served as a missionary in South America and received as a gift a Spanish New Testament dating back 100 years. Miss Comer might be an appropriate subject for either your senior citizens or your religion pages.

In addition, Drew Matthews could make an interesting personality profile for the religion or the entertainment page. The author of over 1,000 magazine articles, he supports himself full time by writing for the Christian market. He also sells photographs professionally.

I'm certain that either of these individuals would be more than willing to be interviewed. If you are interested, contact my office.

Thank you very much.

Sincerely,

Pastor

8 / TO NEWSPAPER ABOUT CLARIFICATIONS

Thank you for publishing on February 2 the front page article in which you interviewed me about First Church's Food Pantry and Clothes Bank. We are delighted to get the publicity, in order that more people who need this kind of help can be informed that it is available.

However, in the fourth paragraph of the article, I was quoted as saying that I knew of no other church which had both a food pantry and a clothes bank available to nonmembers on an ongoing basis. I'm certain I did, in fact, tell the reporter that, but actually there are other churches, perhaps many others, which do have these programs, but they aren't in this city.

When I made the comment, the reporter and I were talking about (name of city), but apparently that was left out in the process of writing up and editing the article, which is understandable.

Therefore, I would greatly appreciate it if you would clarify my comment by putting in your corrections column that I meant in this city, not everywhere. The original statement is quite misleading.

Thanks for your cooperation about this matter. Overall, we thought the article was well-done, and we compliment the reporter for her efforts.

If at any time we can be of help for another article, please don't hesitate to contact my office.

Sincerely,

Pastor

9 / TO NEWSPAPER ABOUT CORRECTIONS

Even though the newspaper was wrong about an important statistic, the pastor here begins by showing appreciation. Then, upon pointing out the mistake, the pastor expresses understanding, yet at the same time, states the necessity of a public correction.

It was extremely gratifying to read the February 2 article on the front page about First Church's Food Pantry and Clothes Bank. This kind of favorable publicity is exactly what we need to get the word out about the services we can supply to those who should have them.

However, in the third paragraph of the article, you quoted me as saying that in the four years we have been operational, we average supplying food to three families per month. The correct statistic is three families per day.

I am certain it is quite easy to have mistakes such as these slip by in the editing process. But, seeing as this one makes a significant difference as far as the reader's understanding of the subject, I would be most grateful if you would put the right figure in your corrections column.

Again, thank you for the coverage, and if I can ever be of further service to you in doing an article, do contact my office.

Sincerely,

Pastor

10 / TO NEWSPAPER ABOUT NEWS RELEASES

It would be greatly appreciated if you would run the enclosed press release about First Church's October 14 Festival of Music on the religion page of the Wednesday, October 10 paper.

If any further information is needed, please contact my office.

Sincerely,

Pastor

Press Release:
For 10-10-XX RELEASE

A Festival of Music will be held on Sunday, October 14, at First Church, 112 N. Main Street. Featuring solos by Walter Miller, Joyce Kincaid, and Tina Walkerman, it will begin at 7 P.M. The adult, youth, and children's choirs, under the direction of Ken Myers, will also be singing, and accompanists include Norma Owens, organ; Nancy Atterway, piano; and Betty Gold, violin. The public is invited.

11 / TO RADIO STATIONS ABOUT CLARIFICATIONS

Your recent interview with Rev. Thomas Johnson on the Bill Howard Show was of great interest to me. His own story of embezzlement from his church was moving, as were the other examples of pastors he knows who have fallen into adultery, alcoholism, etc.

It certainly is true that there is abuse of power, dishonesty, and deception on the part of some clergy, just as in any occupation. However, I was disturbed by the implication that all or at least most ministers are involved in something immoral or illegal. While none of us claims to be perfect, I do not believe that corruption is widespread throughout the profession. I personally know a number of colleagues, and of those, I am aware of only a very few who have been caught in the kind of problems Rev. Johnson describes.

Therefore, I feel your interview was, while not untrue, at best misleading. I believe that you owe it to your listeners to clarify that the interview was only one man's opinion and experience. Overall, clergy are basically devoted men and women of God.

Thank you.

Sincerely,

Pastor

12 / TO RADIO STATIONS ABOUT INQUIRIES AND REQUESTS—TO DISCONTINUE OBJECTIONAL ADVERTISING

For several years now, our family has enjoyed listening to WXYN. In fact, I have often recommended it to members of my congregation who are looking for a good Christian radio station.

However, I was dismayed when listening yesterday to hear a commercial for (Name) Magazine. Having seen this publication in the library and grocery store, I was surprised that a religious station would broadcast such an advertisement. While the content may be decent, just the revealing photos on the cover make this magazine objectionable to me.

I hope that this was some sort of mistake and that it will not occur again. If not, I would ask you to please reconsider your position on promoting a publication which attacks the traditional values the Christian community embraces.

Thank you.

Sincerely,

Pastor

13 / TO RADIO STATIONS ABOUT NEWS RELEASE

Would you please air the following news release on your community bulletin board during the week of October 2?

First Church, 112 N. Main Street, (name of city), is holding an All-You-Can-Eat Pancake and Sausage Supper on Saturday, October 7. Serving begins at 5 P.M. and the cost is $4 for adults and $2.50 for children under twelve. Included are beverage and applesauce. For more information, call 889-0076.

Thank you.

Sincerely,

Pastor

14 / TO TV STATIONS ABOUT ANNOUNCEMENTS

On May 2, St. Mary's Church, 1500 Washington Street, (name of city), will be celebrating 100 years of service. In honor of her Centennial, a number of special events will be taking place, including return visits from six to eight priests who served at St. Mary's during her life, a mass celebrating the anniversary, a program put on by the children in our school, the publication of a commemorative booklet, and a ham dinner open to the public and served in the school.

In an age when the Church is thought of as a declining influence, St. Mary's is alive and well, continuing to minister to the needs of those in the parish. Perhaps you would be interested in providing some TV coverage of the events planned.

If you would like more information and/or a detailed schedule of the activities planned, please contact my office.

Yours in Christ,

Father
St. Mary's Church

15 / TO TV STATIONS ABOUT CORRECTIONS

Thank you for having me last night on your interview program, "Dallas Today." I was pleased to have the opportunity to discuss my views on nuclear disarmament.

I did want to point out, however, one mistake. In the introduction, it was stated that my congregation was established in 1956. In fact, Beth-El was founded in 1926, and it has grown on a consistent basis since that time.

I did not feel the error was significant enough to correct the announcer, but I did want the record to be righted.

Thank you.

Sincerely,

Rabbi,
Beth-El Congregation

16 / TO TV STATIONS ABOUT EDITORIALS— POSITIVE REACTION TO

I was pleased to hear news director Vern Miller's views concerning pornography on last night's editorial (11 o'clock news). His concern about the increase of adult bookstores in our city is shared by myself and many in my congregation. Studies have shown that when pornography is readily available, violent crime goes up. In addition, it is suspected that child abuse also increases in such an environment.

I hope that many others respond favorably toward Mr. Miller's editorial. It is only by working together that we can stop the spread of this unwholesome cancer in our locality.

Again, thank you for taking a stand on this important issue.

Sincerely,

Pastor

CHAPTER 7

Letters to Vendors

The day-to-day functioning of every church involves dealing with vendors and suppliers of goods and services. Since these transactions often involve large sums of money, it's very important that communication with vendors be as specific and clear as possible, and when necessary, very firm.

1 / TO PRODUCT SUPPLIERS
   ABOUT DISENGAGING SERVICES

For a number of years, we have been buying supplies for our photocopier, including toner and paper, from you. However, with the last three orders which we have sent you, there have been problems. The merchandise has arrived damaged or significantly later than you promised. When we have contacted you regarding these matters, we have had little cooperation in rectifying the situation.

Therefore, we have no other option at this time but to discontinue doing business with your firm. With unreliable service, it is extremely difficult to keep the church functioning as it should be.

Sincerely,

Pastor

2 / TO PRODUCT SUPPLIERS
   ABOUT ENGAGING SERVICES

Thank you for your response to our recent request for bids for a new furnace for the church. At the October 16, 19XX meeting of the parish council, your bid of $XXXXX was accepted. As stated in the bid specifications, delivery and installation is to be completed by December 1; if there is any problem on your part concerning this, please notify us at once.

When the unit we want has arrived, contact us to set up a time for it to be put in. We look forward to doing business with you.

Sincerely,

Father
St. Mary's Church

3 / TO PRODUCT SUPPLIERS ABOUT ESTABLISHING CREDIT

Thank you for the recent delivery of office supplies which we ordered from your firm. They were more than satisfactory, and we have every intention of ordering again from you in the near future.

In light of that, please advise us of your policy for opening a thirty-day open account with you. We prefer to do business on that basis, and in the past have opened such an account by filing an application with the company.

We appreciate your fine products.

Sincerely,

Rabbi,
Beth-El Congregation

4 / TO PRODUCT SUPPLIERS ABOUT PROBLEMS— IN DELIVERY OF A PRODUCT

In this situation, an order did not arrive within the usual amount of time the church allowed for delivery. A brief, courteous letter, accompanied by a photocopy of the original order form, should quickly rectify matters.

On December 12, 19XX, we ordered six reams of 8 ½ by 11 inch white paper from you for our photocopier. At this point, we still have not received delivery. As we are nearly out of paper, we are requesting that you immediately look into this situation.

In the past, we have always had good service from your firm, and this current problem is probably due to an oversight. We anticipate a speedy resolution to it.

Thank you very much. We await your reply.

Sincerely,

Pastor

5 / TO PRODUCT SUPPLIERS ABOUT REFUNDS

We regret to inform you that we are not satisfied with the quality of the photocopier paper which we received from you recently. It has proven to be thin and easily torn, and therefore is not acceptable for our needs, in spite of your advertising that it would be perfect for every use.

Inasmuch as you have an unconditional guarantee for all your products, we are requesting an immediate full refund for the six reams of paper we purchased.

We would appreciate your prompt attention to this matter.

Thank you.

Sincerely,

Pastor

6 / TO SERVICE SUPPLIERS ABOUT BIDS

This is to inform you that St. Mary's Church is inviting bids for a new roof, according to the specifications on the attached page. Delivery and installation of the roof must be made by September 1, 19XX.

If you wish to submit a bid, please mail or bring it to church in an envelope marked "Bids on roof" by 5 P.M., Tuesday, March 21, 19XX.

Bids will be opened and recorded at 8 P.M. on Wednesday, March 22, and the awarding of this bid is to be made at a meeting of the parish council within thirty days of the opening of the bids.

Thank you.

Sincerely,

Father
St. Mary's Church

7 / TO SERVICE SUPPLIERS ABOUT INQUIRIES AND REQUESTS—FOR RATES, ETC.

This type of request may be made by telephone; however, by sending a letter, a permanent record is made of exactly what was asked for and when.

Having recently heard about your company, we would like to request your rates for termite extermination. The synagogue is approximately XXX square feet. In addition, please send a copy of your guarantee and how soon you could come to inspect the building, should we decide to hire you.

Thank you for your time. We look forward to hearing from you.

Sincerely,

Rabbi,
Beth-El Congregation

8 / TO SERVICE SUPPLIERS ABOUT TAX-EXEMPT VERIFICATION

This is to advise you of First Church's status as a nonprofit organization. Our tax-exempt number as furnished by our denominational headquarters is XXXXX. Also, enclosed you will find a photocopy of our letter of exemption and of the state form verifying it.

I trust you will find this sufficient. If you have any questions, please contact my office. Thank you.

Sincerely,

Pastor

CHAPTER 8

Letters for Special Occasions

Ministers delight in the many special occasions in which they have the privilege to participate. So that these occasions can be truly special, it's necessary to communicate specific information as to times, dates, and procedures, so that participants can be at the right place at the right time, doing the right thing.

Also, there are those occasions calling for a word of encouragement, congratulations, and affirmation—where the minister shares in the joy of new parents, a new couple, or a significant anniversary.

Whether addressed to groups, couples, or individuals, a positive and friendly note from a caring and supportive minister is always a genuine blessing.

1 / TO COUPLES ABOUT ADOPTION—PLACEMENT OF BABY THROUGH ADOPTION

While many churches send welcoming letters to new babies, they may not think to include those who are adopted. In this example, the pastor can especially share in the celebrating, since he was involved in counseling the parents as they waited. And since adoption almost always takes a long time, rejoicing is more than appropriate.

It gives me great joy to congratulate you on the arrival of your son, (name). In the past, you have shared with me your great desire for a child and some of the anguish you have lived through, waiting for an adoption to occur. We have wept together, calling on the Lord to send that special baby just right for you. At last, we can also share in the thrill of seeing our prayers answered.

This precious gift from God will forever change your lives, as a first child always does. Yet you already knew that, I'm sure, and you are more than willing to make the sacrifices involved to bring up (name) in a godly home surrounded by love.

Please be assured that you are in our prayers as you begin your parenting career, and feel free to contact me if I can help you in any way.

Rejoicing with you,

Pastor

2 / TO COUPLES ABOUT ANNIVERSARY—FIFTY YEARS

On your wedding day, June 12, 19XX, were you apprehensive about how your life would proceed for the next fifty years? If so, you needn't have worried.

Throughout those years, you have achieved what many admire but few reach—a fulfilling, happy, God-centered marriage. Not that things have always been easy. Like couples everywhere, you have certainly had times of pain and sorrow, disagreements and trauma. Yet for you, it's obvious that the good times of laughter and closeness, love and companionship, have far outweighed the dark experiences.

Truly, our heavenly Father must be pleased as you celebrate fifty years together. May He grant you many more. We rejoice with you as you reach this great milestone.

With warmest regards,

Pastor

182

3 / TO COUPLES ABOUT BAPTISM—OF INFANT

We were pleased to minister the sacrament of infant baptism to your son James last Sunday. While he is too young to remember, you will not forget it. In later years, you can tell him of the promises you made in his behalf, promises to raise him in a Christian home, to demonstrate your own faith in your daily lives, and to lead him in the ways of the Lord. And as the congregation vowed before you, we are willing to help and support you in any way we can.

We welcome little James into the family of God and look forward with you to watching him grow in every way.

Because of Jesus,

Pastor

4 / TO COUPLES ABOUT BIRTHS—
ARRIVAL OF FIRST GRANDCHILD

Here is another situation which most churches and synagogues don't think to acknowledge. Yet, sharing in the joy of a new life is just one more way of saying to a parishioner, "We care about you." The letter writer also uses this opportunity to urge the grandparents to do what they can to bring the baby and his parents into the synagogue more frequently.

It was with great joy that I heard the news about arrival of your first grandchild. What a thrill for you both! I am sure you will find being a grandparent is rewarding as well as challenging; you will have many opportunities to share of yourselves with this newest member of your family.

Naturally, one of the most important things you can do is to encourage your grandchild to have a religious life. Your own example is the best place to start. In addition, you can encourage your son and daughter-in-law to be faithful in attending synagogue.

I trust that both mother and baby are doing well, and I look forward to meeting little Seth soon.

Sincerely,

Rabbi,
Beth-El Synagogue

5 / TO COUPLES ABOUT DEDICATIONS—OF INFANT

Thank you for your willingness to dedicate your daughter (name) this past Sunday. You have made some serious promises to God and the congregation about how you will raise your child. Believe me, those words will be tested in the years to come as you face the many challenges of Christian parenting. But knowing your commitment to Jesus and to each other, I have every confidence that you will not fail (name of child).

I appreciate your faithful support of First Church in your attendance, finances, and service. May our loving Heavenly Father bless you and (name) abundantly.

In Him,

Pastor

6 / TO COUPLES ABOUT ENGAGEMENTS— UPON ANNOUNCEMENT OF

Congratulations on the announcement of your engagement! We rejoice with you in this important step.

As you know, deciding on a marriage partner is one of the biggest decisions you will ever make. It is not to be taken lightly, and I am confident that you have both sought the Lord on this matter until you are sure that He has put you together.

Even so, your relationship will not always be easy. But you have the assurance that with each other and with Jesus, you can have the wonderful experience of a great marriage.

You have our prayers as you progress toward the day of your wedding. Treasure the specialness of the bond God has given the two of you.

Joyfully,

Pastor

7 / TO COUPLES ABOUT RETIREMENT— UPON ANNOUNCEMENT OF

A major adjustment for both spouses, retirement can produce a significant amount of stress and depression. In this upbeat letter, the priest points out the good side as well as puts in an appeal for help in the parish, especially important to an individual who needs to feel needed.

Congratulations on Bob's recent retirement from (name of company)! On behalf of the entire parish, I would like to offer best wishes to you both.

Many new opportunities await you as you enter this new stage of your lives. You will have the freedom to pursue interests, friendships, and travel in ways in which you have not found possible before. My prayer is that the two of you will have many good years together to enjoy life.

I also hope that you will find time to devote yourselves to church work. There are many things you can volunteer to do here in your own parish; please feel free to contact me if you would like to know of some possibilities.

Naturally, some adjustments will have to be made in your daily schedules as you get used to Bob's being at home. But I am confident that you will both continue to grow in this part of your lives, and that any problems which do develop will be worked out.

Again, warmest wishes for your future.

Yours in Christ,

Father
St. Mary's Church

8 / TO COUPLES ABOUT SHOWERS—GRANTING PERMISSION TO HOLD IN CHURCH

Thank you for your recent request to use Fellowship Hall for a wedding shower for Tina Johnson and Rob Ortiz. Although we do not usually have this sort of an affair at the church, I am willing to make an exception in this case. Tina and Rob are both quite active in many different groups within the congregation, therefore making them well-known to most of the members. In addition, since you both are willing to take complete responsibility for putting on the shower, cleaning up afterwards, etc., I see no reason why you should not go ahead with your plans. The May 2 date is fine; nothing else is scheduled in the building that afternoon between 2:30 and 4:30 P.M.

I assume that since you are holding the shower at the church, you will be opening it to everyone who wishes to attend. Perhaps a blanket invitation could be put in the church bulletin that week, and another posted in the church office.

I hope the shower will prove to be enjoyable to all who come.

Sincerely,

Pastor

9 / TO COUPLES ABOUT WEDDING—AFTERWARDS

At last, the waiting is over and you are husband and wife in the sight of God and everyone else! The church staff joins me in wishing you the very best as you begin this new stage of one-ness in Christ.

As I'm sure you realize, marriage won't always feel as wonderful as it does now. But in spite of the problems which are inevitable, your relationship can continue to grow more and more special each year as you keep Christ in the center.

It was a great blessing for me to officiate at your wedding; the presence of the Lord was very real.

Again, our most sincere congratulations. If at any time I can be of personal help to you, feel free to contact me.

Yours because of Him,

Pastor

10 / TO FAMILIES ABOUT ADOPTION— ON FINALIZATION

After a child is placed with a family, there is a waiting period, generally about six months, before the adoption is legal. When that point is reached, it's a day almost as special as when the child moved in. A letter such as this is most appropriate.

Congratulations on the recent finalization of the adoption of your children Kimberly and Joshua. It must be a satisfying feeling to know that the court has now declared them to be your offspring. In the past months in which they have resided with you, there have been many adjustments, both for you and for them. A new home, school, church, and life-style take some getting used to. Yet by now, Kim and Josh seem to be beginning to fit into their surroundings.

I'm certain you realize that there will still be problems at times, but no family can avoid the differences that arise in day-to-day living. With Christ as the center of your household, you will be able to cope.

Again, best wishes from me and the parish. May your family continue to grow in closeness and faith.

Sincerely,

Father
St. Mary's Church

11 / TO FAMILIES ABOUT BAPTISM— ADULTS' DECISION TO UNDERGO

I was pleased to hear of your decision to be baptized at First Church. From what I understand, those of you who will be undergoing the sacrament are Dick, Martha, and Kathy.

At this point, a baptismal service is scheduled for Sunday, March 4 at the indoor pool at the YMCA, 1222 North Washington Street. It will take place at 3:30 P.M. Following a brief teaching on the meaning of baptism, those who wish to do so will be baptized by immersion in the shallow end of the pool. We will have use of the locker rooms, so plan on bringing dry clothing. Please also remember to wear something that will not become transparent when wet. Many have come with a swimming suit topped by a large colored tee shirt.

I look forward to your participation in this important step, which is symbolic of the death of the old sinful nature and the beginning of the new life which you have found in Christ. God will bless you as you obey His instructions in the Bible to be baptized.

If for any reason one or all of you cannot join us on March 4, let me know and we will work out something else.

In Christian love,

Pastor

12 / TO FAMILIES ABOUT BIRTHDAYS— CHILD'S FIRST

While a year-old child isn't aware of the significance of his/her birthday, the parents consider it to be a milestone. In this letter, the pastor encourages them to make the church one of their child's early memories.

As Stephanie's first birthday approaches, I would like to take this opportunity to offer the best wishes of myself and the entire parish. Naturally, she is too young to understand the significance of this special day, but you as her family can rejoice in the good memories of this past first year with her.

It is my hope that as the years pass, you will continue to make the Church an important part of Stephanie's life. Though her days are relatively problem-free now, she is bound to face trials and troubles at some point. That's why it's so vital to make one's faith real from a young age; when the difficulties do arise, there is something there to hold things together.

Again, I wish you a pleasant day as Stephanie celebrates her birthday. May she have many more birthdays to enjoy.

Yours in Christ,

Father
St. Mary's Church

13 / TO FAMILIES ABOUT BIRTHS

On behalf of the church staff and the congregation at First Church, I would like to congratulate you on the arrival of your son, (name). It is an occasion for great joy when the little one finally arrives and both mother and child are doing well.

The newest member of your family will mean some adjustments for all of you, as well as greater responsibilities. But with the help of your loving Heavenly Father Who has given you this precious gift, you will be able to handle it.

Knowing your faithfulness in attending and serving at church, I'm certain that we will meet (name of child) soon, and that you will make every effort to raise him in a manner which would please God.

In the meantime, you have our prayers and best wishes as you begin the process of helping him grow physically, emotionally, mentally, and spiritually.

Joyfully,

Pastor

14 / TO FAMILIES ABOUT DEDICATIONS— OF NEW HOUSE

I was pleased to receive your request to perform a home dedication for you. Moving into a new house is always exciting, particularly when you have had it built for you and have watched from the beginning the progression from hole in the ground to completed dwelling.

In such circumstances, I feel it is only appropriate to dedicate the home, and all who reside there, to God's service. I am more than willing to participate in it. Have you decided upon a specific format? If you are interested, I have some material I have used in the past at which you may look.

In addition, please let me know as soon as possible when you would like to do this, so that I may mark my calendar.

I look forward to this special time together.

Because of Him,

Pastor

15 / TO FAMILIES ABOUT GRADUATIONS— OF HIGH SCHOOL MEMBER

As graduation approaches, we are certain you share our pride in your (son/daughter) (name). Completing high school is a big step and an exciting time of life, as the young person plans for his/her future.

First Church will be honoring our graduates and their families during morning worship on May 24. Each youth will be presented with a gift from the congregation, and following the service a time of fellowship over coffee, punch, and cookies will be held.

We hope that you and your family will be able to participate. In addition, if you have older children who are graduating from college, please call the church office. We are also interested in honoring them for their achievements.

Again, congratulations to your graduate.

Sincerely,

Pastor

16 / TO FAMILIES ABOUT HOLIDAYS—EASTER

Coming up with something fresh to say about major holidays is an annual headache for most clergy. Note how this pastor calls upon a personal experience to bring that new element to this Easter letter.

The trial, crucifixion, and resurrection of Christ—every Lenten season we attempt to gain new insight from the same familiar story. Yet how often do we succeed in truly feeling the physical and emotional pain that our Lord bore? Does it really penetrate our apathetic hearts just what Easter means?

Last year, I discovered a renewed appreciation of what Jesus passed through so many years ago. It came by way of a television special about Him, one that I had viewed before. While it was good, it had no long-term affect. But this time, I watched it with my children, who had been too young in other years to stay up to see it.

These little ones, so used to the fighting and killing on TV shows in which the hero wins, sat teary-eyed as they whipped Christ, spat upon Him, and dragged Him to Golgotha. This was different than what they usually watched—this actually happened to their precious Savior. Caught up in their reactions, I studied their young faces, so intent on the gruesome scenes before us. As Jesus's body was placed in the tomb, they were the picture of sorrow and confusion.

I told them to keep watching. When the resurrection was shown, their faces immediately transformed into complete joy and relief. "Jesus is all right!" one said over and over.

I admit to spending more time intent on my children's responses than on the TV show. But what I came away with was a new joy, a new understanding of the reality of the cross and the victory over death that followed.

This Easter, I encourage you to discover anew the Easter story. And once you have, involve your family in helping them to do so too. Read the Scripture accounts after dinner in a version your children can understand. Perhaps act out the story. Decorate your home to celebrate. Mail Easter cards to far-away loved ones. Attend the special services at church.

You can think of other ideas more appropriate for your family. But whatever you do, don't let this Easter pass without getting a firmer grip on what happened over 2,000 years ago in Jerusalem.

May God grant you a truly unique Easter experience this year.

In His service,

Pastor

17 / TO FAMILIES ABOUT RECEPTIONS—PLANS TO HOLD

On Sunday, March 8, First Church is planning a reception in honor of Fred Jones's twenty years in the choir. It will be held in Fellowship Hall from 3 to 5 P.M. I'm sure it would mean a great deal to him to have present as many members of his family as possible.

We are planning a few words from the choir director and some of the choir members, a presentation of a certificate to him, some music from anthems sung over the years he has been a part of the choir, refreshments, and some special surprises. I'm certain it will prove to be an enjoyable afternoon for all.

We are blessed to have someone like Fred as part of our fellowship. His dedication to choir and the other work of the church has been an example to us all, and we are pleased to be able to do something for him.

I sincerely hope that you will be able to join us on the 8th.

In God's service,

Pastor

18 / TO FAMILIES ABOUT THANK YOU— FOR ALTAR FLOWERS

Thank you for the recent gift of altar flowers in gratitude for the successful removal of Marie's brain tumor. We join with you in praising God for His grace in seeing her through the operation, and we continue to pray for her as she goes through the process of recovery.

Your gift was a fitting one; the sanctuary was beautified by the flowers, and as you requested, they were then taken to the home of a shut-in from the church. In this way, they continue to brighten a heart.

Again, we appreciate your generosity, and we ask Christ's blessing on each member of your family.

In Him,

Pastor

19 / TO FAMILIES ABOUT WEDDINGS— DECISION NOT TO ATTEND DAUGHTER'S

In this delicate situation, the pastor carefully chooses his words so as not to generate more negative emotion. Though he expresses understanding of the parents' feelings, he gently urges them to reconsider, on the basis of the overall picture.

I was sorry to hear about your decision not to attend Susan and Joe's wedding. The beginning of their new life together is an important time for them, and naturally, they want you, as Susan's family, to share in it with them. It is causing them great pain to think that you cannot do this.

I know that you too are hurting as a result of this situation. It is always difficult to see your loved one choose to go in a direction you think is wrong, for whatever reasons. Yet I wonder if any cause of disagreement is so overwhelming that it is worth completely breaking off family ties. Susan does not want such a thing to happen, and I believe that in your hearts, you don't either.

For the sakes of all who are involved in this unpleasantness, I am asking you to reconsider your position. Certainly Susan has, is, and will in the future make wrong choices. That is part of the heritage that all of us, as human beings, are stuck with. But she desperately needs you to stand by her, in spite of them.

I realize that attending the wedding will not be easy for you to do, but I am confident that if you can make the extra effort and look at the long-range picture, instead of just what is happening now, you will not regret it. If, on the other hand, you stick with your decision, you may well come to feel it is one of the biggest mistakes you ever made.

If I can be of any assistance, please don't hesitate to contact me. I am hopeful that God will help all parties to reach a place of reconciliation before the wedding date arrives.

Sincerely,

Pastor

20 / TO GROUPS ABOUT ANNIVERSARIES—OF GROUP

Thirty years ago, a small group of women at First Church met to discuss their concern for the denomination's missionaries. While the missionaries' major needs were being cared for, the ladies felt that a number of little things could be done on a regular basis to brighten the days of the workers on the field. Organizing under the name of the Women's Missionary Society, the group committed itself to writing weekly letters, providing remembrances for birthdays and Christmas, and keeping the church updated about the missionaries' personal victories and prayer requests.

From this humble beginning, the group has grown in both size and purpose. In addition to the initial projects, it has taken on year-round fund raising for missions, setting up several missions services a year, and actively recruiting future missionaries from the youth.

All this is at a time when it is increasingly difficult to get volunteers to do anything. Ladies of the Missionary Society, we salute you on this occasion of your thirtieth anniversary. You have spent those many years in faithful service to your Lord, and He will surely reward you as you deserve. If each of the missionaries whom you have aided could do it, I'm certain they would join together in one mighty voice of thanks for all you have done.

May our Heavenly Father continue to bless and guide your efforts on behalf of our missionaries.

With warmest congratulations,

Pastor

21 / TO GROUPS ABOUT AWARDS AND HONORS—
PRESENTED TO GROUP

It is with great pleasure that I inform you that First Church has been selected by the denomination as the recipient of the 19XX Best Sunday School Growth Award. This honor recognizes the tremendous effort that the Sunday school department, as well as each member who has attended, has made in building up our Christian education classes.

As your pastor, I am extremely proud of our department for achieving this accomplishment. Many churches never are able to reach it. But then I've always known there was something special about the congregation here!

Again, thanks to all who have helped make this award possible. May we continue to work together not just to watch our Sunday school grow, but to see more people commit their lives to Christ and mature in that relationship.

In His service,

Pastor

22 / TO GROUPS ABOUT CERTIFICATES—
READY TO BE PICKED UP

Congratulations! You have successfully passed the CPR course you have been attending at CYO. I'm pleased to say that everyone who attended each of the sessions held in the past month did well on the exam. It will be a blessing for the parish to know that in case of an emergency, so many of our youth are qualified in CPR.

A certificate made out in your name is waiting for you in the church office. Please pick it up sometime within the next few weeks. Again, our congratulations!

Sincerely,

Father
St. Mary's Church

23 / TO GROUPS ABOUT FUNERALS—
OF GROUP MEMBERS

The funeral for Clarence and Lydia Green will be held on Saturday, October 3, at 10 A.M. in Leed and Sons Mortuary, (address).

Since you are a part of the Faithful Followers Sunday school class in which Mr. and Mrs. Green were involved, their children and families would like to invite you to a dinner at First Church immediately after the burials at Rest Haven Cemetery.

The tragic, unexpected loss of the Greens is a severe blow to all who knew and loved them. Please remember to keep the families in your prayers. While they may never have answers as to why the car accident claimed the lives of Clarence and Lydia, God can strengthen them as they go through this time of sorrow. And we can all take comfort in the assurance that the Greens are now in the very presence of Jesus, the Lord they served so faithfully.

Sincerely,

Pastor

24 / TO GROUPS ABOUT HOLIDAYS—CHRISTMAS

Christmas is a time of giving. At no other time in the year are we so kind, thoughtful, and generous.

And this is as it should be. Giving helped celebrate that first Christmas, for when the Wise Men found the Baby Jesus, they presented treasures to Him. Throughout the Bible, we have many other examples of generosity and its rewards. Vastly exceeding even them is God's greatest gift to mankind, His son. Subjected to one of the most cruel deaths imaginable, He submitted to it in order that we might live.

At this wonderful time of year, we can follow His footsteps by purposing in our hearts to be generous, yes, to our loved ones, but also to those who are in need, whether or not we call them friends. I challenge you this Christmas to seek out someone like that, a lonely, elderly person, a neglected child, an unemployed father, or a youth far from home. Find out what you can do to make his/her holiday a little brighter. It need not be expensive; time and some thought will mean more than costly gifts.

In helping others who can't pay you back, you are really helping yourself. Giving is one of the secrets of life. It is a basic clue to life's meaning. The grain of wheat cannot release its life unless it dies; the atom cannot give its power unless it is split. In fact, life cannot fulfill itself unless it is generous.

One of the most startling things Jesus said concerned the generosity of life. "For whoever would save his life will lose it, and whoever loses his life for my sake will find it" (Matthew 16:25). In holding onto life, we lose. In giving it away, we keep it.

Christmas is a good time to learn this secret. May you have a rich and fulfilling holiday. I hold you in my prayers.

In His service,

Pastor

25 / TO GROUPS ABOUT RECOGNITION OF SERVICE—OF GROUP

Now that another Easter season is over, I would like to thank all of you in the Pathfinders class who helped in planning and putting on the Wednesday evening Lenten services. I found each one to be meaningful and well-done; they added to my personal celebration of the resurrection of our Lord. While they must have involved a significant amount of time and effort, you have the satisfaction of knowing they went as scheduled, ministering to the congregation as it prepared for Easter.

Again, I appreciate your hard work and dedication. I know I can count on the Pathfinders!

In His service,

Pastor

26 / TO GROUPS ABOUT SHOWERS— THANK YOU FOR HOLDING

On behalf of my wife and myself, I would like to thank you for the recent baby shower you put on for us. The entire Couples Club went to a great deal of work to make it an enjoyable evening for Molly and me, and we will not soon forget the loving expression of caring. The gifts were also much appreciated, and will be put to good use as soon as our child arrives!

We would invite each of you to plan on coming over to meet our new son or daughter. It gives us joy to know that he/she will have such a wonderful group of people with which to grow up.

Sincerely,

Pastor

27 / TO GROUPS ABOUT THANK YOU— FOR MEMORIAL GIFT

On behalf of the staff and congregation at First Church, I would like to thank you for the ceiling fan donated by the Faithful Followers adult Sunday school class in memory of member John Ransom.

I'm certain the Ransom family is deeply touched by this gift, one that will be appreciated by everyone, particularly in the summer months when the sanctuary used to get so hot. Each time the fan is used, we will remember John.

You have chosen a practical and appropriate manner in which to express your sorrow at losing John from your class. We are deeply grateful.

In His service,

Pastor

28 / TO INDIVIDUALS ABOUT AWARDS AND HONORS—SUNDAY SCHOOL TEACHER OF THE YEAR

For a significant award such as this, the letter writer wanted more than just a statement of announcement and congratulations. In this letter, he specifies not only the requirements for the honor and who makes the selection, but adds his personal pleasure at having worked with the recipient. With this much detail, the letter will be a treasured keepsake for her.

It is a great privilege for me to inform you that you have been selected as Sunday School Teacher of the Year. This award is to honor you for the years of faithful service you have given the children of this church, and we hope you will accept it as a token of the gratitude of the church staff and congregation.

The Sunday School Teacher of the Year is selected on the basis of evaluations of myself, the Director of Christian Education, other staff, teachers, and pupils. The winner is to be a person of integrity, consistently demonstrating a Christian life-style. He or she is to be faithful in attendance and show an interest in continuing to develop new and more effective teaching methods. A personal interest in the students which extends beyond the classroom is necessary.

In these and other considerations, you have excelled. Therefore, you are to be congratulated as the 19XX Sunday School Teacher of the Year.

For me, personally, it has been a joy to work with you. Having you as one of our teachers has been an asset to the entire church. May God bless you in every way as you continue to serve Him.

Yours because of Him,

Pastor

29 / TO INDIVIDUALS ABOUT BIRTHDAYS— EIGHTIETH

In addition to acknowledging first birthdays, it's appropriate to do so with those who reach milestones such as seventy-five, eighty, eighty-five and above. The letter writer takes the opportunity to also thank the honoree for the seemingly small contributions she has made over the years to the church.

All of us at First Church want to wish you the best on the occasion of your eightieth birthday. Reaching this milestone is a great achievement, but even more noteworthy is what you have accomplished in that amount of time.

Over the years you have been a member, you have taught Sunday school, sang in the choir, served on the board, and worked at countless church ice cream socials. Numerous visitors have been greeted by your smile, and it's not unusual to see you soothing a fussy baby so its mother can have a break. In short, you have been a faithful servant to your Lord.

Now God has granted you this special birthday. Enjoy it! We are confident that you will continue to minister in His name, and that He will bless your efforts and your life.

Yours because of Him,

Pastor

30 / TO INDIVIDUALS ABOUT CERTIFICATES— VERIFYING DETAILS

Welcome! We were pleased to have you officially join First Church last Sunday, and we trust that membership will result in both ministry to you and from you.

A certificate acknowledging your new status is being prepared for you. In order that it may be filled out correctly, please check the spelling of your name and the other information at the bottom of this letter. If any corrections need to be made, contact the church office at once.

The completed certificate will be mailed to you within the next two weeks.

Again, we are delighted to have you as part of our fellowship, and if there is anything I can do for you, don't hesitate to call my office.

In His service,

Pastor

31 / TO INDIVIDUALS ABOUT ENGAGEMENT— BROKEN

While a broken engagement may not be as traumatic as a divorce, it can cause a great deal of emotional pain. Yet most people don't consider that when they hear of one. Here the letter writer sensitively offers support without prying into the reasons or taking sides.

I was saddened to hear recently that your engagement to David has been broken. Such a step is always difficult, and you will be in my prayers as you adjust to it.

Nevertheless, it is certainly preferable to break an engagement than to later go through a divorce. If the problems in the relationship caused you to wonder about the chances of a successful marriage, then you showed wisdom in stopping now instead of going ahead and risking a disastrous union.

It may not seem like it now, but God will lead you to the right person to marry, whether it means going back to David at some point or finding someone new. In the meantime, He cares about you and will help you through this rough time.

If you feel like talking, give me a call.

Sincerely,

Pastor

32 / TO INDIVIDUALS ABOUT FUNERALS— AFTER LOVED ONE'S

If you are like many other bereaved spouses, you probably have little if any memory of Mary's funeral. That's perfectly understandable, but I did want you to know that it was one of the most moving funerals at which I have officiated. The great number of people who attended could not help but be touched by the obvious Spirit of the Lord. I am certain that even in death, Mary was a tremendous testimony to the hope of life in Christ.

Of course, this does not by any means make up for the heartbreaking loss you have experienced. Life without her will always be difficult to some extent, although your pain will lessen after a time. Yet even so, you can take comfort in that Mary showed her deep faith to those who knew and loved her both before and after she departed from this life.

May the caring and compassion of God reach out to you during this difficult time.

Sincerely,

Pastor

33 / TO INDIVIDUALS ABOUT GRADUATIONS— CONGRATULATIONS TO INDIVIDUAL

Congratulations on this important milestone in your life! We at First Church rejoice with you in this accomplishment.

We will be honoring all of our graduates on Sunday, May 26, in our morning worship service. We will be presenting a gift to each graduate in recognition of their hard work. We hope you can be with us, that we might be able to congratulate you personally.

Sincerely,

Pastor

34 / TO INDIVIDUALS ABOUT RECEPTIONS— INFORMING OTHERS

Can you imagine serving twenty years as Sunday school superintendent? Time after time, dealing with unruly children, curriculum that isn't in when needed, and teacher vacancies would be something many of us would not want to face. Yet Fred Johnson has faithfully served in this position since 19XX.

I'm sure you agree that something special would be in order as this remarkable man steps down. What's being planned is a surprise reception to honor Fred. Set for Saturday, September 9, at 2 P.M., it will be held in Fellowship Hall. Punch and cookies will be served, and we are asking everyone to write down a humorous or inspirational experience about Fred to be read aloud at the reception.

I know Fred would want you to come, so mark your calendar now. But remember, it's a SURPRISE!

See you on the 9th,

Pastor

35 / TO INDIVIDUALS ABOUT RECOGNITION OF SERVICE—CHOIR DIRECTOR

It's not necessary to wait to acknowledge years of service until the person is celebrating a round number such as twenty or thirty years. A simple letter of appreciation like the following might make the difference in whether or not the recipient quits when things get rough or stays with it to reach a round number.

As I was recently checking through some church files, it came to my attention that you have been choir director for thirty-seven years. I had no idea that you dedicated your time and talent to First Church for so long!

Your loyal service is certainly commendable; what a fine example of faithfulness year after year. I am certain that many people in the congregation have also noticed your hard work and determination to always have a prepared choir. Even though it may not be said often, you are appreciated.

Again, my thanks for your years of work with the choir. I trust that you will continue for many more.

In His service,

Pastor

36 / TO INDIVIDUALS ABOUT RETIREMENT

On behalf of the staff at First Church, I would like to congratulate you upon your retirement from (name of company) after thirty years of employment. Your faithful service there has been an example to your fellow employees, your supervisors, and your family. I firmly believe that the Bible teaches that putting in a good day's work and having integrity in one's job are important. You have demonstrated those characteristics consistently over the years.

Now as you enter this new stage of your life, I pray that God would bless and guide you each step of the way. You may be retired, but He still has plenty for you to do!

With warm regards,

Pastor

CHAPTER 9

Letters of Acceptance, Confirmation, Invitation, and Refusal

Ministers are asked to speak before other congregations and groups, and ask others to be speakers at special church functions and services. Ministers also are asked to serve on committees and boards.

Sometimes these invitations to speak and to serve are welcomed by the minister and are easily accepted. Other times, the invitation is felt to be inappropriate, or the minister is just too busy to schedule yet another engagement on a loaded calendar.

Letters of acceptance, and especially letters of refusal, require dignity and tact. Also, letters of invitation must be clear in what is being asked, and convincing that the invitation is sincere. It is equally important that when an invitation has been extended and accepted, a follow-up letter confirming all the relevant details be sent.

1 / TO GROUPS ABOUT ACCEPTING NEW POSITION

Thank you for your recent invitation for me to join the board of the Sandusky County Substance Abuse Program. As you probably know, I have been for some time concerned about the number of people in our community who abuse alcohol and drugs. I have had opportunities to work with some of them in trying to help them deal with their problems, and it has been challenging yet rewarding. Therefore, I am pleased to accept your invitation and join forces with you in helping with a cause which is so worthwhile. I am confident that by combining my efforts with your group's, many more will find the assistance they need to break away from abusive behavior.

Thank you again. I look forward to attending my first meeting.

Yours in Christ,

Father
St. Mary's Church

2 / TO GROUPS ABOUT ACCEPTING SPEAKING INVITATION

An acceptance of this type may be brief and courteous. It's wise to restate the specifics of the offer, so as to be certain they were understood correctly.

Thank you very much for asking me to speak at the Ross High School Commencement at 2 P.M. on June 3. I consider it a privilege to accept your invitation.

As you suggested, I will plan on talking for twenty minutes. Within the next month, my office will forward to you the title of my address.

Again, I appreciate this opportunity. As the date approaches, I will be in touch with you.

Sincerely,

Rabbi,
Beth-El Congregation

3 / TO GROUPS ABOUT ACCEPTING RECOGNITION

I was delightfully surprised to receive your letter announcing that I have been selected as Man of the Year by the city. This is a great honor indeed, one that I did not expect. There are many here who have done much more than I have, but I will always appreciate my having been chosen.

I look forward to the annual banquet on May 16, and as you suggested, I will prepare some brief remarks to make after the presentation of the award.

Again, my deepest thanks to each member of the committee who decided on my receiving this recognition. With God's help, I will do my best to continue to work for the betterment of the city.

Sincerely,

Father
St. Mary's Church

4 / TO GROUPS ABOUT CONFIRMING DATES AND TIMES

It is with great anticipation that I await the coming of Joyful Sound to First Church. We have started publicity for your visit, and the congregation is eagerly beginning preparations for it. Truly, this will be a time of special ministry.

To confirm our plans, you will be appearing at the 7 P.M. service on Sunday, April 28. The group will arrive at the church at approximately 4 P.M., at which time the sound equipment will be set up with help from the men of the church. A potluck supper will be served at 5:30 P.M.

I will open the service, which will then be turned over to you. After your ministry, which should last about an hour, I will close the service.

If you have any questions, please contact my office. Thank you for your willingness to come, and may God bless you as you travel to other churches to sing in His name.

Sincerely in Him,

Pastor

5 / TO GROUPS ABOUT CONFIRMING TELEPHONE CONVERSATIONS

Telephone conversations should always be followed up with a letter; even with the best intentions, it's easy to forget or confuse matters discussed. In this example, the pastor names the person he spoke with, so that if there are any questions about the details worked out, they can be referred to him.

It is with great anticipation that we look forward to your coming to present the play *Man Of God* at First Church on March 30. Having never had professional Christian drama in our sanctuary, we are expecting a great evening of inspiration and entertainment.

As I discussed on the telephone with Joe Masters, your group will plan on arriving at the church at 4:30 P.M. A soup/salad bar will be served to you at 5:30, and you will have the remaining time before the 7:30 service to set up and rehearse. Following the conclusion of the program, members of your group will be assigned to host families in the congregation, where they will be spending the night.

Other details may be worked out upon your arrival. However, if you have any questions, please feel free to contact me. We are eager to have you here at First Church!

Because of Jesus,

Pastor

6 / TO GROUPS ABOUT INVITING GROUPS

Through our members Bob and Jean Brown, I have recently heard about your ministry in music and how God has been using you. I would very much like for Joyful Sound to come to First Church and sing for a Sunday evening service.

If you would be interested, please send me information about the group, including what sound equipment would be needed and what financial arrangements you make. Our policy has usually been to take up a freewill offering the evening a group ministers, with the total amount collected going to them. In addition, they are permitted to sell records, tapes, etc. after the service.

We would also need to know any other requirements your group has, such as for meals or housing. Please send the name and address of your pastor in order that I may contact him if necessary.

The congregation is always enthusiastic about special services, and I am certain that if we can work something out, it will be a great blessing for all of us. I look forward to hearing from you.

In His service,

Pastor

7 / TO GROUPS ABOUT INVITING SPECIAL GUESTS

I would like to extend to you a special invitation to join us for our evening service on Sunday, May 2, at 7 P.M. At that time, Joyce and Howard Wilson of Lima will be sharing their testimony.

Since part of their experience deals with Joyce's loss of over 100 pounds with the help of God and Weight Watchers, I wanted to be certain your weight loss group knew about it. I would encourage as many members of it as possible to come hear this inspiring program.

I hope to see a number of people from your group as our guests on May 2. It will be well worth your time!

Because of Christ,

Pastor

8 / TO GROUPS ABOUT REFUSING NEW POSITION

Thank you very much for your letter of September 19, offering me the position of chaplain at the Ohio Reformatory. While I have been greatly blessed during the times I have come to your facility to visit the inmates, I find I cannot accept full-time employment. I am satisfied with my job as pastor at First Church and currently have no desire to move on to another place.

Again, I do appreciate your thinking of me. Perhaps at some point in the future, God will call me into prison ministry on a regular basis, but for now, I must decline your offer. Naturally, I will continue my monthly visits to the reformatory, and I look forward to working with your new chaplain when he/she is hired.

In Christ,

Pastor

9 / TO GROUPS ABOUT REFUSING A GROUP

It's always difficult to say "no," but unfortunately, it's a task which must be done at least occasionally. This warm refusal candidly states the reasons for the negative response, making it clear that it isn't a personal rejection, and leaving open the possibility of another time.

Thank you so much for the information about your group Living Waters. It sounds like the Lord is truly blessing your ministry.

However, at this time, we cannot ask you to come to First Church. On several occasions during the past year, we have had musical groups share with us, and another one is scheduled for next month. I certainly feel music ministry is important, and our members have always been receptive to them. But I believe that by having too often the same type of ministry, its effectiveness can be lessened.

I will keep your information on file, and perhaps next year we will be able to work out a date when you can come. In the meantime, I pray that God will continue to use you in His service.

Sincerely in Him,

Pastor

10 / TO GROUPS ABOUT REFUSING AN INVITATION

Thank you so much for inviting me to speak at your annual Father/Son Banquet. I would like to accept, but unfortunately, I cannot.

Over the past six months, I have spoken to a number of groups, which has been a great blessing to me. However, I have recently felt God calling me to spend more time with my family. I'm sure you can understand my desire to be with my children while they are young. Because of this, I have decided that I will not accept any speaking engagements for the rest of this year.

If, at some point in the future, you again have the occasion to need a speaker, please feel free to contact me. I may be open to accept at that time.

Again, I appreciate your offer. May God bless you and send you the right speaker for this year's banquet.

In His service,

Pastor

11 / TO GROUPS ABOUT REFUSING RECOGNITION

I appreciate very much your recent letter inviting me to serve as honorary chairman of the 19XX Tourney with the Pros Golf Fund-Raiser to benefit Cystic Fibrosis. It is a great honor for me that you want me to serve in this position.

However, I find that at this time I am unable to accept your kind offer. During the tournament, I will be in California attending a conference, which will not be over until several days after the end of the fund-raiser.

I certainly want to help fight this cruel disease in any way in which I can, and I deeply regret that I cannot accept the chairmanship. But I am confident that you can find someone else even more deserving to take my place. Perhaps in the future I will be able to do something similar to this.

Again, thank you for thinking of me. I wish you all the best as you plan the Tourney with the Pros.

Sincerely,

Rabbi,
Beth-El Congregation

12 / TO GROUPS ABOUT REFUSING SPEAKER

It was with interest that I read your recent letter offering to provide a speaker for one of our men's fellowship meetings. However, upon sharing your proposal with our board, it was decided that we will be unable to schedule such a program at this time. While hearing about energy conservation would prove to be helpful, it is not in line with the type of meeting that we attempt to provide for our members. That is, the thrust of the evening is to offer spiritual enrichment.

Nevertheless, I will keep on file the information sheet you sent. If circumstances should change, I will contact you. Again, thank you for your interest.

In Christ,

Pastor

13 / TO SPEAKERS ABOUT CONFIRMING COSTS

Thank you for your letter of May 2, 19XX, specifying the terms under which you will be speaking at First Church in July. We will be more than happy to provide the $50 you requested for travel expenses, as well as allow you the opportunity to sell your book after the service. In addition, we will provide a meal for you upon your arrival at the church, approximately 5 P.M.

We are excited about your coming and are confident that God will use you in a mighty way as you minister to our congregation. If you have any questions, feel free to contact me.

Because of Jesus,

Pastor

14 / TO SPEAKERS ABOUT CONFIRMING DATES AND TIMES

It was with regret that we received your letter indicating that you will be unable to speak at First Church on August 6 as planned. However, the alternate date which you mentioned as a possibility for your coming, August 20, would suit us very well. Why don't you plan on ministering to our congregation on that Sunday instead? All the arrangements can remain the same; the service begins at 7 P.M., and you will have thirty minutes for your presentation.

While it is unfortunate that the original plans will not work out, we understand the situation and feel confident that the new date will be just as satisfactory for all involved. I appreciate your promptness in informing me of the change, and I anticipate a good time of fellowship with you upon your arrival.

Sincerely,

Pastor

15 / TO SPEAKERS ABOUT CONFIRMING SPECIAL EVENTS AND FACILITIES

As the time for you to speak to First Church approaches, I join the congregation in a sense of growing excitement. Truly, we have a wonderful evening in store for us!

I wanted to inform you that I did talk to the church council about the possibility of renting the high school auditorium for your program. The members agreed with me that a large crowd could be expected to attend and that our own sanctuary just would not be big enough. Therefore, we have arranged with the school to use the auditorium, located at 55 S. Washington Street (the south end of the school).

As we discussed before, the time for the service to begin will remain at 7 P.M. All other arrangements will also stay the same.

We are confident that this larger location will provide a superior setting for the presentation you will be making. We look forward to an opportunity for great ministry.

In His service,

Pastor

16 / TO SPEAKERS ABOUT CONFIRMING SPEAKERS

While this letter is enthusiastic about the speaker coming, its rather formal tone stresses the importance of the guidelines for his visit. Numbering them adds emphasis.

We are glad of your willingness to share with us at First Church on Sunday, January 7 in our 10:35 morning worship service.

We have sought to have your ministry here because we feel it is compatible with our vision and will be strengthening to the Body. Please allow us to help you make your visit a memorable one. You will love the First Church people and find them very responsive and kind.

To make your ministry most effective, we ask that you observe the following five guidelines:

1. The pastor will be in full control of the service. At the conclusion of the ministry, the guest will turn the service back to the pastor for final announcements and the closing of the service.

2. Since the First Church worship is a complete service, each service will include a time of singing and worship. It's our desire for the guest minister to be present, on the platform, from the beginning of the service. (Our people will not respect dramatic entrances just before the ministry.)

3. The pastor is the only person authorized to receive offerings. The guest minister will not take any offering. This must be strictly adhered to. First Church is a generous church and we will bless you.

4. It has been popular not to be strict concerning time limitations. This is not our belief. We are considerate of our people, the hour, and the many babies in our nursery. The pastor and the guest minister can discuss these things and work together on them.

5. We feel it is the wisdom of the Holy Spirit as well as the years of practical experience that has helped us develop these guidelines. We thank you for working together with us to have a great meeting.

Sincerely,

Pastor

17 / TO SPEAKERS ABOUT CONFIRMING TELEPHONE CONVERSATIONS

It was a joy for me to talk to you over the telephone last week. I'm sure that having you here will be a great blessing for the congregation.

To confirm what we agreed upon, you will speak for about thirty minutes during the 7 P.M. worship service on Sunday, April 21. A freewill offering will be taken to go toward your expenses in coming to First Church, and a table will be set up for you to use after the service to sell copies of the book you have written.

Please send a bio sheet/press release with a photo of yourself as soon as possible, in order that we may begin publicity.

Should you have any questions, contact my office.

Again, thank you for your willingness to minister to us. May God bless and guide you as you prepare.

In His service,

Pastor

18 / TO SPEAKERS ABOUT INVITING SPEAKERS

After hearing you speak at Faith Memorial Church recently, one of our members suggested to me that we invite you to come address our church as part of a Sunday evening service. If you would be interested, please let me know so that we may select an appropriate date. Also, what do you charge for speaking engagements?

I understand that you are an inspiring speaker, and I would like very much to have you come here in the near future. I look forward to hearing from you.

May God bless you in every way.

Sincerely in Him,

Pastor

19 / TO SPEAKERS ABOUT REFUSING SPEAKERS

I recently received your resume and your request that you be considered for a possible speaking engagement at First Church. While I would like to be more positive, I must tell you frankly that, at this time, I do not feel that your presentation would be of interest to the majority of our congregation. The average age of the members is twenty-eight, and only about five families who regularly attend First Church are nearing the retirement age. Therefore, while I am certain that your talk about "Planning Your Retirement" would prove to be helpful and interesting to people in older age groups, our church would not be open to such a ministry.

Nevertheless, I will keep your letter on file, and if in the future circumstances change, I will not hesitate to contact you. Thank you, and may God bless you as you present your talks.

Sincerely,

Pastor

20 / TO INDIVIDUALS ABOUT ACCEPTING A NEW POSITION

Thank you for your letter of June 12, 19XX, offering me the position of professor of New Testament at Faith Bible College. It is with great anticipation that I accept your invitation. For several years, I have had a strong desire to get back into the role of a full-time teacher, and being part of the faculty at your institution will be an answer to that prayer.

Naturally, my family and I will be relocating to your area as soon as possible. I have submitted my resignation to First Church, effective August 15. By the start of the school year, I shall be more than ready to begin my new duties.

Again, I appreciate the opportunity to serve God in this new and challenging calling, and I look forward to working with you and the other staff.

May God bless you.

Because of Him,

Pastor

21 / TO INDIVIDUALS ABOUT ACCEPTING SPEAKING INVITATION

Thank you for inviting me to speak to your sixth grade class about my recent trip to Mexico. I would be happy to accept. Would you also be interested in my bringing some of the slides I took while on the trip? If so, I can plan on bringing those as well as some of the interesting things I purchased there.

As far as the dates you mentioned, either Wednesday, January 4 or Thursday, January 5 would be fine with me. Please have your teacher contact me and we will set up the details.

Again, I'm glad you wrote me. I look forward to speaking to your class.

Yours in Christ,

Father
St. Mary's Church

22 / TO INDIVIDUALS ABOUT ACCEPTING RECOGNITION

I was touched by your letter requesting permission to nominate me for West High School's Hall of Fame. Certainly there are many more deserving in the community than I am, but if you wish to do this, go ahead.

In the years in which I have worked with youth, especially those in trouble, I have found great satisfaction. Not only has it been exciting to see the successes in which someone totally turns his/her life around for the good, but the so-called failures have been a lesson in perseverance to me. From them, I have learned never to give up—that God can reach even the toughest heart.

Again, I truly appreciate your kind gesture to acknowledge my ministry in the school. While I certainly didn't devote all those hours with teens merely to gain recognition, it's still nice to have some!

Sincerely,

Pastor

23 / TO INDIVIDUALS ABOUT CONFIRMING COSTS

It is only several weeks from when I will be addressing the Father/Son Banquet at First Church, and I am very much looking forward to coming. I trust that the bio sheet/press releases which I mailed you last month are sufficient for your publicity; if you need more, please contact me.

Thank you for your willingness to accommodate me financially. The $XX for my travel expenses plus the opportunity to sell my book following the service will be more than adequate in providing for my needs.

Again, I am expecting an enriching evening with your congregation on March 30, and I appreciate your confidence in me as shown by your inviting me to come.

Because of Christ,

Pastor

24 / TO INDIVIDUALS ABOUT INVITING SPECIAL GUESTS

I would like to take this opportunity to invite you to join us for worship at First Church on Sunday, October 3, at 10:30 A.M. At that time, Fred Jones will be recognized for twenty years of service as Sunday School Superintendent. I know it would mean a great deal to him if as many as possible of his children and grandchildren could be present.

It is quite an achievement to have faithfully served the church in this position for so long, and we want to do everything possible to honor him. Following the service, an informal reception will be held for him in Fellowship Hall.

We look forward to seeing you on the 3rd.

Sincerely,

Pastor

25 / TO INDIVIDUALS ABOUT REFUSING NEW POSITION

Thank you for writing to me concerning your desire to do more to fight pornography in our community. I certainly share that desire—we desperately need to eliminate the adult book stores and convenience store sales of soft-core porn in order to return to the type of community in which we can raise our families in traditional values.

However, at this time I must turn down your offer to join you in forming a new task force to combat pornography locally. I feel that with several branches of national organizations active in our city, it would be counterproductive to have another group with the same goals. It makes more sense to me to join forces even more with the existing organizations than to begin something new.

I hope you understand that I am totally sympathetic with what you want to do; I just differ with you as to the means to accomplish that goal. Again, I'm grateful that you contacted me. May God bless your labors for Him.

Because of Jesus,

Pastor

26 / TO INDIVIDUALS ABOUT REFUSING INVITATION

Handling this delicate situation isn't easy, because the parents are almost bound to be upset by the rabbi's refusal, no matter how well he handles it. But in cases like this where it's strongly felt that there is no possibility of compromise, one can only explain his rationale, and hope the recipient will at least eventually understand.

I recently received your request that I come speak to your daughter about her alcohol problem. Your confidence in me is appreciated, and normally I would be more than willing to help in situations like this. However, in dealing with substance abuse, success in breaking the cycle is possible only when the abuser herself is to the point of acknowledging the difficulty. Thus far, I have seen no evidence that Ruth wants to change. You have made the call for help, not her.

Therefore, I must refuse your request. When she herself is ready to recognize the problem and asks for my assistance, I will be more than happy to respond. But until that time, I believe the best course of action is to wait.

May I recommend that you consider attending Al-Anon, meetings for those who live with an alcoholic? The people there can help you learn how to cope with your daughter, and I am sure you would find it helpful. If you are interested, please contact me and I will supply you with the time and location of the nearest meeting.

Again, I am grateful to you for asking for my aid, and I hope you understand why I must refuse. If I can be of service to you any other way, please let me know.

Sincerely,

Rabbi,
Beth-El Congregation

27 / TO INDIVIDUALS ABOUT REFUSING RECOGNITION

Thank you for your recent letter expressing your appreciation for my efforts to help your son. I am certainly grateful for all your kind words, and I join you in rejoicing that Ryan has made definite steps toward progress. Breaking away from the cycle of drugs and alcohol he has been chained to for so long is extremely difficult, but I am confident that with God's help he will continue to rebuild his life in the right direction.

As to the suggestion you made to establish a scholarship at the high school in my honor, I do very much appreciate the idea, and I can understand your wanting to do something to show your joy in Ryan's turnaround. However, I must ask that you not name the scholarship fund after me.

In my work with troubled youth, it is important that they see me as a friend on their level, not one linked with the police, school officials, etc. Having my name on the scholarship fund might jeopardize this trust in at least some of the teens' eyes. I want to keep my role in helping kids low-key, in order to make it most effective, and while I would normally welcome the chance to have some recognition of my efforts, in this case I feel it might prove to be detrimental.

I am confident that you will understand my feelings and respect them. Again, my thanks for your gesture.

Yours in Christ,

Father
St. Mary's Church

CHAPTER 10

Letters to Raise Funds

While businesses rely on the sales of goods and services to produce income, and government survives on taxes, the church must rely on the goodwill of others for its funds.

Fund-raising is especially sensitive, since many may be skeptical of the good a church can provide. Asking for money must be done in an open, straightforward, and honest manner.

When asking for contributions, it is important to be specific about the need and how the funds will be used. The minister should always be ready to provide a complete and detailed financial statement showing exactly how much money the church has taken in and given out. A good steward need not be ashamed asking for support from members and from businesses and the community at large.

Churches provide valuable and needed services to their communities, and the minister should be bold in asking those who can help to share from their bounty by contributing to the needs of the church.

1 / TO BUSINESSES ABOUT CHURCH MINISTRIES—FOOD PANTRY FOR POOR

Greetings!

As you may know, St. Mary's Church has run a food pantry for the poor for several years. We average helping five to ten families and individuals a week, and since we are the only group in the city putting on this type of ministry, the need is great.

In the past, we have solicited contributions and donations of food items from members of our parish. However, within the past six months, the number of people coming to the pantry has almost doubled. Therefore, we find ourselves in the position of requiring additional supplies.

As a local business, you have been generous in helping our community in the past. Your assistance now would be greatly appreciated. Donations of canned goods, paper products, etc. are welcome, as are cash contributions.

Thank you for anything you can do at this time to aid the hungry in our area.

Sincerely,

Father
St. Mary's Church

2 / TO BUSINESSES ABOUT EMERGENCIES—FAMILIES LOSING HOMES TO FIRE

As you may know, two families in our community recently lost their homes and possessions to fires. Both of these families are members of our congregation, and we are making every effort to help them recover from this tragedy.

Although we are receiving a great deal of clothing, food, etc. from within the church, we would also like to be able to give them some new things. Perhaps you would welcome the opportunity to be a part of recreating their lives.

Especially needed are the following: drapes/curtain rods, meat, toys, paper goods such as toilet paper and facial tissues, bicycles, shoes, and underwear. In addition, almost anything in the way of furniture could be put to good use.

If you would like to make a donation in the name of community service, please call the church office to arrange delivery. We would appreciate very much whatever you can do.

Gratefully,

Pastor

3 / TO BUSINESSES ABOUT SPECIAL PROJECTS— FUNDS FOR ORGAN TRANSPLANT

In the following letter, notice how the letter writer uses an informal personal appeal. Especially effective are giving the businesses the option of a pledge or of refreshments, and having the youth actually do something to raise the funds instead of merely requesting donations.

If you're like most people in (name of city), you have noticed the recent newspaper stories about little Ryan White, the six-year old boy from our area who is in need of a liver transplant. Unfortunately, his condition has continued to deteriorate, and if he does not get a new organ soon, he will not survive much longer.

Naturally, this type of surgery requires a large amount of financial backing. Through car washes, bake sales, etc., over $XXXXX has already been raised for Ryan. But much more is needed.

In an effort to bring in some more of this money, the youth at St. Mary's have determined to hold a Rock-a-thon on Saturday, February 3, from 7 P.M. until 7 A.M. Over thirty young people have committed themselves to this and are currently gathering pledges for each hour they rock.

Since you are a community-minded business, we want to offer you the opportunity to get involved in this worthwhile project. We would appreciate any donations of food for the youth to eat as they rock all night, or, if you would prefer, a pledge for cash to go to Ryan.

Thank you for whatever you can do.

Yours in Christ,

Father
St. Mary's Church

4 / TO CHURCH MEMBERS ABOUT CHURCH MINISTRIES—TV MINISTRY

This letter in regard to a church's TV ministry employs a useful technique—a testimonial from someone who directly benefited from the thing for which funds are being raised. And because she is from outside the church, even more credibility is established.

Recently I received the following letter:
Dear Pastor,
Lately things in my life had not been going well. My husband and I didn't have much of a marriage left, and our oldest child was causing us a lot of grief. I really wondered if there was any reason to go on living. Then I happened to tune in your TV program on channel 33. At first, I

thought I would turn it off, since I have never had much use for religion. But I kept listening anyway. You made the love of God sound so real and personal that I got tears in my eyes. I knew that with God's help, I could keep going and that He would work things out. So far, my husband and child don't seem any different. But I am, and I thank you for it.

What a marvelous testimony of God reaching someone through the television ministry at First Church! Who knows what might have happened to this dear lady, had she not turned on the TV that night?

And when she expresses her thanks, it's you whom she's addressing. Each person who has contributed to the fund for the TV ministry is directly responsible for changed lives like the woman who wrote that letter.

A number of letters like this one have been sent to the church. While the individual circumstances may vary, each person has one thing in common: he or she has been touched by Jesus as a result of the TV program.

In addition, I understand that for each person who takes the time to write, about ten times that many are equally ministered to but don't get around to writing.

Yes, the TV ministry is making a difference in our city, and that's why I want it to continue to air each week. In order to do that, we need your prayers and your financial help. Although the camera operators and technicians donate their time to tape the programs, there are still expenses: for the air time and for supplies and equipment.

Please carefully consider how you might help in this ministry. How many others are out there like the lady whose letter I received? How many more are there who need the love of Christ and can find it as near as their own living room, if we continue to be faithful in this calling?

Thank you.

In His love,

Pastor

5 / TO CHURCH MEMBERS ABOUT DEBT RETIREMENT

As the new year approaches, the church council has felt led to set a specific goal for 19XX, that being, eliminate our indebtedness. At this time, we owe a total of $XXXXXX. If our regular schedule of payments is continued, the bond issue will be paid off in two years and the mortgage will not be paid off until six months afterwards.

Beginning on January 1, we would like to start making a monthly deposit of $XXXX for the Bond Issue. If this schedule is abided by, we can expect the debt to be paid back by (date).

We would keep on paying our mortgage payment at the same rate we have been.

As I'm certain you realize, being debt-free would be a wonderful testimony to our community of God's faithfulness. I believe that He would have us unite our hearts in this worthy goal, that we might go on to bigger tasks in the year following this one, unhindered by debt.

How can you help? There are three ways. First, consider a special gift in your Christmas offering. You may mark it to go toward debt retirement. As you know, we will be sending a portion of the offering to our missionary office and to the local shelter for victims of domestic violence, but all gifts designated for the debt will go directly to that fund, as well as a third of undesignated gifts.

A second way you can help us reach our goal is to pledge to give $1 per week especially for this cause. If each adult in the congregation gave this small amount each Sunday for a year, so marking on the envelope, we would achieve great progress toward our goal.

Finally, you may prefer to give a one-time gift of any amount to this fund.

I appeal to you to prayerfully consider the preceding options and do your part to help us reach our goal of debt retirement in the coming year. Thank you.

Serving Christ,

Pastor

6 / TO CHURCH MEMBERS ABOUT EMERGENCIES— FAMILIES WHO LOST HOMES IN FIRES

Most of you are already aware that during the past week, two families at First Church lost their homes and possessions in fires. Can you imagine how you would feel to never again see your children's baby pictures, your great-grandmother's handmade quilt, or your wedding gown? And what about all those familiar things that made your house special, like the mounted fish you caught when you were ten, the autographed copy of a book by your favorite author, and the picture you embroidered?

While we cannot replace these things, we can help supply the basic needs of these families who have lost so much. At the moment, the greatest aid would be cash donations to be used to locate housing for the victims. Please ask God if He would have you contribute to this fund, and if so, how much. Then make out your check to "First Church—housing need" and mail or bring it here as soon as possible.

In the near future, we will be collecting clothing, food, and household items to donate to the families as they begin to get established in new locations. Perhaps you can start to save now for this.

Most importantly, do keep the Millers and the Brandons lifted up in prayer. Though I'm certain they are thanking God that there was no loss of life in the fires, they are going through a very difficult time. Very few of us will ever really understand what it means to lose all material goods.

You have my heartfelt thanks for your generosity.

Sincerely in Him,

Pastor

7 / TO CHURCH MEMBERS ABOUT EVANGELISM OUTREACH—CHRISTIAN CONCERT

As you probably know, contemporary Christian musician (name) is coming April 21. We have been greatly excited about this opportunity to reach out into the community with the good news about Jesus.

But as the planning committee has met and prayed about the concert, it became clear that First Church might not be the best location. Many people automatically ignore the invitation to attend anything held at a place of worship. If our major goal for (name's) coming is to expose the unchurched to the Gospel message, then it seems plain that the place to do it is somewhere neutral.

With that in mind, we have tentatively reserved the high school auditorium for the concert. We feel that many more people will come to the school who would not enter a church.

However, in planning expenses for the concert, we did not anticipate having to pay rent for the location. We need your help! Please seek God and, if you can, join us in financially supporting this endeavor.

There are so many out there who are living empty, hopeless lives. If they knew of the abundant life that Jesus has for them, they would embrace it. Let's do our part to see that they do hear about it.

Thank you.

With Christ's love,

Pastor

8 / TO CHURCH MEMBERS ABOUT EXPANSION

Plans for a new building are almost certain to raise controversy. In this example, possible objections to the program are brought up and refuted, and the dubious are reassured that the main focus of the church is not changing.

Exciting things have been happening at First Church! One of them is that for the past six months, attendance at the morning worship service has been averaging over 300. Praise God!

While having large numbers of people is not a prime objective for us, it is encouraging to see that more and more are finding a church home which ministers to their needs.

However, you may have noticed that it is extremely difficult for a congregation of this size to fit into our sanctuary. Every Sunday, chairs have to be set up in the aisles, which is inconvenient as well as uncomfortable.

In discussing this problem with the council, we have determined that it is time to begin plans for a new, larger building. A committee is being formed to investigate the matter, and they will be checking into the possibilities of buying a building or constructing one.

Although actually being in a new location is not going to take place for some time, the council has voted to set up a building fund. If each of us would faithfully give just a small amount to this project on a regular basis, we would have the finances when they are needed.

I realize that a new building is not a priority for some. They would rather see the money going to helping the poor or reaching out to those who don't know Jesus. Their feelings are certainly justified.

On the other hand, the church cannot carry out its ministry if the building is not large enough to hold the congregation. First Church must have a bigger sanctuary, although not at the cost of funneling all donations into this, nor at the expense of our current ministries.

But I'm praying that God will speak to your heart about the importance of the building fund, and that you will be able to contribute to it, even if all you can give is a small amount.

The real mission of our church—to lead people into a personal relationship with Christ and to help them grow in this relationship—is still our focal point. Yet in order to do it well, we must have adequate facilities.

I enclose a building fund envelope for your convenience. Thank you for your help.

In Him,

Pastor

9 / TO CHURCH MEMBERS ABOUT MISSIONS

How much do you spend a week on coffee and on soda? Perhaps a dollar or two?

If you're like me, you don't think too much about that cup of coffee you grab at the drive-through on your way to work or that soda you pick up after an evening meeting. After all, it doesn't add up to much money.

But if you were to take that same amount and give it to missions each week, how much more it could accomplish! Even only five dollars a month totals $60 annually. If every family in the church would commit itself to that figure for missions, we would have over $12,000. Just think how many people could be helped with that amount of money—churches built, Bibles purchased, pastors trained, all this and more.

Wouldn't you like to be a part of the ongoing work of God's kingdom? At $5 a month, it's the bargain of the century. I challenge you now to purpose to find that extra few dollars and give it to the church's missions program. Perhaps it'll mean a couple less sodas or maybe one less night out at McDonald's. But the long-term results will be heavenly!

Giving for Him,

Pastor

10 / TO CHURCH MEMBERS ABOUT PLANT MAINTENANCE

As you may have noticed lately, First Church has had more than one occasion when raindrops literally were falling on our heads, as the song goes. The board has had the roof inspected, and based on the opinion of several experts, a decision has been made to replace it.

Although we have repaired the roof before, it has now reached the point where the work required is so extensive that it can no longer be patched. Not only is it awkward to have to place buckets around the church to catch the rain, but the more water which leaks down through the ceiling, the more permanent damage is done. We simply cannot hold off any longer on this much needed maintenance.

After much discussion and prayer, the board had felt led to go ahead and advertise for bids for a new roof for the entire building. It is expected to cost in the area of $XXXXX. The problem is that currently, money available for this project totals only $XXX, only about one-third of the estimated expense.

I realize that it's much more gratifying to give to missions or needy families or a new organ. All of us like to see what our dollars accomplish, and merely putting on a roof isn't that exciting. In addition, we still need your regular tithe to carry out the ongoing expenses of the church.

But I sincerely hope that you will ask the Lord how you can help finance this important project. The board would like to see the new roof installed before winter's rains and snows, which would further damage the old one.

Personally, I would rather see this sum of money used to increase the outreach of the church. Yet all the many ministries we have cannot function if the building is not properly maintained.

I enclose an envelope for your contribution. If you have any questions, please contact my office or any board member.

Thank you for your help.

In His service,

Pastor

11 / TO CHURCH MEMBERS ABOUT SPECIAL EVENTS—VISITING EVANGELIST

We have before us an exceptional opportunity. When you hear about it, I hope you will be as excited as I am!

On April 4, the renowned evangelist (name) will be speaking at Faith Memorial Church in (city). Perhaps some of you were planning to attend the service. On April 5, (name) had planned to go to Maple Grove First Church. But because of various circumstances, he will be unable to speak there on that date. His office has contacted me, indicating that if we are interested, he would instead come here.

Several years ago, I had the great privilege of hearing (name) preach at a conference I attended. His message was one of the most powerful I have ever heard. I am absolutely convinced that having him here would be a tremendous blessing to our congregation as well as to the community. It's very unlikely that we would ever again have this chance to have him in our church, since he is so busy that he usually only addresses conferences or large fellowships.

However, if we were to have (name) at First Church, there would be a financial investment of approximately $XXX. We do not have this money in the budget.

I am asking you to seek God about whether or not we should take advantage of this opportunity. (Name) must know within two weeks if we want him. If you feel this would be an asset for our congregation, please have your contribution mailed or brought to the church in the enclosed envelope by Sunday, November 15. If we have raised one-third of the required amount by the time, I will know that your answer is yes.

I pray that it will be.

Gratefully,

Pastor

12 / TO CHURCH MEMBERS ABOUT SPECIAL PROJECTS—HOUSING FOR NEEDY MEMBERS

For many of us, winter is not a season to which we look forward. The snow and cold are inconvenient; the heavy coats awkward. It's a time we could just as well do without, or at least shorten to only a month or two.

Yet for some, winter is much worse. To those in inadequate housing, the storms and low temperatures are near torture, as the icy fingers of the season penetrate into each room. Hands and feet are never quite warm enough.

Perhaps you did not realize that one of our own members at First Church is in this very situation. She simply cannot spend another winter in her present location, and the Love at Work fund has decided to find her another house which will keep her and her family warm during the coming cold months.

Because this need is quite a bit larger than most that the fund handles, there aren't enough funds available at the present time. I'm asking you to make a special sacrificial gift toward the housing project, in order that our sister can be moved in time. Yes, the amount of money needed seems great, and of course the church continues to need finances for the usual ministries. But I know the generosity of First Church when something like this arises, and I am confident that the amount will be available in time.

Thank you.

Sincerely in Him,

Pastor

13 / TO COMMUNITY ORGANIZATIONS ABOUT CHURCH MINISTRIES—CRISIS PREGNANCY CENTER

For several years now, First Church has felt a special concern for women facing crisis pregnancies. Several of our members have taken young women into their homes until their babies have been born, and we have helped place a couple of babies into adoptive homes.

But in the last six months, we have decided that we would like to get more involved in this type of work. Therefore, we are in the process of opening a home for unwed mothers-to-be. Tentative plans call for this home to open in May, 19XX, with facilities for four to six women.

To this end, we are in need of just about everything to outfit the house where these young women will be staying. As an organization committed to helping within the community, we wanted to give you a chance to be a part of the work we are beginning. Would you consider being one of the original sponsors of the home?

Your assistance may come in the form of a one-time gift or an ongoing commitment to be paid monthly, semiannually, or annually.

May we hear from you as soon as possible?

Sincerely,

Pastor

14 / TO COMMUNITY ORGANIZATIONS ABOUT PLANT MAINTENANCE

As you have probably noticed, the furnace has not been working well in our building for some time. We recently called a repairman to evaluate the situation, and were dismayed to discover that the work needed is so extensive that the only thing to do at this point is to replace the entire unit.

A new furnace of the size and type required will cost approximately $XXXXX. Although we had been aware for some time that the heating unit was old and not working properly, we did not think it would need to be replaced for several more years. Therefore, the money is not currently available.

However, we do not feel it is fair for the children attending our school to have to try to learn in a chilly environment, so we are going ahead and ordering the replacement unit.

We have asked the families within the parish to make a special gift at this time to help finance it. Since your group meets in our building, we thought you too might be willing to consider a donation for this purpose.

Thank you.

Yours in Christ,

Father
St. Mary's Church

15 / TO COMMUNITY ORGANIZATIONS ABOUT SPECIAL EVENTS—SUBSTANCE ABUSE SPEAKER

Even in as small a town as (name), drug and alcohol abuse exists. In fact, if the truth was to be known, the number of youth and adults in our community who are involved in it is significant.

As a congregation, we are concerned about this problem and wish to do something about it, as I'm sure your group does. It appears that one of the steps to decreasing substance abuse in any area is education. When our youth are informed about the dangers and misconceptions of drugs and alcohol, they are better able to resist the pressure to try it themselves, and they may even influence family and friends to stop.

Therefore, we would like to bring Buddy Young to (town) to put on an assembly for the high school this spring. An alcoholic since the age of twelve, Buddy spent three years in prison for crimes committed as a result of his habit. But while there, his life turned around, and he now travels across the nation, speaking about his experiences with drugs and alcohol and urging youth to avoid them. He is a powerful speaker, and as one who has been there himself, he is respected by young people.

However, the expense for bringing Buddy here is $XXXX, more than what we as a synagogue can afford. Would your group consider making a one-time contribution to this special assembly? Any amount would be helpful.

Thank you in advance for anything you can do.

Sincerely,

Rabbi,
Beth-El Synagogue

16 / TO INDIVIDUAL BENEFACTORS ABOUT EVANGELISM OUTREACH—CHRISTIAN MOVIES

As you know, First Church has always attempted to share the love of Christ with our community. This has taken different forms, including a concert at the high school and a gym/swim day at the YMCA. These activities held outside the church building have been highly successful in bringing into the family of God people who would not come to a regular worship service.

With this in mind, we have scheduled a series of movies on the family to be shown Tuesday evenings beginning on April 4. The series features well-known Christian physician William Watkins, and is in four parts. Because many people are interested in bettering their family life, we are hopeful that this too will bring a number of unchurched people in contact with the Lord Himself.

As you can imagine, expenses for this type of outreach are high. In addition to the cost of the movie rental, we are paying to use the high school auditorium and have purchased literature to pass out after each presentation. While there is money in the church budget for this type of project, we do not have enough at this time. We have described the need during morning worship, and a number of members have come forth with special gifts for the movie series.

However, in order to meet the bills which we know of (movie and auditorium rental), we still must have additional funds of $XXXX. If you feel this is a worthwhile project, please send your gift marked "movie outreach" to the church.

We appreciate anything you can do.

In Christian love,

Pastor

17 / TO INDIVIDUAL BENEFACTORS ABOUT EXPANSION

Those who attend regularly would be aware of the problems of meeting in too-small a facility, but by listing each one by itself in a set-apart format, they are emphasized. Recipients might find themselves saying, "I knew about all those, but I didn't realize there were so many. . . ."

As you may know, over the past two years we have been seeking God's direction for a worship center. Let us consider some of the needs which are not being met by our present location:

Sanctuary too small,

Cramped quarters for music ministry,

Poor parking,

Sunday school rooms too small and not enough,

Poor heating system and lighting,

No church office,

No storage.

Obviously, there are many areas which are woefully inadequate for our congregation. But in order to take a step forward—either by buying and converting an existing building or constructing one ourselves—we will have to have a great deal more than is currently in the building fund. May I personally challenge you to consider making a gift for this purpose?

In the past, you have helped us several times with large contributions on occasions on which they were badly needed, and your generosity has been much appreciated. This would certainly qualify as one of those situations; your assistance would be gratefully received.

Should you have any questions or wish to discuss the issue in more depth, I would be happy to meet with you at any time.

Sincerely,

Pastor

18 / TO INDIVIDUAL BENEFACTORS ABOUT MISSIONS

Two years ago, the board of deacons established a program to help people in our area. They called it the Meal-A-Week Offering; the idea was that each member would forgo one meal a week and give one dollar that would have been spent to eat to this offering. In this way, the deacons could give money to various agencies in the city to aid local families and individuals. Agencies selected to receive these funds were Samaritan House, Rescue Mission, and Salvation Army.

Since March, 19XX, we have received approximately $XXXXX through the weekly offering to Meal-A-Week. In addition, a number of small gifts have been made to go specifically to one of the agencies. You can see that just a small regular gift has made a significant difference in caring for the needs of the people in our area.

I am writing to you at this time because, currently, the Meal-A-Week fund is very low. While members of our congregation have continued to be faithful in giving to it, the money is being spent on a regular basis. In order to keep up this important mission, we need to build up the fund.

This letter is being sent to you and just eight other people. If you feel that what we are doing is important, I would ask for your gift to be sent to the church, marked "Meal-A-Week."

I know there are many calls upon you for your donations, and you alone must decide which are worthy of your interest. I hope that you will prayerfully consider this mission's project.

Thank you.

Sincerely,

Pastor

19 / TO INDIVIDUAL BENEFACTORS ABOUT PLANT MAINTENANCE

Occasionally, it's appropriate to ask individuals with the financial means to donate to a specific project. Note in this example the matter-of-fact tone, which doesn't beg, and the specific details of the situation, so that the recipient can make an informed choice as to whether he/she will support the project.

As you may have recently noticed, a major problem with the church's roof has developed. It is now in such a state of disrepair that when it rains, buckets to catch leaks have to be placed throughout the building in at least twenty locations.

Two experts have come in to check over the roof, and they are in agreement that it can no longer be merely repaired again. Based on their opinions, the board has made the decision that a new roof must be installed before the winter comes.

However, estimates for the job run approximately $XXXXX, and money currently available for the project amounts to only $XXX. We have issued a plea to church members for funds, and as you have been kind enough to donate to such projects before, we thought you might be willing to do so at this time.

I realize that contributing for a roof is not nearly as rewarding as it would be to construct a new building or to feed the hungry. But the mission of the church is hindered in facilities such as we have now.

On behalf of everyone at First Church, permit me to thank you in advance for anything you can do to help with this need. God will bless you for your generosity.

Sincerely in Him,

Pastor

20 / TO NONMEMBERS ABOUT EMERGENCIES— LOCAL TORNADO

As you know, clean-up in our neighboring community of Deshler is now beginning in earnest, following Monday's destructive tornado. Many of the residents there lost everything they owned, and the process of rebuilding virtually the entire town will be a lengthy one.

In light of this tragedy, which left us untouched, a number of our citizens have joined together in an attempt to help Deshler during this crisis. Beth-El Synagogue has been designated as the collection center for food, clothing, and furnishings. If you would care to donate any of the above, please bring them to the synagogue. Or if you need pick-up for larger items, call and we will arrange it.

While we cannot begin to replace the great loss of sentimental possessions for our Deshler neighbors, we can reach out with caring to lessen, even if only a little, the terrible trauma in which they find themselves.

Thank you for your generosity.

Sincerely,

Rabbi
Beth-El Synagogue

21 / TO NONMEMBERS ABOUT MISSIONS— CHRISTMAS OFFERING

Have you ever thought about why the wise men bowed down and worshipped the Baby Jesus when they found Him in the stable? Here were men of wealth and power, respected for their wisdom, used to people honoring them. Yet they put aside all that at the sight of the Infant King.

The reason for their homage is obvious: they knew who Jesus was. Their actions and gifts were expressions of their adoration.

Today, we also come to worship the Holy Babe, and we, no less than they, bring of ourselves. Recognizing Who He is, we can do no less.

But around the world are many who can honestly say they don't know Jesus. Millions exist in an apparently hopeless world which reflects little of the peace and joy that we experience. This Christmas, I hope that you will bring a special gift for the sakes of these who long to find Him.

Our denomination is beginning a project to send missionaries, Bibles, and other Christian literature to South America, where so many live who need them. At First Church, we have committed ourselves to a goal of $XXXXX toward it. Although you are not a member of our congregation, you have attended upon occasion, and we wanted you to be aware of the project. We hope that you will also want to be a part of it.

When you bring your contribution, please mark it "Christmas Offering," so that we will know where to put it. And as you do, think of your act of generosity as a gift to Christ Himself.

Sincerely,

Pastor

22 / TO NONMEMBERS ABOUT SPECIAL EVENTS— CONCERT BY LOCAL TALENT

We are delighted to inform you of a special opportunity. On March 16, First Church will be holding a benefit concert put on by Andrea Pell. Many in our community are aware of the vocal talents of Mrs. Pell, and you are invited to spend an hour listening to her sing a variety of songs, from old-fashioned hymns to contemporary Christian.

While no admission will be charged, a freewill offering will be taken, with the funds going to send Mrs. Pell to a week-long conference in Colorado for Christian musicians. This will enable her to further develop her talents.

If you cannot attend the concert but would still like to contribute towards Mrs. Pell's trip, send donations to the church, marked "Pell Trip."

Thank you for your help, and I hope to see you at the concert. You won't be disappointed!

In His service,

Pastor

CHAPTER **11**

Letters to Colleagues

It is only logical that a minister will have to communicate on various issues to colleagues and superiors. These model letters will help the minister to communicate a competent and positive image necessary for productive interactions with ministerial colleagues.

1 / TO COMMUNITY PASTORS ABOUT INQUIRIES AND REQUESTS—FOR PARTICIPATION IN COMMUNITY SERVICE

This year, I am in charge of planning the community Thanksgiving service, and I was wondering if you would care to participate. It is to be held at Faith Memorial Church on Wednesday, November 26, at 7:30 P.M.

At this point, I need someone to give the call to worship, the Scripture reading, and the closing prayer. If you would be interested in doing any of these, please contact my office as soon as possible.

We are anticipating a large crowd and a meaningful service. I do hope you can be part of it.

In His service,

Pastor

2 / TO COMMUNITY PASTORS ABOUT MEMBERSHIP TRANSFER

(Name) has asked to unite with First Church, and therefore has requested that we contact you in order that his/her name be removed from your church roll.

We are pleased to receive (name) into our fellowship, and are certain that he/she will be an asset. Thank your for your prompt compliance with his/her desire to transfer membership.

In Christ,

Pastor

3 / TO COMMUNITY PASTORS ABOUT PROBLEMS— CONFRONTATION BETWEEN YOUTH

In this touchy situation, the pastor takes care not to insinuate any blame while urging the recipient to join with him in getting the conflict resolved. While the tone is serious, it has underlying optimism that things will work out.

I recently became aware of a situation of which I feel sure you would want to be informed. At the city-wide youth rally last week, Brian Gatz from our church became involved in a fight with Fred Young and Jeff Majors from your congregation. The result was a broken nose for Brian.

At this time, I do not know exactly what started this confrontation, although I am certain that it was not entirely either side's fault. I am attempting to get to the bottom of this unfortunate situation. Perhaps you will want to do the same. The parents of all these boys have been notified about the fight.

Whatever caused the problem is really not the main issue in my eyes. I find settling a disagreement in this way to be totally unacceptable, particularly in the context of a Christian event like the rally. This is not the kind of witness I want to present to the city.

Please call me at your convenience so that we can discuss what action should be taken at this point. I am convinced that as believers, we can work out this problem in a way acceptable to all involved.

Sincerely,

Pastor

4 / TO COMMUNITY PASTORS ABOUT RELOCATION—OF SENDER

I would like to inform you that as of September 1, I will no longer hold the position of pastor at First Church. Having decided to go back into teaching full-time, I accepted an offer from Trinity Bible College to serve as professor of New Testament. My family and I will be relocating to that area sometime during the month of August.

As pastor here, I have had the opportunity to work together with you on a number of occasions. I would like to thank you for your cooperation with me, and also for your support and friendship. You share my desire to extend the Gospel to those who have not heard it, and I appreciate that.

Although I look forward to the new challenges that await me, I will miss many aspects of the work here, and particularly the people, like you. I pray that God will continue to richly bless your ministry and your church as you work for Him. May I ask that you make welcome my successor and help him in his adjustment to his new position? I am confident that I can depend on you.

With warmest regards,

Pastor

5 / TO COMMUNITY PASTORS ABOUT WELCOME

Welcome to (name of city)! As you begin your ministry at Faith Memorial Church, I pray that God will guide and bless you.

Several times in the past, First Church has joined with your congregation in hosting a speaker or concert. It is my hope that such ventures will continue. There are many people here who need to know the good news about Jesus, giving us great opportunities to reach out. May we unite with the other local pastors in doing the work that He has called us to do.

I look forward to meeting you soon. In the meantime, I hope that your adjustment to your new responsibilities will be smooth, and that your family's relocation will be as easy as possible.

With warm regards,

Pastor

6 / TO NATIONAL DENOMINATIONAL OFFICERS ABOUT INTRODUCTION—OF SENDER

Greetings in the Name of the Lord!

I am pleased to have recently been ordained in the denomination, and am looking forward to a long and good relationship with you. Already, I have heard many favorable things about how the leadership in the church really cares about each individual pastor and makes every effort to help him.

In addition to my position as pastor at First Church, I do some writing for Christian magazines. I have been asked to write a brief history of the denomination for (name of magazine), and I would like to ask for your assistance.

In the five years that I have been submitting manuscripts for publication, I have sold over thirty of them to *Decision, Leadership, Key to Christian Education*, and others. I enclose copies of several of my published articles. Also, I have attended two nationwide Christian writers conferences, and am active in a writers' club which meets in this area.

My wife Laura and I met at Purdue University, from which I received a degree in journalism before going on to seminary. We have been married for four years.

Now that I have told you a little about myself, I would appreciate it if you could forward some information to me about our founder and the early years of his ministry. I have a June 1 deadline for this article, so I need your help as soon as possible.

Thank you again for anything you can send me. If you want to check out my credentials any further, feel free to contact my bishop, Dr. Ken Upton, or my seminary advisor, Dr. Paul Beeker, (address).

Sincerely,

Pastor

7 / TO NATIONAL DENOMINATIONAL OFFICERS ABOUT PROBLEMS—LACK OF COOPERATION WITH SENDER'S MEMBER

One of the members of my congregation, Randy Kincaid, is in the process of writing an article about homosexuality for publication in a national Christian magazine. As part of his research, he is contacting a number of denominational headquarters to discuss this issue with some of the leadership of various churches. Although he has tried to reach you on several occasions, he has had no success.

Might I ask for your cooperation in this matter? I realize that you have a great deal of responsibility in your position as general supervisor of the denomination, and that you are extremely busy. However, what Mr. Kincaid wants would only take ten minutes on the phone. A faithful member of our church, he is trying to do his job well, and I know his motivation is to bring glory to Christ through his writing. His credentials as a writer and as a believer are excellent.

In addition, I feel that his including our denomination in his manuscript would give us some favorable publicity. I do hope that you can cooperate with him; it would mean much to both him and myself.

Thank you.

Sincerely,

Pastor

8 / TO NATIONAL DENOMINATIONAL OFFICERS ABOUT REPORTS—ATTENDANCE

Enclosed you will find First Church's Monthly Report.

Church Monthly Report
March, 19XX

First Church   Church Code Number 1641

112 Main St., (City, State, Zip Code)
Rev. Harold J. Fox, Pastor, 44 North St., (City, State, Zip Code).
Marilyn A. Rosenberger, Church Secretary, 1919 N. Monroe (City, State, Zip Code).
Michael T. Post, Church Treasurer, 53 Yellow Creek Road, (City, State, Zip Code).

Church Ministry Record

Church Services	Day	Time	Average Attendance
A.M.	Sunday	10:30	612
P.M.	Sunday	7:00	402
Midweek	Wednesday	7:00	367

Christian Education

| Sunday School | Sunday | 9:15 | 246 |
| Youth Fellowship | Thursday | 7:00 | 56 |

Men's Ministries:

| Prayer Breakfast | Saturday | 7:30 | 95 |
| Monthly Meeting | Tuesday | 7:00 | 146 |

Women's Ministries:

| Bible Study | Tuesday | 10:30 | 39 |
| Monthly Meeting | Thursday | 7:30 | 165 |

Evangelism:

Approximate number of calls made through visitation outreach: 79

Responses to Church Ministry:

Decisions for Christ: 41   Water Baptisms: 12

Church Membership:

Members Previous Month: 897

New Members: 59   Deaths/Withdrawals: 23
Active Members: 701   Inactive Members: 232

Total Members: 933

Date of last membership meeting: December 6, 19XX.
Date of last council meeting: March 12, 19XX.

In His service,

Pastor

9 / TO OTHER DENOMINATIONAL PASTORS ABOUT INTRODUCTION—RESPONSE TO

Thank you for your recent letter introducing yourself. I am delighted to have you as a welcome addition to our conference, and I am certain that you will find our denomination to be a framework in which you and your ministry may blossom.

Concerning your question about area resources, I can offer you little help in the areas of substance abuse or domestic violence. You might want to contact Rev. Charles Walker, (address), pastor of the Lima First Church, who has worked in these areas for some time.

As far as fighting pornography, I have been quite involved in this for the past several years. After organizing a local group called CUT (Clean Up Toledo), I served as president for the first year and now am on the board of directors. I have also been asked to serve on a state task force studying the results of pornography, and I have done extensive research into the problem, its effects, and possible solutions.

With this background, I do a good bit of speaking on the subject, and would be more than willing to come to your city if you are interested. Another possibility is that I could forward some information to you. Please let me know what you want.

Again, let me say how pleased I am to have you join the denomination and also our conference. In my eighteen years in this area, I have received nothing but encouragement from the denominational officers with whom I have worked. I am confident that you will have the same experience.

In Christ,

Pastor

10 / TO OTHER DENOMINATIONAL PASTORS ABOUT INQUIRIES AND REQUESTS

Since many might not be familiar with the difficulty of adopting a healthy infant nowadays or with the concept of private adoption, this letter goes into a good bit of detail. Another less personal way to handle some of it would be to include a brief résumé of the couple. In that case, the pastor's letter would be one of recommendation and perhaps a short explanation of private adoption.

I am hopeful that you will be able to help me with an important request.

A couple in our church, Jim and Mary Williams, are looking for a baby to privately adopt. Perhaps you know that adopting an infant these days is extremely difficult, due to the small number given up for adoption. These dear people have been trying for over three years to bring a child into their family through adoption, but they have had no success. At this point, they are turning to their brothers and sisters in Christ to help them.

Maybe you have an unwed mother-to-be in your congregation or you know of one. Has she considered private adoption? Legal in our state (and almost all others), it is handled through a lawyer with no agency involved. The adoptive parents pay for the mother's medical expenses as well as the legal costs, and the birth mother has the assurance of knowing her child will be brought up in a loving Christian home by parents who very much wanted him/her.

The Williamses have been active members of our congregation for eight years, during which time they have been involved in youth ministry, teaching adult Sunday school, and serving on the church council and several committees. I feel they have a stable marriage, good jobs, financial security, and I can highly recommend them as excellent prospective parents.

If you know of anyone who might be willing to consider giving up a baby for adoption, or you would like more information about private adoption or the Williamses, please contact me.

This couple has gone through a difficult time waiting for God to bring them the desire of their hearts. I believe it is very much in order to seek the child for them within the Body of Christ; as we minister to each other's needs, we are all helped.

Thank you for your consideration.

Sincerely,

Pastor

11 / TO OTHER DENOMINATIONAL PASTORS ABOUT MEMBERSHIP TRANSFER

Recently, we were saddened to lose Keith and Mary Monroe as active members of First Church, due to their move to Bristol, Connecticut. However, they have informed us that they now desire to unite with your fellowship in their new location.

We are pleased that they have found a church with which they feel comfortable, and we trust that they will prove to be a blessing to you as they have been to us in the past. This letter officially terminates their membership with us, and we gladly leave the Monroes in your hands, trusting that their joining with you will advance the Gospel.

Because of Jesus,

Pastor

12 / TO OTHER DENOMINATIONAL PASTORS ABOUT RECOMMENDATION—GIVING A FAVORABLE ONE

The letter writer's enthusiasm shows through here. Note how the candidate's achievements both in the classroom and in her personal life are highlighted.

I understand that you are considering Mrs. Barbara Woods for the position of teacher at your nursery school. I would highly recommend her.

Mrs. Woods served as our teacher for three-year olds for a period of four years. During that time, she demonstrated a deep love for children, sensitivity in dealing with parents, and ability as an educator. She is innovative and dynamic in the classroom, and she patiently and skillfully handles each situation in a flexible manner. In addition to being popular with the children, she is well-liked by the rest of the faculty.

Perhaps more importantly, Mrs. Woods is a committed Christian who has been a faithful servant to her Lord for a number of years. She is truly an example of how to live for Jesus. Although she taught full-time at the school, she was also quite active in the church, singing in the choir, leading a youth Bible study, and serving as an officer in the women's group. Had she not relocated due to her husband's transfer, she would continue to be employed by us.

If you have any further questions, I would be happy to discuss them with you.

Sincerely in Christ,

Pastor

13 / TO OTHER DENOMINATIONAL PASTORS ABOUT RELOCATION—OF RECIPIENT

I recently heard that you are being reassigned to First Church in (name of city). Congratulations on your new assignment! I am certain that it will prove to be a challenging and rewarding experience for you.

Naturally, I am sorry to hear that you will be leaving our area. I have enjoyed working with you on the projects we have done together, as I have been encouraged by your friendship.

May God continue to guide you as you pursue new fields of ministry, and may He bless your life in every way. If ever I can be of any service to you in your new location, please don't hesitate to contact me.

With Warm Regards,

Pastor

14 / TO STATE/DISTRICT DENOMINATIONAL OFFICERS ABOUT RECOMMENDATION— REQUEST FOR

We are considering the application of Rev. Kevin Baker for the position of youth pastor at First Church. Would you please forward to me any information you have on his years as youth pastor at First Church in Winona? We are particularly interested in knowing the following:

1. His relationship with the senior pastor—was he cooperative and supportive? Did he tend to get problems out in the open or keep them inside?

2. His relationship with the district—was he active in district youth activities and did he encourage participation of the youth? Did he seem to uphold the beliefs of the denomination? Is he well-regarded in the district?

We have already received a reference from the senior pastor he served under, and so far, we believe that he might be the one for the job. Nevertheless, several board members wanted more information from a source outside of the church where he previously ministered. Therefore, we would appreciate your response as soon as possible.

Thank you very much.

Sincerely,

Pastor

15 / TO STATE/DISTRICT DENOMINATIONAL OFFICERS ABOUT REPORTS—FINANCIAL

Here is our monthly financial statement as you requested.

First Church Financial Report

Checking Accounts Beginning Balance _____

Income

Tithable to District

    Church offerings _____
    Sunday school offerings _____
    Bequests & Gifts _____
       Total   _____

Non-tithable

    Missionary offerings _____
    Special offerings/visiting speakers _____
    Building Fund offerings _____
    Bible college offerings _____
    Designated Fund offerings _____
    TV Ministry _____
    Music Ministry _____
    Tape Ministry _____
       Total   _____

Grand total of all incomes   _____

Expenses

Missions:

    Church Extension Tithe _____
    Bible Colleges _____
    Camp Offerings _____
    Local benevolence _____
       Total   _____

Facilities:

    Loan payments: principal/interest _____
    Property insurance _____
    Taxes _____
    Equipment and Furnishings _____
    Church Facilities _____
    Rent _____
    Utilities _____
    Telephone _____
    Building Improvements _____
    Maintenance _____
       Total   _____

Ministry

    Children, youth, adult ministries _____
    Sunday school _____
    Radio & TV programming _____
    Office operation _____
    Advertising _____
    Church vehicle operation and maintenance _____
    Church vehicle insurance _____
        Total   _____

Personnel

    Sr. pastor salary _____
    Other salaries _____
    Payroll taxes _____
    Personnel insurance _____
    Retirement/social security _____
    Allowances _____
    Staff housing _____
        Total   _____

Miscellaneous

    Designated Funds _____
    Visiting Speakers (honorarium and expenses) _____
    Other _____
        Total   _____

Grand total of expenses _____
Ending Balance _____
Total of above two amounts _____

Savings

Name and address of bank _____
Beginning balance _____
Deposits _____
Interest added to savings _____
Withdrawals _____
Ending balance _____

Combined Checking and Savings Balances by Department:

Church _____
Sunday school _____
Children, youth, adult ministries _____
Convention fund _____
Building fund _____

Total combined balances _____

Indebtedness
Accounts payable _____
Property and notes _____
Total _____

Sincerely,

Pastor

16 / TO STATE/DISTRICT DENOMINATIONAL OFFICERS ABOUT WELCOME—TO NEW SUPERVISOR

Congratulations on your recent appointment as our district supervisor! I am delighted to welcome you to our area, which I am confident you will find to your liking. In this district, there are plenty of devoted pastors, dedicated church members, and enthusiasm for the Lord's work. We are eager to press on with it under your leadership.

I enjoyed a good relationship with your predecessor Rev. Charles Bishop, and I am anticipating developing the same sort of relationship with you. With your extensive background in ministry and administration, you will certainly add much to the district.

Again, let me welcome you and add that if I can do anything to help in your adjustment to your new position, don't hesitate to call. I look forward to meeting you and your family in the near future.

In His service,

Pastor

CHAPTER 12

Letters of Policy and Doctrine

Each church offers unique qualities, and these characteristics need to be communicated clearly in statements of policy and doctrine. This allows for a successful match between church and individual, eliminates confusion, and protects against disharmony and troublemaking in the body.

To be effective and active members in a church, individuals need to know exactly what is offered to them, and what is expected from them. These letters will help you achieve these ends.

1 / TO GROUPS ABOUT AVAILABILITY OF SPECIAL SERVICES—NURSERY

We are looking forward to your congregation joining us for the community Thanksgiving service to be held on Wednesday, November 26, at 7:30 P.M.

For your convenience, during the service we will be operating both a nursery for babies under the age of two and one for toddlers ages two through five. Each will be staffed by First Church nursery workers. We hope you will feel free to make use of them.

Thank you, and we anticipate a meaningful joint service as we unite to show our gratitude to our great God.

Sincerely,

Pastor

2 / TO GROUPS ABOUT BUILDING AND KEY USE RULES

An established set of guidelines for outsiders who use the church or synagogue is helpful to have in writing. While this example has a cordial tone, it is also clear in exactly what is expected.

Thank you for your recent request to use the church building on Saturday, October 2, 19XX, for a craft bazaar to take place between the hours of 10 A.M. and 5 P.M. We are happy to grant you permission to do so, under the following conditions:

No smoking in the church.

Unused areas of the building are to be roped off so that no one goes into them.

Food and drinks are not to be taken outside of Fellowship Hall.

A certificate of liability insurance must be filed.

A fee of $50 will be charged to pay for the extra custodian work.

No one will be permitted in the church before 8 A.M. or after 7 P.M. on the day of the bazaar.

We would appreciate your cooperation in these matters. May you have great success in your endeavor.

Sincerely,

Pastor

3 / TO GROUPS ABOUT CHURCH POSITION ON ISSUES—NUCLEAR ARMS RACE

In light of the current debate about the nuclear arms race in the denomination, we would like to present to you the enclosed proposed resolution reflecting the view of our congregation.

Whereas, as Christians, we believe in peace which brings real freedom to persons of every nation; and

Whereas, as citizens of the Kingdom of God as well as of the United States of America, we pledge proper loyalty to both; and

Whereas, our government, having received God's blessing, has served us well over the years of its existence; and

Whereas, the U.S. Constitution provides separation of church and state; and

Whereas, the President of this country, congressional representatives, and other elected and appointed officials have the responsibility of providing security and common defense of the United States, as well as the mandate to work for world peace; and

Whereas, the Soviet Union persists in expanding nuclear, strategic, and conventional military forces, the U.S. has the clear responsibility to maintain peace and freedom by deterring such actions; and

Whereas, it is not in the best interests of this nation to have a comprehensive test ban treaty, as long as there is need for nuclear deterrence, thereby requiring a structured test program which will ensure the safety, reliability, and effectiveness of such weapons; and

Whereas, the government has the resources, intelligence, and scientific knowledge available to it, as well as the best interests of and the information concerning the mindset and activities of the U.S.; and

Whereas, we have both the opportunity and the responsibility to pray for our government officials as they fulfill their obligations to strive for world peace;

Therefore, be it resolved that First Church of (city) commends the President, Congress, and other officials for steps they have taken, as well as will take, to pursue peace through nuclear arms reduction agreements, a test ban treaty, etc., to assure U.S. security and that of the rest of the free world, with the objectives of achieving peace and freedom for people everywhere. Further, be it resolved that as members of this Body and of this nation, we vow to renew our commitment to Jesus Christ and to the United States, lifting up our leaders to God each day in prayer.

We trust that you will take into account our sentiments. Thank you.

Sincerely,

Pastor

4 / TO GROUPS ABOUT JOB DESCRIPTIONS FOR VOLUNTEER STAFF—SUNDAY SCHOOL TEACHERS

Greetings in the name of the Lord to all Sunday school teachers!

As another year begins, we are looking forward to new opportunities as we strive to bring our students into a closer walk with God. For the benefit of those who have recently accepted their positions, as well as to remind those who have held them for a while, here is your job description:

1. In both your teaching and your personal life, you are to radiate Jesus, so as to minister to the needs of each of your students.

2. You are to attend the monthly teachers' meetings with the pastor.

3. You are to be at the teachers' workshops, which will be tentatively held in early November and March.

4. You are to visit each student in his/her home at least once during the fall quarter.

5. You are to commit yourself to spending adequate time to prepare your lesson each week so that the presentation of it will go as smoothly as possible.

6. You are to use as many visual aids, attention-getting devices such as puppets, drama, etc. as possible in order to make your lesson as interesting as you can.

7. Orders for curriculum must be into the superintendent by the first of the month preceding the month the material is needed.

8. If you know you cannot teach on a specific Sunday, you are to find a substitute and contact the pastor a week in advance. If unexpected circumstances arise, please notify him as early as possible. Your students are counting on you being present!

Thank you for your cooperation in these matters. I am certain that by working together, we will see a year of great personal growth, both for ourselves and for our students.

Because of Him,

Pastor

5 / TO INDIVIDUALS ABOUT ACCOUNTABILITY— OF STAFF

In answer to your inquiry, the following should clarify our position:

An associate pastor at First Church is to be accountable to the senior pastor in consultation with the Church Council. He/she shall be elected by the vote of the congregation, with the call to be approved by the district office.

The pastoral relationship between the associate pastor and the church may only be dissolved by the district. He/she may request such action and must also state his/her intention to the Church Council, who will then call a congregational meeting to act on the request. If the congregation and the pastor agree, the district will so move. In cases in which the congregation does not want the dissolution, it may state its case to the district, who will rule one way or the other. Should the congregation wish to dissolve the pastoral relationship, a similar process will be followed.

To summarize, the associate pastor is directly responsible to the senior pastor, in cooperation with the Church Council and the District office.

If you have further questions, feel free to contact my office.

Sincerely,

Pastor

6 / TO INDIVIDUALS ABOUT MEMBERSHIP REQUIREMENTS

This fairly informal letter concisely lists the membership requirements in an easy-to-follow format.

Thank you for your interest in investigating joining First Church. We have the following membership requirements:

at least ten years of age,

evidence of having personally asked Jesus Christ to be Lord and Savior,

baptized by water,

evidence of living a godly life-style,

participate in membership classes led by the pastor, and upon their completion, have a private conference with him.

If you feel you can meet these criteria, please contact my office for information about the date of the next series of membership classes.

Please feel free to contact me if you have any questions.

Sincerely,

Pastor

7 / TO INDIVIDUALS ABOUT QUALIFICATIONS FOR VOLUNTEERS—SUNDAY SCHOOL TEACHERS

Thank you for your recent inquiry about the possibility of teaching Sunday school. We have the following qualifications:

member of the church,

regular attendance of Sunday school for at least the past year, attend the basic teacher training seminar and then go to the teachers' workshop scheduled several times a year,

agree to be at monthly teachers' meetings held with the pastor,

demonstrate a love for the age you will be teaching,

be of the highest moral character, living a life-style consistent with Biblical standards.

If you feel you can meet these requirements, please contact my office. We are constantly looking for dedicated individuals willing to commit themselves to teaching in our Christian education department.

In His service,

Pastor

8 / TO INDIVIDUALS ABOUT STAFF ABSENCES

For your information, the revised policy of staff absences is as follows:

1. Absences due to a death in the immediate family (defined as spouse, child, parent, or other member of household) will result in up to one week's paid leave.

2. Absences due to a death of a relative other than immediate family will result in up to three day's paid time off.

3. If an employee is called for jury or witness duty, he/she will be paid for the time off and is permitted to keep any compensation received for such duty. However, if such duty does not require the entire day, the employee is expected to report to the church for work during the remaining hours of the workday.

4. Absences for personal business are permitted if approved by the department head in advance. A maximum of three such days per year will be allowed.

5. In the case of personal illness, an employee has up to ten days sick leave per year. The church office should be notified prior to 8:30 A.M. on the first day of such absences, as well as on each succeeding day the illness continues. A doctor's statement may be requested after the third day off. In some cases of serious illness in the immediate family, the supervisor may classify it as personal illness.

6. Leaves of absence will be granted if recommended by the department head and approved by the senior pastor.

Absences, as much as possible, are to be reported in advance to the department head. A week's notice is preferred, but a minimum of forty-eight hours is strongly suggested.

Unexcused absences will be dealt with by the senior pastor first, then referred to the Personnel Committee of the Session if needed, and finally handled by the Session itself if there are further problems.

I hope this is clear to you. If you have any questions, feel free to ask.

In His service,

Pastor

9 / TO INDIVIDUALS ABOUT STATEMENT OF DOCTRINE

Enclosed you will find First Church's Statement of Doctrine.

Statement of Doctrine

1. The Bible is the divinely inspired Word of God. It is truth untarnished by any degree of error, it will endure forever, and it is the standard by which all conduct, creeds, and opinions are to be tried.

2. There is one God, the Maker of Heaven and Earth, holy and just, Who is expressed in three equal Persons, the Father, Son, and Holy Spirit.

3. Man was made in holiness but, by his choice, fell into sin, thus resulting in a sinful nature of all, in that each voluntarily go astray and are therefore under condemnation to eternal separation from God.

4. God has graciously provided a way out through His Son, who freely took on human nature, was born of a Virgin, lived tempted in all manner of sin, but remained sinless and died for our transgressions. He rose from the dead and is now enthroned in Heaven.

5. In order to be saved, sinners must personally invite Jesus Christ into their hearts, repenting of their sins and intending to walk in newness of life with the help of God.

6. The Christian who has thus experienced salvation is to persist in personal prayer and Bible study, freely sharing the faith with those around him/her, regularly fellowshipping in a Bible-believing church, and participating in every sort of good work for the advancement of the kingdom of God.

7. In obedience to the Word of God, a believer is to undergo the Sacrament of Baptism, symbolizing the death of the old man and the birth of the new in Christ. The Sacrament of Communion, by which the members partake of the bread and wine in memory of Jesus and His atoning work on the cross, is to be celebrated on a regular basis.

8. The end of the age is approaching, and with it, the personal return of Jesus Christ, the bodily resurrection of the just and the unjust, the everlasting blessedness of the redeemed, and the everlasting torment of the lost.

If you have any questions or concerns, please contact my office.

Because of Him,

Pastor